MAKING SOAPIES IN KABUL

MAKING SOAPIES IN KABUL

Hot days, crazy nights and dangerous liaisons in a war zone

TRUDI-ANN TIERNEY

ALLEN&UNWIN

SYDNEY · MELBOURNE · AUCKLAND · LONDON

Certain names and details have been changed to protect the innocent and guilty alike.

First published in 2014

Copyright © Trudi-Ann Tierney 2014

Allen & Unwin
83 Alexander Street
Crows Nest NSW 2065
Australia
Phone:(61 2) 8425 0100
Email: info@allenandunwin.com
Web: www.allenandunwin.com

Cataloguing-in-Publication details are available
from the National Library of Australia
www.trove.nla.gov.au

ISBN 978 1 74331 427 2

Internal design by Christabella Designs
Set in 11/19 pt Cambria by Bookhouse, Sydney
Printed and bound in Australia by Griffin Press

10 9 8 7 6 5 4 3 2 1

The paper in this book is FSC® certified.
FSC® promotes environmentally responsible,
socially beneficial and economically viable
management of the world's forests.

To my amazing mum, who sent me off to Kabul with her blessing,
and my wonderful Afghan friends,
who welcomed me with warmth and love

Contents

1.
The Den and my Knuckle-Dragger Friend

The whistling dog woke me up again, for the sixth morning running. Despite having not hit my pillow until 2am, I smiled when I heard his feeble toot-tooting just after five. My mangy Labrador alarm clock didn't exactly belt out a tune (although I had picked out a solitary bar of 'Sweet Caroline' two mornings before), and as I watched him sitting alone under my window, serenading the first signs of sun, I couldn't discern any actual lip-pursing or puckering-up. But he was most definitely whistling.

I had never encountered a whistling dog before, but then the past month had been a rollcall of phenomenal firsts; my entrée into life in Afghanistan in April 2009 had been nothing short of mind-blowing.

Hundreds and thousands of expats had made this journey before

1

me. Soldiers ordered here to fight the bloody war; aid workers committed to cleaning up the mess; doctors and diplomats; money-hungry entrepreneurs who'd sniffed out the scent of a quick buck to be made in the battle zone. Amongst them, I felt uniquely out of place in my mission to Afghanistan; I had come to Kabul to manage a bar and restaurant—'The Den'.

I spent my entire three-hour flight from Dubai into Kabul pressed up against the plane's window, marvelling at the alien new world below. I gazed in wonderment as the plane cruised over chocolate-brown mountains, their tops sugared with snow, and then dipped into barren valleys where the only hints of habitation were tiny perfect grids of crude mud fencing. I was an unabashed, window-licking, mouth-breather, and I was not even particularly disconcerted when the turbaned fellow in front spent minutes at a time staring back at me through the gap in the seats. As we skimmed over the NATO base next to the airport and landed alongside military choppers standing to attention on the tarmac, I fumbled for my headscarf and recalled the extraordinarily easy journey that had brought me to this place.

It all began late in 2008 over dinner with my brother Adam, one of my life-long friends, Paul, and his partner, Jose. Paul had just been appointed as the head of production for Afghanistan's largest and most successful television broadcaster and was back in Australia trying to assure his family that moving to Afghanistan was a sane and sensible life choice. My TV career in Australia was kind of at a standstill. My business partner, Muffy, and I had recently had a comedy show optioned by an international production house and an Australian network was showing genuine interest in funding the series in the new financial year. Muffy also had a documentary in early development with another company. We were playing the waiting game and I was in need of a new adventure. Much to Adam's horror, I farewelled Paul that night with a commitment that, if ever there was an opportunity for me to join him in Afghanistan, I wanted in.

Over the next few months Paul and I emailed back and forth; he wasn't in a position to offer me a job but, if I could somehow get myself into the country, he was certain that I would pick up work. Then in March he called me with a proposition—a new bar and restaurant had just opened in Kabul and it was owned and operated by friends of his, Sue and Don. They were going on four weeks' leave and needed an expat to manage the local staff in their absence.

Fifteen minutes later Sue, a chipper Australian woman with a smile in her voice, was on the phone to me. They would cover my airfare, arrange a work visa and pay me the not-too-shabby sum of US$3000 for a month of my services. I could eat and drink whatever I wanted and would be living in an apartment above the bar with Paul and Jose, plus a Swedish chiropractor, Jenny.

Two weeks before my departure, I tumbled into a romantic relationship with Nick—a man I had known for years and who had just returned to Australia after a stint living and working in the UK. While our shameless love fest at my farewell party (played out to a backing track of calls for us to find ourselves a room) might have suggested otherwise, we had decided that our fledgling coupledom could withstand a few months of apartness.

So within four weeks of my initial conversation with Sue, I was on a plane and launching into my new adventure. Sue had sent me instructions on how to navigate my way through the airport:

1. Wear a long-sleeved top and trousers (loose fitting) and put on your headscarf before you get off the plane. You're better off being as inconspicuous as possible and it's not worth offending the locals.

2. Immigration can be quite chaotic (Afghans have no concept of queuing). The men can be very pushy, but just stand your ground and try not to make eye contact. And the word for 'thank you' is *tashakor*.

3. There will be porters at the baggage carousel who will take your luggage to the car park for you. The going rate is US$1. Don't let them talk you into paying any more than that.

4. Get them to take you to Car Park B. I'm attaching photos of Don and myself but, if all else fails, I will be the woman wearing the big, red scarf.

The airport experience was everything Sue had described and, after a protracted stand-off with the porter over his insistence that I pay him five dollars, I was left alone to wait. The plane had landed a little ahead of schedule so I sat on my over-stuffed suitcase and took in my new home. Guns—big guns, everywhere. Local guards stationed outside the terminal. Three surly officers manning the car-park gate. A whole lot of fit-looking westerners rounding up their expat arrivals and herding them into armoured vehicles.

A raucous, bosomy American woman, wearing a tight T-shirt and with her blonde hair flowing free, stationed herself next to me as she waited with her group to be collected. The gate guys couldn't take their eyes off her while a troop of turbaned elders, hovering close by, eyed her off less conspicuously, clearly passing judgement in between furtive peeks at her ample rack. I made an obvious show of turning away from her, but then I felt all indignant and abandoned when her ride arrived and she jiggled off with her posse to the car, leaving me as the only foreigner in the car park.

After about an hour, I began to wonder if there'd been some kind of miscommunication about my arrival time. Even if this was true, I was powerless to rectify it, as I didn't have Sue's number. She had sent it to me, of course, but not being a particularly smart traveller and, according to my mother, sorely lacking in common sense, I hadn't printed it out so it was still sitting on my laptop, in an email that I was quite unable to access. The address of my new home was uselessly hanging out in that same vicinity.

I had placed all my faith in a woman in voluminous crimson headgear, whom I had never met, turning up on time to collect me, but clearly something had gone wrong. As the afternoon wore on, I figured I needed a cunning plan to get in touch with her. With my eye firmly on my suitcase, I marched out of the car-park exit and spied some taxis in an adjoining lot. I knew there was a four-star hotel in town called the Serena, as there had been a tragic bomb attack there the previous year that I'd heard about. I'd go there, get on the internet and track down my quarry.

I approached the first taxi driver I happened upon and stated my destination. There really aren't that many ways to pronounce 'Serena', but it took me around eight attempts before something finally twigged and he enthusiastically nodded and smiled his under-standing. I was hurrying back to retrieve my luggage, loving myself stupid for being so resourceful and likening myself to an urban Bear

Grylls, when a car came roaring up behind me. I turned to see a red scarf flapping wildly out of the passenger window.

Sue and Don were effusive with their apologies as they loaded my luggage into the boot and we left the car park. There had been some mix-up with their driver and he had taken the car to go shopping; then they tried to call him and his phone was off . . . But I was too absorbed in the world beyond the airport to take in much of what they were saying.

The place was uniformly brown and dusty; simple mud houses clung to the sides of crowded hills. Women in burqas strolled down the footpath. Two filthy children rode by on a wooden cart, piled high with rubbish and being drawn by a donkey with coloured ribbons and bells woven into its mane. We stopped in traffic and child beggars knocked persistently on the car window, chasing us along the road when we finally moved off. Local police, armed with machine guns, manned a roadside checkpoint. When a convoy of armoured trucks and tanks passed by on the opposite side of the road, Don pointed at it. 'You never want to travel too close to a military convoy; they're prime targets for insurgents. If you're in a car and the driver is sitting behind one of those, tell him to pull back.'

'Right.'

'If anything happens now, while we're driving home, you are to stay in the car. Do not move from the vehicle. If there is an incident with an IED or VBIED, just remain where you are. All right?'

'Yes . . . No . . . A what? I'm sorry.'

'Okay. If there is an explosive device, gunfire, a traffic accident . . . a bloody earthquake, just stay in the car.'

'Got it.'

Despite all the guns I'd seen at the airport, Don's advice gave me my first real sense of being in a war zone and I casually slid away from the window, positioning myself in the middle of the back seat on the pretence of listening more attentively to my new, knowledgeable friends.

When we finally slowed in front of The Den, I initially thought we were making a pit stop. We had arrived in a neighbourhood where the houses were comparatively modern—bricks and cement, windows, doors, tiled and tin-clad roofs—partly concealed behind barbed-wire fences and heavy iron gates. There was no signage to indicate that we had arrived at a bar, and it wasn't until Sue announced, 'We're here!' that I grasped we were home. The gates to the small compound were opened from the inside by two local guards (more big guns) and Don instructed me to stay put in the car until they had securely locked the gates behind us.

It being a Friday, the Islamic day of prayer, the bar was closed; so Sue and Don were able to take their time showing me around. It was a small set-up but cosy, and Sue had done a splendid job of creating a shabby-chic feel to the place. There was a garden and a small terrace, a tiny kitchen and a storeroom with fortified walls and a heavy steel door, which doubled as a safe room in case of an insurgent attack.

We were just going over the menu when I heard my second Aussie accent for the day. 'Hello, darls. Thanks so much for this. Steve's coming over for dinner tonight and I reckon the old fanny might be opening up again for business!'

I turned to see a lean, tall, forty-something woman striding through the door. She did a double-take when she saw me, before stopping short and raising her hand to her open mouth. 'Ooh ah. Sorry, love, I didn't realise . . . Oh God! How embarrassing!'

Sue quickly introduced me to Marg. As we shook hands, she said she'd heard I was coming to town and confessed relief that it was a fellow countryman she had revealed her genital re-launch to. She was there to pick up a bottle of wine to help facilitate the event and informed me that she would be helping me behind the bar the following evening, before hurrying off to gussy herself up for her date.

Sue's assurances that I would love Marg were unnecessary; I already did and was delighted to learn that she was down for two nights a week on a roster of expats who would work behind the bar for free food, booze and fifty bucks cash in hand.

Don felt compelled to warn me that their clientele consisted mainly of 'Knuckle Draggers'. I nodded my head, but really had no idea what I was affirming. I was scanning my brain for some suitable reference point when Sue stepped in and explained that 'Knuckle Draggers' were western private security contractors. Of course The Den had female patrons as well—otherwise, why would the blokes bother to show?—but the bar was usually packed tight on a Thursday night with big beefy guys who were liable to get punchy after too many ales. But all customers were frisked at the door and made to check their weapons, and the local security guards had been trained up by Don (himself a Knuckle Dragger) to deal with any trouble, so I had nothing to worry about. Apparently there were other bars in the city that catered to 'Do-Gooders'—aid workers, NGO employees and the like—but it seemed that the two camps rarely mixed. When it came to night life, Kabul was clearly a tribal town.

But the factions didn't end there. The bar staff were all Pashtun cousins; the kitchen staff were mostly Hazara. I knew enough about Afghanistan to understand the implications of this. Pashtuns are the largest ethnic group in the country and historically have been politically dominant. The Hazaras have been the most disadvantaged and persecuted group and were brutally oppressed under the Taliban. Apparently bar demarcation disputes were common, ranging from the divvying-up of tips to who should light the fire on the terrace each evening. Don explained that they had a tendency to 'carry on like girls', behaviour that constituted bitching, gossiping and sulking. It rarely got out of hand, but I wasn't to buy into it.

In the event of a police raid or an insurgent attack, I was to lock myself in the safe room and call one of Don's security mates, Colin. Colin would also take me to pick up my alcohol supplies each week, retrieved from a house across town belonging to an advisor for an international consultancy firm and stacked from floor to ceiling with booze. 'Grog runs' were highly illegal and, if the police caught us, we would undoubtedly end up in jail. In which case I was to call their Afghan business partner, Abdullah.

Staff aside, I was never to allow Afghans into the bar. Embassy security guards were the only people permitted to bring their weapons in. Oh, and could I possibly find a good recipe for mango chutney?

By the time Sue and Don settled me into my room, I was starting to wonder what exactly I'd taken on.

The next day I officially began work. The first of the kitchen staff arrived at noon. Their English was limited, and my lonely *tashakor* could only get me so far in conversation, so we settled on a couple of rounds of smiling and nodding before I retreated to my room to scour the internet for chutney recipes.

The bar staff started dribbling in mid-afternoon. The manager, Tamim, spoke impeccable English. He proved to be charming and funny and, in between showing me the ropes, offered a lowdown on all the regulars who would soon be arriving. It was a basic assessment. Dave was a good man. Ron was a good man. Trevor bad. Chris good . . . Bad—good—good—good . . . The only deviations from this simple scale were Inge, a Dutch woman who worked with us on Wednesdays and was 'mad', and Al. Al was a great man—he was Tamim's best friend; Al was his brother.

I heard Al before I actually laid eyes on him. I was in the kitchen, ostensibly checking on dinner prep but merely pointing at pots of bubbling gruel while doing the nod and smile, when a low booming, American voice arrested me mid-pantomime.

'Tamim! Your retarded cousin here just served me a warm beer! Get me an ice-cold Corona right now or I'll bend you over that bar and fuck you till your hips snap!'

It was 4.30pm. We didn't open for another thirty minutes and so I hurried to the bar, steeling myself to eject some menacing interloper who was threatening to violate my manager in a most unsavoury and sadistic manner. I arrived to see a huge, hulking, bearded fellow, undoubtedly a Knuckle Dragger, holding Tamim in a headlock. But Tamim was laughing, and the other boys who had gathered to watch the spectacle all looked highly amused.

Then, without releasing his grip, the early-bird assailant turned to me and smiled. He had one of those smiles that are impossible to resist—killer, incongruously cute and all-consuming. It radiated from the tips of his size-seventeen feet to the top of his faraway head.

'Hey!' he said. 'Al. You must be Trudi.'

He let Tamim go and swivelled his full frame to face me. It was like staring up a mountain and I had no doubt that he could indeed snap his best friend's hips if that was his bent. He made an obvious show of looking me up and down.

'Nice. You got a boyfriend?'

'Umm . . . yeah. He's back in Australia.'

'What a waste. Welcome to hell, gorgeous. You need anything, just come to me.'

He reached across and grasped my hand in his massive paw, switching on that excessively brilliant smile again. I was hooked. I instinctively knew then that Al would become my best friend too.

I wonder now how I would have managed those first few weeks without him. Al turned up every afternoon at four-thirty. He took his usual spot at the end of the bar and didn't leave until closing time. He drank all night but never seemed to get drunk, and it was only in recounting his horrendous hangovers that he gave himself away.

'Took some Koreans up in a Black Hawk today. I was so twisted, I was hurling chunks inside my flak jacket.'

He was a Knuckle Dragger and served in the US army for twelve years before moving into private security. He was making an obscene amount of money and couldn't comprehend why I'd chosen to come to Afghanistan to manage a bar. Still, he was immensely happy that I had and was pleased that I wasn't a Do-Gooder. 'Those stuck-up bitches are happy for me to guard their lives during the day, but completely brush me off if they see me out at night.'

He wasn't exaggerating; I watched it happen. One evening a group of gorgeous, well-groomed girls turned up to the bar demanding cocktails. Al recognised two of them from a job he had recently done

11

and, after a couple of bracing beers, bounded up to the ladies to say hello. He was, in fact, quite charming—polite as he greeted them, with that smile just so. He took a seat at the edge of the group and engaged in some banter with the two women he knew . . . before they both resolutely turned their backs on him and continued chatting with their friends. He stared into his beer for a few minutes as Tamim and I struggled to contain our mirth, then he got up, casually made his way back to the bar and threatened to set us both on fire if we ever mentioned the matter again.

Paul was also rather underwhelmed by my new buddy and was at a loss to fathom my friendship with the 'big, loud, scary guy'. I simply would reply that he was a good man. Al only served to reinforce my refusal to see the world in black and white: I was perfectly happy to float in the silty, grey waters, where a steroid-abusing man carrying a gun was the sweetest person I knew.

Al spoke excellent Dari (the most widely spoken language in Afghanistan) and the staff all loved him. He gave them lifts home from work, regularly hung out with Tamim after closing time, and spotted them cash when they were short. Their devotion to him was only marginally eclipsed by the adoration of the kids who lived or lingered in our neighbourhood. There was a handful of them who begged outside the bar each night, haranguing rich foreigners for loose change, and others who resided in the rundown mud houses on the edge of the suburb. My bedroom was at the front of our building and, if I wasn't otherwise occupied, I'd station myself at the window to watch his arrival.

Kids would emerge from everywhere, calling his name as they raced towards him. He spoke to them in Dari so I didn't really know what he was saying as he squatted down beside them in the dirt, but they listened to him like he was a prophet, edging closer and closer until he disappeared inside a ring of tiny, lice-riddled heads.

One day he turned up in his jeep. On cue the kids came running and he piled them all into his car before speeding away. When I asked Tamim about it, he told me Al was taking them to buy new shoes. Apparently he regularly bought clothes for the kids; also he dragged them home if they were still begging outside at midnight and had negotiated with many of their parents to pay for their schooling. He was a one-man aid agency, but when I tried to talk to him about it, he just shrugged it off and asked me when I was going to finally give in and fuck him like a porn star.

Al was a complex jumble of contradictions. He'd expose me to photos of his robustly erect penis on the pretext of showing me pictures of his pet monkey then, ten minutes later, confide in me across the bar about wanting to find true love, get married and have a dozen children. Sometimes he left the bar without saying goodbye because I had rebuffed one of his exceedingly lewd advances, but would text me an apology the very next morning with assurances that I was his best girl and that he would always be there for me.

He could be menacing and threatening (particularly to expat men who took to wearing the salwar kameez—a traditional Afghan outfit of loose pants and a long tunic), but his concern for me, his innate need to protect me, was genuine and touching.

My first Thursday night in charge of The Den was enormous and overwhelming. Patrons stood four deep at the bar as they waited to be served and we struggled to keep up with the endless cries for drinks. One very drunk man started hurling abuse from the back of the pack—just general venom about the standard of our service. I ignored him, but to little effect; then, when he started up again, Al drew himself up to his full height before turning to address him.

'Hey buddy. You keep that up and I swear I will follow you out of here, hunt you down and blow your fucken head off!'

Al turned to me and winked, but I was too stunned to respond. I was genuinely horrified by this brutal declaration, but oddly moved by the sentiment that drove him to make it.

On another night, a first-time patron turned up, perched himself on a bar stool and downed two shots of vodka before slowly lowering his head and promptly passing out. Tamim was surprised that the guy had got drunk so quickly, but I figured he had more than booze running through his veins, and Al confirmed my suspicions.

'He's a smackie, gorgeous. Works for a security company down the road. If the police catch him in here like this, you'll be in all sorts of trouble.'

He revived him with a couple of slaps around the face before dragging him back to his compound. Once there, Al demanded to see the guy's boss and threatened to go to the police if he didn't take charge of his junkie employee and sort him out.

'It's people like that who fuck it up for the rest of us,' he later explained as I handed him a complimentary Corona by way of thanks. He looked warily at it—'I fucken hate that shit'—before downing half of it in a single swig.

Once, when Colin got stuck in Kandahar, Al escorted me on the grog run. He had broken up fights, warned off lecherous men and showed stumbling drunks the door when they refused to accept it was closing time. But his finest moment came one evening when the police showed up at The Den.

I had no warning that they had even arrived. Using the staff entrance, two Afghan men in suits and two uniformed officers had sauntered into the bar and taken a table at the back of the room. Tamim quickly conferred with our sheepish security guard, who had trailed them inside before hurrying over to speak with them. I quietly implored Al to tell me what to do.

'Do nothing. The guy with the beard is the local commander, but it's obviously not a raid. He's probably just trying to rattle you, hoping you might pay him to clear off.'

'Shouldn't I go and talk with him?'

'No. In fact, don't even make eye contact with him. Just keep doing what you're doing.'

What I was doing was completely freaking out so I chose to wipe down the counter instead. Tamim hurried back to retrieve cans of Red Bull.

'You right, buddy?' Al asked him.

'I think so.'

'Just relax, brother. They'll get bored and soon leave.'

But they didn't leave. They just sat in stony silence as most of our customers quietly slipped away. Tamim was seated with them. I tried to call Abdullah, but his phone was switched off, so, when Tamim came back to fetch another round of energy drinks, Al stepped up.

'Here, let me carry those for you, brother.'

As he deposited the cans on their table, Al amped up the smile. Hand to his chest, he bowed and introduced himself, and they all actually stood to make his acquaintance. Al then settled himself into their sombre circle and proceeded to hold the floor.

I have no idea what tales he was telling that night, but the laughter never stopped; the commander continually gripped Al's shoulder in an obvious show of appreciation. Finally they took their leave and as they stopped briefly at the bar to hug and kiss their new friend, the commander handed Al his business card. I poured myself a generous voddy and ensured there was a beer waiting for my saviour when he returned from the gate.

'That old commander, Shakib, offered me a job. Can you believe that shit?' Al laughed as he guzzled back his reward.

The kitchen boys would start arriving soon and I was still in bed, dozing off the morning's dog-whistling wake-up call and last night's late bedtime.

Al had been determined to take me out; I hadn't been anywhere since my arrival and he figured that I needed a taste of Kabul nightlife beyond The Den. I'd resisted his overtures all evening but, after cashing up and locking the takings away in the safe, I discovered that he and Wayne—his new buddy, who had just started working with him—were still seated at the bar and waiting for me.

Tamim agreed that I should go, but he felt obliged to issue a few kindly instructions to Al before we jumped into the taxi.

'You be a good man tonight, Al. Don't start fighting and getting yourself into trouble. I am trusting you to look after my Trudi.'

'*My* Trudi, buddy.'

'You wish, Al.'

We headed to a Do-Gooder bar across town and the difference in clientele was markedly noticeable. Slight, fresh-faced fellows sipped on spirits and talked earnestly about their work, while posses of pretty young things gossiped and giggled and strenuously avoided making eye contact with the male members of my troupe. I was out on the ran-tan with my mates and my new life finally felt normal . . . But then it all turned a tad sideways.

On our way out, a French guy sporting a salwar kameez attempted to steal our taxi. Al grabbed him by the arm.

'Listen here, you French fucker. I have to get this lady safely home. So you either back away from the taxi or I will crush your windpipe until your fucking eyes pop.'

As the poor bewildered chap scuttled back inside the bar, Al made an elaborate show of opening the car door and ushering me inside. He lowered his eyes and smiled like a child, expecting a pat on the head for his remarkable gallantry.

I thumped him on the arm instead, but still thanked him. Grey is grey is grey . . . and I'd accepted I couldn't have him any other way.

2.
Sticky-tape, Spit and String

I felt like the oldest person in the world. Just four weeks into my new life in Afghanistan, Paul came good on his promise of television work and I was now spending my days surrounded by youngsters, barely out of their teens, who positively skipped and giggled as they went about creating and producing some of the most successful shows on Afghan TV. If it weren't for Paul's greying sideburns, offering me some assurance that I wasn't hopelessly out of place in this land of relentless youth, I would have most certainly considered high-tailing it home again, where I would take to a rocking chair and find contentment by boring all and sundry with my fabulous tales of managing a bar in Kabul.

I was now working for the country's largest and most successful media company, Moby Media Group, established in 2003 by the Mohseni family. The three brothers and one sister who owned and primarily ran the business had no background in media and all had had successful careers in other fields back in Australia, before returning to Afghanistan soon after the fall of the Taliban with a view to helping rebuild their homeland.

I could only marvel at the balls and bravado it must have taken for these people to enter into a market where television had been banned for a solid decade and create their company from scratch. They started with a solitary radio station and now boasted two television channels, catering to both their Pashto- and Dari-speaking audiences (Pashto and Dari being the two official languages of Afghanistan), plus two radio stations, a production company, an IT company and some print media.

The first time I met Jahid Mohseni, the CEO, he was perched on top of a six-metre-high rickety bamboo ladder, adjusting the lights in the news studio—he was instant-crush material. I would label it a schoolgirl crush, but at 38 years old even he was younger than me.

There was a head office in Dubai but, from what I could gather, all the action happened here in Kabul. Jahid regularly worked sixteen-hour days, only returning to Dubai on the weekends to spend precious time with his family, while his brothers, Saad and Zaid, regularly flew in and out to help run the operation.

Paul told me tales of the death threats and government intimi-dation they endured for maintaining their progressive brand of television. When a young woman dared to let her headscarf slip and chanced a slight bum wiggle during an episode of *Afghan Star* (a singing show loosely based on the *Idol* franchise) there was a terrific uproar—conservative Afghans demanded that she die for her sins and the poor girl was forced to go into hiding. Journalists had been beaten and kidnapped; actresses were harassed in the streets. The Mohseni family's worthy vision of a free and unfettered media landscape came at a high and terrifying price.

There were around a dozen expats working here for their enterprise and most of them were in business development. Paul, Jose and I constituted the production contingent and the remaining few were scattered across IT, finance and technical services. We represented a tiny foreign drop in an ocean of close to a thousand Afghan employees, with an average age of just twenty-four.

I had been hired to write an eight-part drama serial that was being funded by a foreign embassy. There were a lot of people interested in 'changing the hearts and minds' of the population through the media. Various embassies, the US State Department, aid agencies, ISAF (the International Security Assistance Force, the official name for the NATO-led mission), different arms of the UN and the Afghan government all used radio and television to preach about—amongst other things—corruption, good governance, reconciliation, security, insurgency, education, democracy, health and women's rights.

This new serial, called *Salam,* was a vehicle for counter-narcotics messaging. A basic narrative had been written: in it a young man, addicted to heroin, was unwittingly used to blow up a bus and so killed his sister. He did a runner to his father's home village and, with the guidance of a mystical, all-knowing elder, found redemption. But that was as far as the original writer ever got with it. When I came on board the project was lagging just a little—in truth it should have been broadcast six months before. During the weeks when I was transitioning from working at The Den to working at Moby, Paul and I developed the storyline further, spending our evenings plotting out the serial on large pieces of paper taped to our living-room wall. I was now on board full time, and had roughly one month to script the entire show or we risked losing our funding altogether.

To me, Kabul appeared to be held together with sticky-tape, spit and string. There were brassy, glassed-in office blocks here and there and the odd paved road. There were even a couple of sets of traffic lights that I never saw working; but by and large it was a ramshackle, crumbling, red-hot mess. For some reason I expected the country's premier television broadcaster to have a little more shine, a tad more finesse. But I was sorely mistaken.

On my first day of work I shared a car with Paul and Jose. As our jeep idled at the boom gate and we waited for the security guards to allow us through, I tried to figure out exactly what I was looking at. I was staring down a short, potholed street lined with rundown buildings. Armed guards buzzed around everywhere and armies of kids, who looked just out of high school, alighted from HiAce vans, chatting and laughing as they ambled in to work.

'Is . . . Is . . . Is . . . Is this it?' I managed with a newly acquired stammer.

Jose giggled.

'Oh darls, you haven't seen anything yet!' Paul offered as we rumbled along the road.

There was no formal orientation, no meet-and-greet. Instead, after having my bag searched by a smiling, moustachioed guard—and my camera, perfume and USB stick confiscated—Paul guided me along a labyrinth of uneven pathways, past grubby, paint-flaked buildings, to a tiny office that would normally be regarded as rather snug, even for a single person.

There were two Afghan men already stationed on the right with their backs against the wall—Raouf, the Pashto-language channel manager and Rashid, the Dari-language channel manager. Paul's desk was wedged into the left-hand back corner of the room, positioned at a slight angle so he could slip in behind it, and he laughed as he indicated that my official workstation was at one end of it, so that the back of my chair was jammed up against Raouf's desk.

Paul also took great delight in informing me that I had to share his laptop. For security reasons I couldn't bring in my own personal computer, but he assured me that he would be running around for most of the day, overseeing various productions and the construction of our soon-to-be state-of-the-art news studio. This meant there would be joyous hours at a time when I could embrace the full length and width of our joint desk and indulge in uninterrupted scripting. Jose was closeted next door with around twenty other producers, sharing a handful of bulky beige PCs of a circa 1997 vintage, so I felt quite privileged.

There was an air conditioner clinging to the back wall but, with its constant dripping, its primary purpose seemed to be to keep the carpet next to Raouf's desk permanently wet. We kept the door closed to retain what little cool air it begrudgingly emitted and I was grateful that both my colleagues were deodorant devotees.

Working at The Den had spoilt me. While I spent my time there getting around in T-shirts, shorts and dresses, my new public persona required considerably more coverage. Jenny the Swedish chiropractor and Sue had donated a veritable wardrobe of long-sleeved tops, trousers and full-length skirts to supplement my meagre booty of 'acceptable' attire, and Jose had done a run to the bazaar to top up my paltry headscarf collection. The headscarf came off as soon as I entered work and I spent my days at my desk with my pants rolled up to the knee and my sleeves shoved back as far as they would go. Paul questioned the appropriateness of this, but I was too bloody hot to care.

The toilet was directly across from our office. A single unit that catered to the needs of around forty people and, with the water going on and off all day and the cleaners not overly keen to attend to it, it was a stinking, heave-worthy affair. There was a sign on the wall with diagrams indicating that people should not stand on the seat, wash their feet in the toilet bowl or perform some ambiguous routine that appeared to involve cocking one leg and urinating on the door.

My mantra became 'It smells like somebody died in there!', but I had to desist from saying this when, one night, an employee from our dubbing department actually did die in there. The story went that he had a brain aneurism, but with fundamental Islamic law holding that the deceased should be buried within forty-eight hours of death and that autopsies constituted a violation of the human body, there was no way of knowing for sure what really happened to the poor fellow.

Rashid (the Dari manager) spent most of his time with his head-phones on watching Hindi music videos, so there was no real room for meaningful dialogue there. Raouf (the Pashtun manager) seemed to do little more than sit cross-legged on his chair, chewing tobacco and smiling at me. Occasionally he went into a frenzy of mouse activity, but a quick peek at his computer revealed that he was merely clicking all over his screen saver. It all made perfect sense when, a few days into my job, he bashfully asked me to show him how to send an email.

I really dug Raouf, and early on I figured that he liked me too when he flagged the possibility of taking on a second wife. Paul had warned me to expect this type of attention, so naturally I assumed Raouf was referring to me. Not wanting to offend my new friend, hand on heart I told him that I was extremely flattered, but that I wasn't really on the lookout for a husband.

'Not you, Tooti. You too old!' came his tactful response.

Paul thought this was hilarious, but he still cautioned me against being too familiar with the male staff and suggested that I stop calling Raouf 'darling'. I call everyone 'darling'—babies, old men, teenagers and dogs, but I promised to try to excise the term from my vocabulary. Of course it proved impossible.

So, instead, I explained to my Afghan colleagues that everyone in Australia used the word in the same way that they used the word *Jan* (dear) when they were talking to one another. They instantly bought that, although I couldn't help laughing the first time a hulking great security guard, wielding an AK-47, greeted me at the gate with a laboured but chirpy 'Hello, darling. How are you?'

Raouf was very keen to improve his English and, seeing as I was writing a show for his channel, I figured he could help me come to terms with Pashtun culture. We were a match made in Jannah.

While Rashid spent his days bumping and grinding to the latest hits from India, Raouf and I started to get into a groove of our own. His favourite cartoon was *Popeye*, a morning staple on his channel and although my first priority should perhaps have been coaching him to master the pronunciation of my name, I opted for teaching him the words to the theme tune. I couldn't exactly envisage a time when he would be moved to utter Popeye's grammatically challenged declaration about the body building benefits of spinach munching but after a week he was able to growl out a semi-recognisable rendition of the song and we high-fived our success.

Raouf's lessons for me had a more practical flavour and I was soon able to say 'Hello. How are you?', 'Have a great day!' and 'You are very beautiful!' in Pashto. However our lack of a common language meant that his assistance on the drama serial was almost negligible. We gave it a bloody good go though. I drew diagrams for him on my white board and felt I was quickly becoming a dab hand at charades.

But I effectively threw in the towel the day I was trying to ascertain from Raouf what types of animals Afghan farmers keep. I commenced my enquiry by drawing a big fluffy ball on four legs and bleating out my best 'Baa'.

'Chicken?' was his serious response. We laughed a lot, but it was clear that I was really getting nowhere, so I was assigned a script consultant.

Habib, my script consultant, was a middle-aged Afghan poet living in Scandinavia. He was a song lyricist and political cartoonist who was granted asylum in the West in 1998. Undoubtedly an intelligent and courageous man— he was badly injured in a politically motivated knife attack on a trip back to Kabul in 2002—he unfortunately knew very little about television.

Habib and I conducted our script sessions over Skype and, whereas I simply wanted to know whether Pashtun villagers sat on chairs at tables, he was fixated on the symbolism and imagery of the show. He wanted to add a scene with two ants fighting, and another that featured a goat with burning gold coins for eyes, drowning in a river. I struggled to convince him that filming warring insects was not a possibility and that I was not prepared to drown a goat, particularly as I didn't really get the symbolism. His response was always the same: 'You're not Afghan.' No, I most certainly was not.

I finally succeeded in creating in English something resembling a drama series, and blessedly it was approved by our patient and long-suffering client. And then the real job began, as the whole shebang had to be translated into Pashto.

Fortunately I was assigned a lively, quick-witted man who was kind, wise and unflappable. Khan had attended university in India and travelled extensively throughout the region, but I still managed to fascinate him. It only took him a week to ask the question that I have been asked a hundred times since: 'But why aren't you married?'

My answer was always the same: 'Because I don't have to be.' But the way Khan sadly shook his head signalled the genuine pity and sorrow he felt for his ageing buddy, who could only resort to some feeble platitude to defend her shameful spinsterhood.

Khan's regular job was to provide translations for English-language films. With no intellectual property laws in Afghanistan, he simply would go to the local bazaar, pick up a pirated DVD and then write the script in Pashto for our dubbing department. *Voila!* Two hours of TV programming done and dusted. In fact, the first time I saw *Avatar* was on our Pashto-language channel.

Khan had to be particularly careful about the films he selected. They couldn't contain any sex scenes—even a kiss was considered taboo—and any untoward sexual content had to be edited out. Our in-house censors judiciously took the axe to other sensitive material as well—divorce, illegitimate children and extra-marital affairs all found their way to the cutting-room floor and the films were regularly hacked to the point where they didn't make sense anymore.

But violence never seemed to be an issue—I watched *Die Hard* at ten in the morning in Kabul. He also tried to avoid films that featured too much flesh as our editors had to painstakingly pixelate any female skin visible between the head and feet.

Khan had an excellent grasp of English but, at times, we had to resort to the diagrams and charade routine. *Caves, coffins, crestfallen*—so many words and concepts had to be explained or simplified, and Habib's comparatively progressive contributions to the script all had to be carefully reviewed. It seemed that behaviour that would be deemed acceptable TV fodder for an urban Dari-speaking audience just wasn't going to cut it with our more conservative, rural Pashtun viewers. One scene that I had written in and that had passed Habib's filter without question had two of our characters hugging. They were a married couple, were fully clothed and were embracing in their bedroom following the husband receiving some good news about a job promotion. Khan was adamant that I should amend the scene, and I laughed when he suggested that perhaps they just briefly grip each other's shoulders to mark their joy. After much debate, I decided to keep it in; the censors could always knock it on the head if they deemed it too amorous and racy.

Khan couldn't type and so did all of his work by hand. Once he completed a script, one of the writers on our Pashto-language channel, Sapa, bashed it out on a keyboard for him; Khan then did his edits before Sapa again typed up the revisions. We were just nearing the end of this laborious process for the *Salam* script when it was brought to my attention that a further translation of the scripts was required. Inevitably, most of the crew would be Dari speakers and the Pashto version would make as little sense to them as the

English version. They would need a Dari version so they could follow what was going on. I had hoped that Khan would have time to do the translation, but he was simply too busy with his own work to assist and so we needed to start from scratch. The only consolation was that my Dari translator could actually type.

I was despairing of ever emerging from this soupy, word-muddled mire. But when I finally did come up for air, I was hit with a proposal that took my breath away all over again.

Paul wanted me to produce the series. I was to oversee the entire production, mentor the crew and live in Jalalabad—a rural Pashtun town three hours outside of Kabul—for the duration of the ten-week shoot. I had worked in television for twelve years but had never produced a drama serial and the idea seemed utterly preposterous. But I was stupid and blindly adventurous, and so, with my boyfriend Nick's blessing, I agreed to extend my stay in Afghanistan.

My friends back home told me that I was crazy, and indeed I was. I was bat-shit crazy. Crazy in love with this country I was in . . . with Raouf, Khan and the inexperienced kiddies who Paul had started to crudely assemble into some kind of crew.

Nick wondered how I'd cope as a woman supervising an all-male team in an Islamic country, but I assured him that I'd manage because I was old, forty-five years old, and verging on ancient. I was older than most of their mothers, who they uniformly loved and respected with a passion that was fanatical beyond religious persuasion.

In a country where around forty-seven per cent of the population was under the age of fifteen and the life expectancy tragically stood at just forty-four, I was practically an elder.

3.
The Search for Salam

I had managed to fit the huge, wooden bowl into my luggage when I left Kabul. But after a full day of shopping in Bangkok resulting in a healthy haul of shoes, tops, dresses and some saucy underwear that barely fit where it touched, I just couldn't seem to squeeze it in anymore. I briefly considered leaving this beautifully carved object in Thailand, but that was a shameful notion, which I instantly dismissed. The bowl had been given to me as a gift for my mum by Sidique, one of my lovely young producers on the *Salam* shoot, and I'd promised to email him photos of her holding it. I ended up stuffing into it a single sandal, a top and my newly acquired lacy bras and knickers (which all seemed a little wrong and distasteful, considering the bowl was a present from a devout Muslim boy to a seventy-eight-year-old woman) and then I managed to zip my suitcase shut while sitting on it.

I had left Afghanistan with a swag of get-well gifts from my team for Mum—bracelets, scarves and said bowl (which was roughly the size of my head)—together with promises that they would pray daily to Allah for her recovery to good health. It was October 2009 and I was heading home to nurse her, following open-heart surgery; she was to be released from the rehabilitation centre in two days' time.

When I'd first headed to Afghanistan, I'd assured my family and friends that I was only a day away; if I ever needed to come home for any reason, I could be on the first flight out. I was proven to be a big, fat liar on a Friday, five weeks before my Bangkok stopover, when my brother called me to say that Mum had been hospitalised following some general pain in her chest and was having triple bypass surgery the following Monday. The operation was fairly routine—well, by Australian standards anyway—but her doctor had carefully outlined all the risks inherent in a woman of her age going under anaesthetic and I desperately wanted to see her before she went into surgery.

We were shooting in Jalalabad and I immediately got online and began checking flights. Factoring in my three-hour trip back to Kabul, a quick pack and a brief transit in Dubai, I could be back in Sydney at nine-thirty on the night before surgery. Then I made a call to Shafi, our wonderful, accommodating assistant to the CEO, and began outlining my itinerary. He stopped me before I'd even got to the flight details and reminded me that I didn't have a passport—it was currently with the ministry because I was having my visa renewed. There was no way he could get it back in time for me to travel. I felt physically sick, and it took me a good hour to compose myself and call my brother to deliver the news.

The surgery was a success and a family decision was made that I should stay on in Afghanistan to finish the shoot and arrive back in Australia in time to look after Mum once she was released from hospital. The plan was to stay in Sydney for six weeks before returning to Kabul to supervise post-production on *Salam*. In truth, my team still had two days of filming to go when I deserted them, but I felt that I needed to decompress in a luxury hotel in Bangers for a few days before I hit home.

After close to seven months in Afghanistan, I needed to tend to cracks in my heels you could slip a five-cent piece into and a strip of hair regrowth the width of my arm. I wanted to reward my stomach with something other than rice and kebab and street-stall chicken, and I longed to slough off the dust and dirt accumulated in eight weeks of tramping all across the Nangarhar countryside.

For three days running I allowed firm, expert hands to massage away the stress of perhaps the most exhausting, but also the most exhilarating, job I had ever undertaken. And I was not worried about abandoning my team to go it alone because I was leaving them in the capable hands of Aleem, my senior producer, who had just turned nineteen.

When Paul had first introduced me to Aleem, I honestly wondered why there was a fourteen-year-old kid working for the company. I could literally count the wispy, soft hairs on his chin (four) and, as he stood quietly telling me about his love of television, I was considering the very real possibility that my tiny hands could comfortably encircle his slight little waist. But he was, in fact, eighteen, had been with Moby for six months, had never worked on a drama production and would be one of my producers on *Salam*.

Twenty-year-old Sidique had already been assigned to me and, having been with Moby for two years, was a veritable TV veteran. Again, no experience in drama but he was sassy and smart and he knew his way around the company, which was an unwieldy beast that I still hadn't learnt to properly navigate. And soon after Aleem came a clever and gorgeous Hazara girl, Zahra, but she would have to divide her time between working on *Salam* and producing a cooking show.

As we began making props lists and costume lists and plans for Jalalabad, I eagerly awaited more appointments—maybe a production assistant or two, an enthusiastic young runner, a set dresser who could maybe double as a wardrobe consultant. To his rascally credit, Paul spent a good two weeks deflecting my queries about extra staff and only finally addressed the issue one night over dinner and after a bottle of wine.

He offered me one of those good-news-bad-news scenarios. The good news was that Paul's partner, Jose, was coming on board. Hooray! A hairdresser by trade, Jose had been working as the company's resident stylist before he'd moved into production. He, too, was a TV newbie, but he'd quickly made his mark as a leader of men, by virtue of being street smart (as you would expect from a worldly, well-travelled Colombian) and a good few years older than the other producers. Plus I loved him and would have a fellow expat and friend to tread this strange new terrain with. The bad news was that Jose would be the final addition to my production team. *Boo . . . hoo-hoo-hoo-hoo.*

In the following weeks, I managed to convince a gutsy friend of mine, Tiggy, to come across from Australia as my first assistant director in exchange for food, accommodation and a modest monthly allowance. She claimed she was after adventure, but I still maintain that what got her across the line was my declaration that the ratio of men to women in Kabul was a solid nine to one.

Between all of us, we would cover casting, wardrobe, set-dressing, location scouting, props buying, scheduling, budgeting, catering . . . and any other random tasks associated with making an eight-part drama series. And when Zahra left the company early into the shoot to study full time at university, our pitiable little tribe dwindled to five. My two directors were also thoroughly green but enthusiastic, and I was genuinely freaked out about being the 'expert' on set.

Our first job was to hold auditions for the main roles. Tiggy was still making her way over, so Aleem, Sidique, Jose, Zahra, Raouf and myself would travel to Jalalabad to hold the casting. We made a general call for actors on local radio and television and within two days we had at least fifty males signed up to try out for a twenty-something drug addict and a forty-five- to fifty-five-year-old mystical elder, plus miscellaneous police officers, insurgents, a mullah and a couple of kids.

Our actresses all needed to be imported from Pakistan as Afghan Pashtun women were traditionally forbidden by their families from appearing on TV; we would select them through photos, CVs and the recommendations of one of Raouf's mates.

I had chosen audition pieces for each of the male characters, but was told by Aleem that we had no way of getting them to the actors beforehand—very few of them would have access to email and almost none of them to a printer—so we would simply ask them to improvise something appropriate on the day. I had my doubts about this, but Raouf assured me there was nothing to worry about. He was a native of Nangarhar Province, where filmmaking was apparently prolific; the capital of Nangarhar, Jalalabad, had even earned itself the moniker 'Jallywood' for its abundance of producers, directors and actors: 'These good actors. These best actors. These actors too perfect!'

Who was I to argue against such a stunning recommendation?

We were holding our auditions in the 'reception hall' of the hotel where we were staying—a gloomy, cavernous room that smelt like wet towels and fresh wee. We had called the actors for 10am; by 9.30am there were close to one hundred men milling around outside, waiting for their moment to shine. Zahra was stationed at the door taking names and making ID cards; inside, Jose manned the camera while Aleem and Sidique played warm bodies in scenes where actors demanded one. Raouf assessed their ability to speak Pashto, and I was primarily on acting watch. We had imagined it would be a seamless, conveyor-belt operation, but it quickly became a dog's breakfast.

Our actors had no idea what parts they were auditioning for so, as they stepped up to the mark, we gave them a quick once-over—we made a brief round-the-room assessment as to whether they looked like an insurgent, a policeman or a drug addict—and then threw them some kind of improvisational bone to gnaw on. Following each performance, another round of nods, winks and mutterings sealed our appraisal of their work before we sent them on their way.

I smiled brightly every time I relegated an actor to the trash heap: 'Yeah ... no. Maybe he could be a village extra,' I'd offer in hurried

English, cracking my best face-splitting grin. Raouf, on the other hand, relishing his role as dramatic arbiter, would scowl, shake his head with unnecessary animation and usually offer a hearty double thumbs-down to indicate his disdain for their performance.

Aleem and Sidique weren't far behind in the ruthlessness stakes, constantly stifling giggles and groaning mid-routine. At one point, after a 'drug addict' made a particularly poor show of going through withdrawal, snarling and crawling around on the floor like a rabid dog, Raouf approached him and appeared to give him a solid dressing down. When I asked Aleem to translate, he explained that he was telling the unfortunate sod that he had shamed himself by acting so badly.

I convened a quick meeting before the next lamb was led to the slaughter, suggesting that we all perhaps show a little more respect for our thespian friends. But Jose was the only one to agree with me; the others all thought that demeaning hapless actors was an eminently acceptable sport, the general consensus being that they shouldn't be auditioning if they didn't have the chops.

'You not Afghan,' Raouf declared, by way of closing this argument, and once again I had to concede that I most certainly was not.

We came away from our first excursion to Jalalabad with a handful of sound, worthy actors and a local fixer, who undertook to scout locations for us while we were back in Kabul. But we still hadn't found our lead character, Salam. Most of the young actors whose performances we had suffered through at the casting had clearly learnt their 'craft' watching Bollywood films, but what might have been 'too perfect' for some cheesy Hindi song-and-dance routine just wasn't going to cut it on our drama serial. Admittedly, I'd hardly written a modern-day *Macbeth*, but it was at least worthy of a leading man who could indicate 'feeling tired' with a tad more subtlety than vigorously rubbing his eyes with balled-up fists and mock yawning.

We decided to start fishing around for our lead actor in Kabul, and Jose and Sidique put a call out over TV and radio and began the audition process all over again. We agreed that Jose would only show Paul and me footage of truly promising candidates, but after close to a week of castings we had yet to sight a single frame.

I can't recall now what I was doing when Jose phoned me and demanded that I immediately make my way to the audition room. We were both feeling a little jaded by that stage and had taken to wickedly re-enacting some of the poorer performances we had witnessed in Jalalabad. 'Snarling Dog Man' was a particular favourite, as was the 'Psycho Insurgent' who had wandered around the room mumbling to himself for about five minutes before pulling out an imaginary knife and stabbing himself repeatedly in the chest.

So I hurried over, half-expecting to see some terrifying routine that superseded all acting atrocities that had come before. Instead, Jose introduced me to Atiqullah, a striking young fellow whom I could instantly picture playing Salam. He had studied acting at university and was part of a local theatre company. As Sidique once again put him through his paces, we all knew that we had our man.

Paul got on board with our decision rather quickly: he was consumed with multiple broadcasts covering the upcoming presidential elections and was happy for us to make the call. The only other person we needed to convince was my old mate Raouf.

'No, Tooti. This no good,' he declared after watching the audition tape.

'No, Raouf. This very good. Very, very good!' I countered.

Raouf had been gunning all along for a mate of his to play Salam. His candidate was some minor Jallywood celebrity whose depiction of 'anguish' over killing his sister involved him ripping open his pink satin shirt, dropping to his knees and beating his fists on the floor, so I was a little sceptical about Raouf's appraisal of Atiqullah's performance. However, with the assistance of Aleem, I discovered that the problem wasn't with Atiqullah's acting but with his accent: it seemed he spoke excellent Pashto, but it wasn't *Nangarhar* Pashto and that would put him out of kilter with the actors we had already cast.

I was already across the Pashto-accent-dilemma as our Pakistani actresses were all going to have their voices dubbed for the very same reason, but I was determined not to lose Atiqullah. I called him back into the office that same day and explained the situation. He understood completely and promised to present himself to us the next afternoon with a perfect Nangarhar Pashto accent.

I excitedly divulged this latest development to Raouf but, after indulging in a lengthy stretch of tobacco chewing, followed by the ceremonial spit into the bin, he declared that it simply couldn't be done. I explained to him that actors often have to modify their accents for certain roles and then demonstrated to him all the different ways, in accented English, that I could say 'Hello, Raouf. How are you?' I did typical British, Irish, American and a guttural German, plus a poor facsimile of Indian, complete with a head wobble.

But he just laughed at me. 'You just say: "Hello, Raouf. How are you?" What you saying? This all you saying, Tooti: "Hello, Raouf. How are you?"' My finely nuanced performance was completely lost on him.

The next day we all gathered in the audition room to watch Atiqullah perform. I spent the entire time with my eyes fixed on Raouf, but he was inscrutable. Afterwards he engaged Atiqullah in some serious-sounding banter before finally turning to me with a smile: 'He good, Tooti. This very good Pashto. Little, little more learning but he be very good Salam.'

I held up my hand for a high-five, but Raouf left me hanging—he felt it was more of a double thumbs-up moment.

Four weeks after our first visit to Jalalabad, we ventured back, to check on our fixer's progress. Nick was visiting me at the time and, posing as my husband, came along for the ride. Tiggy had also just arrived in the country and was excited to meet the team and get cracking.

Despite being paid handsomely for his services, the fixer had basically done bugger-all. Our requests to see his recommendations for the school, the village, the police station, the mosque . . . were all met with a vacant stare followed by frantic phone calls as he attempted to line up something—anything—for his impatient employers.

The man was a friend of Raouf's, so his lack of location-scouting chops didn't attract the ire that I thought it quite rightly deserved. But, after a day of trudging around in forty-five-degree heat with absolutely zero results, Tiggy unleashed a spray at him that was completely justified, boldly articulated and would have been perfectly fine if it had not been publicly delivered by a beautiful young woman to a proud Pashtun man.

'This is fucking ridiculous! You haven't done a thing! You are incompetent, lazy and completely disorganised! What the fuck have you been doing for the past month?'

Although the meaning of her rant was lost on him (and no doubt most of our entourage), her intention was abundantly clear, and the shocked silence that followed the tirade indicated that it wasn't terribly well received.

'This no good. She loud woman. She angry woman,' Raouf warned me as we made our way back to the van.

And that evening, when most of the team turned up very late for a production meeting that Tiggy had called and she cut loose again, I quite literally had a revolution on my hands. After the meeting was over, an indignant delegation cornered me to inform me that they were not willing to stand by and be shamed by this angry little western woman.

Tiggy, a very attractive thirty-six-year-old, looked a good ten years younger. Apparently she wasn't going to be able to pull off the revered elder–mother persona that I had so effortlessly managed to foster for myself. My pang of jealousy was sharp but fleeting.

As Nick lay in bed reading a book, I was up and down all night; I joined Aleem and Sidique on the balcony, Raouf in the garden and Tiggy in her room. It was like a classic French farce, with doors opening and closing all over the joint, complete with covert entrances and exits, and whispered conversations in the dark.

During the course of this interminably hot evening, I made it perfectly clear that I wasn't going to accept the 'You're-Not-Afghan' argument anymore. We were attempting to make television to western standards, and it required discipline, commitment and everyone generally doing their jobs. I was quite prepared to shame anyone who wasn't prepared to work.

When it came to Tiggy, my argument was simple and succinct. I warned her that, if she didn't dial it down a bit, she'd probably get shot.

On the streets of Kabul, shooting *Salam* with Tiggy and the team. We were always guaranteed to draw a crowd: 'Quick everyone! There's a crew and some old, foreign bird making a TV show in our street!'

On the road with the boys in Jalalabad, about to shoot a car chase scene.

The team at work on *Salam* in Jalalabad. We were filming in the grounds of our hotel as a security threat had closed down most of the city.

Turning a blind eye to OH&S practices—our cameramen were often forced to improvise to get the shot.

A security guard on duty at my guest house. Guns are very handy for lots of reasons.

A rather inventive and original solution for shooting on *Salam*.

The infamous 'boy-down-the-well' shoot, with some of the child actors I forbade to go to school. *Inset:* The boy down the well.

The glamour of making TV. On set, in a tiny, airless, mud hut in 37-degree heat. At least I didn't have to 'sleep' under a woollen blanket, like our child actor.

Shooting a scene for *Salam* in the village. A motorcycle, an actor who couldn't ride it, excited children and a man leaping onto the road—yep, that looks safe.

How to create a gunshot wound in Afghanistan. Not the way they normally do it.

With the *Salam* crew, in the mountains of Nangarhar. I found out a few days later that the area we filmed in hadn't yet been properly de-mined. Whoops.

Setting up on my final day on the *Salam* shoot. Once again, flagrantly ignoring accepted OH&S practices (and child-labour laws).

Filming our Army TV spots in Mazar-e-Sharif. I think the gun I'm posing with was unloaded.

Front-row view of a Buzkashi game in Mazar-e-Sharif. It's not really wise to be this close—these guys have serious attitude.

Hero shot. The Army shoot, Jalalabad. The safest I've ever felt filming in Afghanistan.

Just hanging out on a helicopter and manning the machine gun. As you do.

4.
Jallywood

The start of the *Salam* shoot coincided with the Afghan presidential elections of August 2009 and, one week before we were due to travel to Jalalabad, our head of security, Ahmad, told us that it was too dangerous to go. Our client had already cut us considerable slack and we couldn't possibly delay any longer, so we selected a series of scenes that we could shoot locally and moved production to Kabul until it was safe to travel. A bombed-out palace on the outskirts of the city would become our junkie den and one of the security guards at work generously offered up his house (essentially relegating the nine family members who lived there to an out-building at the back of the small compound) as the location for our lead character's home.

Our Jalalabad actors were excited to come to the capital; our Pakistani actresses not so much. While they were prepared to hop illegally across the border and make the short trip to Jallywood, travelling further west into Kabul was a whole other scene. As the only Pashto speaker in our troupe, Aleem was quickly dispatched to Peshawar, their home base in Pakistan, to negotiate with them. He sat with their husbands, fathers, mothers and brothers, drinking endless cups of tea and attempting to smooth things over. In consultation with myself and management, he renegotiated the terms of their contracts, ensuring them a third of their pay upfront and the rest when filming wrapped. And when one of the actresses ultimately refused to come, he held a hurried audition to find a replacement.

When the women finally arrived, Aleem was their confidant, protector and friend, and every concern or complaint that they had (of which there were many) was conveyed to me through that darling slip of a boy. They didn't like the food and they were unhappy with their costumes. Because Ahmad was convinced they were all sex workers, he had forbidden them from leaving their guest house at night. They turned up on set each day with a fresh list of complaints and teary declarations that they would abandon us altogether if the situation didn't improve. It took a considerable amount of consoling, cajoling and some hardline negotiating with our security chief to keep them on board.

The actress we had chosen to play Fatema, the progressive, university-educated and unmarried sister of our lead character, arrived in Kabul looking considerably larger than when I had viewed her in photographs a few months earlier. Cool bananas, it wasn't necessary for our shining star of Afghan womanhood to be a size six. Then, four days after she arrived, Aleem was called up in the middle of the night to take her to hospital. She was vomiting, she was feverish—she was five months pregnant. She didn't seem bothered by this development and nor did her mother, whom we had selected to play her on-screen mum. Fortunately Fatema was going to be blown up in a bus explosion in episode one, so we didn't have to recast the role.

By the time we returned to Jalalabad three weeks later, Aleem had established himself as the father of the whole tribe. And when, just a week into the shoot, Jose, Tiggy and I relocated to the only western guest house in town due to our rather precious distaste for cold showers, rats and being gawked at by turban-wearing men every time we left our rooms, he assumed this role with supreme authority. He stayed up late at night; he ran through the lines for the next day's scenes with the actresses; he lectured the other boys about keeping it down when they partied and played poker in their rooms; and he woke up an hour earlier than everyone else so as to get the crew organised and to work on time. When they finally all made it to the set each day, it was with great relief that he handed the reins over to me.

We had two security guards assigned to us for the duration of the shoot. Zarhawar, who was a native of Nangarhar, stayed with us on a full-time basis while various other guards came and went throughout our time in Jalalabad. Zarhawar was a habitually smiling Pashtun man who had me sussed out from the get-go; he made it his personal mission to keep an eye on me. Through Aleem he issued my security briefing: 'No singing, no dancing, no clapping in public.'

I thought this was an odd directive. But he had observed me in Kabul for months before the shoot and his prohibition only made me realise how often I do, in fact, sing, dance and clap. I would tunelessly break into any little snippet of song that entered my head; I would jig with the sound man to the latest Hindi hit blaring from his phone and I would clap with joy after a particularly good take. My impulses were endless, but it only took one stern look from Zarhawar to shut them all down.

By the end of each shooting day, I would be like a mad street dog that had been tied to a fence all week; so, as soon as we were settled into our van, I would lead the team in a rousing rendition of the 'Zarhawar Song' to his immense embarrassment. The lyrics were simple and the tune consisted of only a few ascending notes; however, we would belt it out with gusto, clapping and swaying and jigging all the way back to our guest house: 'Zarhawar, Zarhawar. He's the king of Afghanistannnnn!'

And repeat. And repeat. And . . . repeat. Lame? Sure. But after a ten-hour shooting day in the middle of summer, it didn't take much to amuse us.

The guest house where we were staying, The Taj, was a heavily fortified affair and the other occupants were a mix of NGO workers, government advisors and their western security contractors. About a week into our stay, after we had rumbled into the compound in our battered HiAce van at the end of a long day of shooting and Zarhawar in his simple salwar kameez had casually walked us to the gate, one of the security contractors, Amy, hauled me aside to express her serious concerns about my personal safety. She believed that Jose and Tiggy, with their raven hair and olive complexions, could both easily pass as Afghan, but I was a stand-out fair-skinned blonde and an obvious target.

Amy was a scary bird—she had muscles where I didn't know muscles could exist. She would grab me around the waist with one arm, hoist me off the ground and carry me around the bar, and she had taken to calling me 'Pussycat'. She was head of security for one of the world's largest accountancy groups and, with another contractor, was safeguarding an auditor, Scott, who was working with local government.

Scott's entrances to The Taj were finely tuned events. Two armoured jeeps in convoy would roar down the driveway, stopping directly outside the gate to the guest house. Amy and her cohort would stride from their cars in perfect formation, guns drawn, before opening the door for their flak-jacketed client and marching him inside.

When I assured her I felt perfectly safe in Zarhawar's hands, she almost exploded. 'Are you fucking mad? Your life is in the hands of some local, dopey git wearing man jammies. Does he even have a gun?' I confessed that I wasn't entirely sure and she grunted more disgust. 'Oh, Pussycat, you are seriously fucking demented!'

Over the next two hours, and in between doing push-ups on the bar, she alternately interrogated and lectured me on security. No, I didn't own personal protective equipment, nor had I ever taken part in any drills on kidnapping-prevention techniques. No, I didn't have a 'proof of life' question. What was a 'proof of life' question, anyway?

I quickly learnt that I, too, was a 'dopey git' and that a 'proof of life' question is a personal question about yourself that hostage takers are asked to provide when they need to prove that you are still alive.

'Oh, like my date of birth,' I offered.

'No, you daft twat! It can't be something they can find on the internet! Something like: what was the name of your first dog.'

'Okay, that can be my "proof of life" question.'

'It's no use having one if nobody in your company is going to ever fucking ask it!'

By the end of our session she had given me a cover—I was now married with three children back in Australia to support, because my husband was terminally ill (apparently this might engender some sympathy from my captors). I had a silver ring for my wedding finger, to back this claim; even more effectively, I had a small, innocuous-looking hand torch with a base that was covered in tiny ridges of saw-like teeth. Amy showed me how, with a savage thrusting and twisting motion, I could use it to take out an eye. I asked her if she'd get me out of Jalalabad if the shit went down.

Hmmm . . . She wasn't really interested in looking out for some silly, blonde, western woman, but she'd consider it if I let her carry me upstairs to my room. I declined the offer but, quite powerless to resist, I was scooped up and carted to my door anyway.

Despite Amy's misgivings, I felt genuinely safe with Zarhawar. He was a local lad who clearly knew his way around and I personally believed that trundling around town in a local vehicle and hanging with my large Afghan posse made me comfortably inconspicuous. Plus, through Raouf's connections, we also had a small team of police officers who escorted us around each day, although most of them seemed to be permanently stoned. Because they would regularly desert us—to go and eat, to pray at the mosque or to do some real policing—Jose and I devised a game called 'What Would You Do if the Taliban Turned Up?' Our options were always limited, but we could be pretty creative.

'I'd grab a bamboo stalk, jump into that river, hide underwater and use the stalk as a snorkel.'

'I'd run over to those goats and crouch down in the middle of the herd.'

'I'd jump into the lighting box and close the lid.' (I had actually tested the lighting-box trick and found that I fitted inside quite nicely.)

What began as a game became a little more serious as the shoot wore on. Over time our police grew weary of the novelty of making television and, despite their regular demands for 'fuel money' always being met, they would often abandon us in the wilds of Nangarhar after only an hour or two of filming. Thankfully, we never got a chance to test any of our strategies. I strongly suspect that, if the Taliban had ever shown up, I'd have been capable of little more than wetting myself before completely passing out.

Our three weeks of shooting in Kabul had been manic and, at times, utterly shambolic. But Paul and Massood, the head of our production company, had ensured that we had all the resources and assistance needed to muddle our way through the last-minute change of tack. Khan came to the set each day, to coach the actors through their dialogue; if some piece of equipment or an important prop had been forgotten, members of staff back at the office would be hastily dispatched to bring it to us; a diligent, young producer, Merzad (who was already stretched thin overseeing a weekly soap opera) was delegated the task of arranging our transport to the set each day and making sure that all the crew arrived on time. But once we hit Jalalabad, our bare-bones team was on its own and I quickly realised that my various crew members worked strictly to rule.

The sound guy just did sound. If the lighting guy wasn't required to set up lights, he stayed in the van, snoozing away his hash hangover. Our cameraman had a rigid policy that he wouldn't carry anything else besides his lightweight camera as we trekked up mountains or waded across streams; he refused to contemplate that his free hand might possibly accommodate a tripod or a part of the crane. But with such a small team, this way of working was simply not feasible.

I initially thought I could lead by example. 'Hey, look at your boss! Watch me as I lug a beach umbrella and a make-up kit up a hill in 40-degree heat!' But, because I didn't have a specific role on set, they all thought it entirely reasonable that the 'boss' should earn her keep as a packhorse. Fair cop.

I coaxed, I wheedled, I joked, I jabbed . . . and finally, I yelled. I screamed my heart out—my throaty baritone reverberating around the Jalalabad basin. Fortunately, Zarhawar didn't consider 'bellowing like a fishwife' to be a security issue but, after about a week of this, Aleem confided to me that the crew got very scared when my eyes grew big and my face turned red. I gleefully told him to pass the news on that 'If they don't like it, then they shouldn't do anything to make me get like that.'

But it wasn't just the crew who copped it, I yelled at actors too. At times it was completely justified, even necessary.

One particular scene called for our drug dealer to get angry with his henchman and to slap him hard across the face. In rehearsals, he delivered a freakishly solid hit to the poor man's jaw and I quickly called a conference. I have never been a fan of method acting and I demonstrated how the slap could be realistically delivered on camera, while explaining that the *crack* could always be added later in post-production. But, with great artistic conviction and a liberal dose of derision, the actors explained through Aleem that this was the Afghan way—the drug dealer *would* be delivering a genuine slap, and the henchman was enormously happy to receive it.

So we shot the scene. Nine times. The drug dealer kept fluffing his lines and, after ten takes of being savagely beaten around the head, the henchman not surprisingly lost his love of method. He grabbed the drug dealer by the shirt, and an aggressive push and shove ensued. The director just stood back and let them vent, while the crew were delighted by the unexpected argy-bargy. It was only Mother's booming voice that settled the fracas down.

But there were times when my yelling shamed me beyond belief.

Another actor, Insurgent #1, stumbled through his very first scene for eighteen takes. It was thirty-seven degrees; we were surrounded by at least fifty noisy, excited spectators; and we were desperate to get the scene done before we lost light. I confess to also being pre-menstrual. So when, on the nineteenth take, he fumbled his words five seconds into the scene, I completely spat the dummy.

'You've had the script for three weeks! How can you not know your dialogue? This is completely unacceptable!'

He didn't speak a lick of English, but he totally got the gist. With his head bowed, he mumbled to Aleem and explained that he couldn't read. My bad. Our ingenious improvisational casting process hadn't factored in that eighty-six per cent of Afghans are illiterate. He was a major character, who we couldn't simply replace, so the incredibly dedicated Aleem volunteered to spend his nights coaching him for the rest of the shoot.

But my most mortifying moment was something that still makes me cringe and that Tiggy vowed she would never allow me to forget. Another stinking hot day, another huge scene, this time involving a boy being rescued from a well. Apart from Well Boy (a patient, sweet little fellow, who spent most of the shoot sitting at the bottom of a stinking, muddy, two-metre hole), we had fifteen child extras; it seemed that everyone in the village had come out to watch their son, brother, nephew or cousin perform for the camera. The well rescue also included a donkey, which was skittish and stubborn and was constantly trotting out of shot. Between the mental donkey, the noisy crowd and every second take being marred by some starry-eyed child looking directly at the camera, we were doing it tough.

Then at 1pm, as we were setting up for only our third shot of the day, all our child actors started drifting away. I frantically called to Aleem to find out what the story was and he returned to tell me that they were all going to study. There was a UNICEF school just over the hill—a huge white tent that I had noticed in passing. It was time for their lessons and they had to go. As I watched the last of the children ambling out of the village square, I yelled as I had never yelled before: 'NOBODY IS GOING TO SCHOOL TODAY!'

I wish I could say I was pre-menstrual, or that my immediate recall of the child labour laws in Australia softened my resolve. But

I was a deranged woman, blinded by the rigours of production, and all integrity just simply vanished.

I can honestly say that I instantly regretted my demand, but am embarrassed to admit that I did not retract it. No children went to school that day and when, at the end of the shoot, I tried to get a photo of myself riding the donkey, it bucked me off. Instant karma.

Once everyone had grasped the 'all-for-one-and-one-for-all' ethos, our little team really hit its stride, and I was constantly amazed by just how innovative and adaptable they could be. A motorcycle chase saw our lead cameraman lie spread-eagled on the bonnet of a car to film it, while two other crew members hung out the windows, holding him down by his ankles. When he decided he needed some height for a shot in another scene, our lighting guy held him up against a wall for a solid twenty minutes. A gunshot wound, complete with blood splatter, was created using a small plastic bag filled with red dye and attached to a tiny firecracker, which was then fitted underneath our actor's shirt. A piece of cardboard was taped to the poor man's chest, offering him some protection against the small explosion that would dramatically disperse the 'blood', and I was exceedingly impressed by how authentic it looked.

The shoot was far from easy-going. My crew stood waist deep in streams to get the best camera angles, trudged up mountains at 4am to film sunrises, climbed into sewerage drains, hung out of trees and off the sides of cliffs, and would work late into the night to get a scene right despite knowing that they had an 8am start the following day. There was no overtime, no bonuses and clearly little regard for occupational health and safety practices. But it was Sidique and Aleem, in particular, who did the hardest yards.

Tiggy prepared meticulous call sheets for our shooting days, setting out all the scenes we would be filming, but things rarely ever went to plan. Actors would simply fail to show up, or call Aleem on the night before the shoot claiming illness or some family crisis. An important prop car would suddenly have been sold to a cousin in Mazar, or a location that we'd been using just the previous day would mysteriously be no longer available (or available at four times the agreed daily rate). One week our actresses couldn't make it back into Afghanistan because the border with Pakistan had been closed, and security threats were constantly shutting down various parts of the city.

Aleem would phone us up at 6.30am each day to discuss our shooting plan and to advise us of any late-night or early-morning developments that would necessitate revising it. More often than not, the schedule would need some serious rejigging. Tiggy and I would then scramble through scripts, trying to cobble together a feasible, full day of filming before handing it over to Aleem and Sidique to make it all happen. While the rest of the crew showered, ate breakfast and smoked their morning cigarettes, Aleem and Sidique would be frantically trying to lock in actors, find new locations and gather together essential props.

At night, after the rest of the team had retired to their rooms to play cards or watch TV, Aleem would trudge back to our guest house, where we'd sit together and go over the budget. Finance would only release our money in dribs and drabs, and we needed to give them three days' notice to have funds transferred from Kabul to Jalalabad.

So, along with providing them with daily expenditure reports, we would also have to devise some kind of estimate regarding upcoming expenses. It was a time-consuming, brain-wilting exercise, but at least I could have a wine or two to take the edge off it, and it was always a great relief to finally hit 'Send' on our accounting emails to Kabul.

I think back now to October 2009 and the last day with my crew in Jalalabad. Tiggy and Jose had long gone by then, both headed off on overdue leave, and our already minuscule production team was down to just three. We were filming a huge party scene with around twenty-five actors—it was a flashback to our main character, Salam, as a teenage boy and meeting his future wife for the very first time. Our casting had failed to uncover a 'Young Salam', so Aleem had stepped up to take on the role.

We arrived at the location at 5am to dress the set. I clambered over roofs and Aleem and Sidique climbed trees as we struggled to hang huge tarpaulins over the yard. We swept and cleaned, moved furniture and placed props, and by the time the rest of the team lobbed in at 8am, demanding to know where their Red Bulls were, we already felt as if we'd done a full day's work. We were all tired by then, sick of living and working together and eager to get home. The day dragged on into infinity.

The last shot was of Young Salam laying eyes on his ladylove for the very first time. Aleem, who had never acted before in his life, needed to smile, look suitably coy and generally enamoured of her, but by that stage of the game he was barely able to stand up. It didn't help that the actress playing his love interest was already on her way back to Pakistan and, with nobody to play off, he was struggling to summon up any real passion. Finally our director, Sayed, suggested that I stand behind the camera to give Aleem someone to interact with and provide him with an eye-line.

Sure, I was the only woman on set, but the thought of flirting with a boy who called me 'Mum' was a trifle off-putting. I couldn't hold eye contact with him; I fidgeted and laughed and exasperated the bejesus out of everyone. Finally, when we took a short break so our cameraman could change his battery, Aleem approached me.

'I'm so sorry. I'll be good, I'll do better,' I quickly offered.

But he just hit me with a stern, solemn look. 'Mum, do you know that you are shaming yourself in front of us all?'

Whoa. I was mortified and I finally got the whole shame thing—I was a disgrace to my team and unworthy of my tribe. It was an absolute killer! The wink and smile Aleem threw me before heading back to his mark only marginally tempered my acute embarrassment. I immediately transformed into a coquettish fifteen-year-old girl, and we scored the shot in the very next take.

That night I shouted what remained of the team to dinner at an open-air restaurant on the river and thanked them all for their overwhelming awesomeness. They, in turn, each made short, shy speeches declaring their fondness for me, their hopes that they would have the opportunity to work with me again when I returned from Australia and their regrets over any mistakes they might have made.

Sidique had to translate most of it, so I'm guessing there may have been a fair bit of gilding by the time it reached my ears but I cried like a baby anyway. Their obvious discomfort over my copious tears alerted me to the fact that I was probably shaming myself for the second time that day. But, whatever—I had a good six weeks back in Australia before I would see them again to live that one down.

5.
Propaganda
and
Production

It was my first ever chopper ride. I hitched a lift home from a shoot in Jalalabad on an ageing, Afghan army helicopter that rattled and wheezed its way through the mountainous vista, and I copped hell for it that night from one of my expat mates. Over dinner he cited numerous examples of mechanical failure, pilot error and inevitable crashes, his diatribe punctuated by the words 'silly' and 'reckless'. But after a few bottles of wine and a couple of rounds of single malt whisky, my irresponsible exploits had seamlessly morphed into some hilarious caper and I was being celebrated as 'crazy' rather than just plain old dumb.

To be honest, the chopper ride was a glorious ending to a month of production hell, which began soon after I arrived back in Afghanistan in late December 2009. My chief purpose for returning at that time was to supervise post-production on *Salam.* Mum had fully recovered from her surgery and the broadcast of the series was looming, so I left a perfect Sydney summer to return to the biting cold of a Kabul winter. Then mid-January, I was hauled into an emergency meeting with business development and management and advised that I would be executive-producing a series of nine thirty-second TV and radio spots intended to counter the use of improvised explosive devices (IEDs; basically home-made bombs). The strategy around the campaign was to promote security, good governance and develop-ment. It was a huge contract with an important external client; every element of the project needed to be produced and broadcast by the end of February.

It was at the conclusion of this same meeting that I learnt that my future with Moby would almost exclusively be based around this type of work. Ostensibly, I was the head of drama; but in truth, I was nothing more than a propaganda merchant, paid to oversee production of TV and radio content that contained messaging for Afghans. The majority of Moby's programming was self-devised, original and funded through advertising revenue, but there were particular projects fully financed by interested outsiders.

The official term for what I was facilitating was 'Psychological Operations', better known as PSYOPS, which basically equated to identifying target audiences and influencing their values and behav-iour to suit the objectives of, in the case of Afghanistan, NATO and its allies. I must confess that, up until a month before I started this role, I had been completely ignorant of the whole PSYOPS scene. I know now that Psychological Operations have been extensively utilised throughout the history of modern warfare and that it encompasses a whole raft of initiatives that fall into three types of propaganda— White, Grey and Black.

White PSYOPS is where the source of the propaganda is fully acknowledged—think leaflet drops and loudspeaker missions over Viet Cong territory during the Vietnam War. With Grey PSYOPS, the source of the propaganda is not acknowledged and it can actually appear to originate from a non-hostile or indigenous source.

Black PSYOPS is freaky business. It's unashamedly deceitful and the propaganda is actively ascribed to a source that is not at all responsible for it. It's generally used to stir things up. When I was still working at The Den, there was a rumour doing the rounds that a prominent and well-respected mullah in Kabul was, in fact, a Jew. All the Afghan staff had been talking about it, but nobody could really tell me where the information had come from. In hindsight, I'm guessing this was some clever Black propaganda.

Salam was an exercise in Grey PSYOPS and most of my work would fall into that area, with a bit of White here and there.

The PSYOPS media industry was big business and we operated in a highly competitive market. Although there was no television at all under the Taliban, there were now forty-seven TV channels and one hundred and fifty radio stations in Afghanistan, along with an abundance of small local production houses. So the bidding process on the various projects on offer could be fierce. We had an entire arm of the company dedicated to sniffing out requests for proposals and potential grants, and writing up and submitting the formal applications. They effectively managed the project in terms of client liaison, while my team did all the creative and production work.

Most of our clients had PSYOPS units attached to them and these were the people who we ultimately answered to. Many of them had no background in media and most of them rarely left their heavily guarded compounds. A lot of them came in and out of the country on high rotation—I was told that in the space of a year it was possible to deal with three different people, each of them eager to make a personal mark on 'their' project—and a lot of my time would inevitably be spent in managing unrealistic expectations or convincing the client that its 'revolutionary new concept' was in fact old or impossible to pull off in the allocated time frame, or that it simply wouldn't be palatable to an Afghan audience.

The project I was assigned to had been floating around for months. Our newly formed creative team in Dubai was developing the idea and I really had no knowledge of it; somehow it had managed to slip through the cracks and suddenly it was panic stations. The client had approved the basic concepts but we still had scripts to write, storyboards to draw, actors to cast, locations to scout, props and wardrobe to be sourced and purchased . . . and I didn't have a team. I immediately pulled Aleem on board to assist. The official project manager was an American guy, Virgil, but it was Nilu, an Afghan–American woman who had only recently started with the company, who was doing most of the legwork on behalf of business development.

Nilu and I hadn't really known each other previously; in fact, it was only through arranging the shoot that we came to be friends. We had just two weeks to organise everything, from casting to costuming, and the fact that Nilu managed to laugh her way through the madness made me realise that I had been blessedly yoked to a kindred spirit.

An older, experienced Afghan director, Mirwais, had started with us just that week. I hadn't even met the man and our first face-to-face saw me delivering the news, through Nilu, that he would be responsible for directing every component of the campaign. He just laughed and asked Nilu if I was insane. She apparently told him that I was, but that my directive was quite genuine. He laughed again, I laughed, Nilu laughed . . . and then I reached across the table, shook his hand and welcomed him to the company.

Three of those thirty-second spots were vehicles for promoting the Afghan army. Our first spot was to exalt the warriors of old—the turban-wearing, sword-wielding men on horseback who fought the British in the nineteenth century.

We were to shoot it in the hills of Mazar-e-Sharif, a city in northern Afghanistan. Our crew would consist of fifteen Afghans, most of them freelancers who I had never met before, and we would all be travelling the seven hours to Mazar on a bus. The trip entailed our travelling along the Salang Pass, a stretch of road built by the Russians in the 1960s. Reaching 3400 metres, it is one of the highest roads in the world and includes a two-lane, 3.2-kilometre tunnel. Avalanches along the Salang Pass are devastatingly common in winter. The tunnel itself has no exhaust system and people have died from carbon monoxide poisoning during traffic delays.

One look at the bus told us it was dodgy—it was a banged-up old beast and its chassis was peppered with patches of rust. Still, it looked adequate for an afternoon jaunt through the countryside.

We were late heading off from the office but our best estimate was that we'd reach our destination by 7pm.

It took us about fifteen minutes to realise that the bus had no heating. It had been a fairly mild winter and the skies were clear as we rumbled out of Kabul, so we weren't overly perturbed by this discovery. We were all in good form, excited to be out of the city and quite dazzled by the brilliant white landscape that lined our route. We stopped after a couple of hours, so I could take photos of the first real snow I had seen in Afghanistan. I romped off to the side of the road to stand knee-deep in it, but I was quickly stopped in my frolics by horrified shouts from our security guard, Omar—apparently the area hadn't yet been de-mined and it seemed there was a distinct possibility that I would blow myself up.

Three hours into the trip, the weather conditions turned nasty; the pretty, soft snow was falling quite heavily by then and our trusty chariot became thoroughly bogged. While Nilu and I hugged each other for warmth by the side of the road, the rest of our team sweated and grunted for a good thirty minutes as they manually pushed and dragged the bus out of the snow.

At this stage, the bus driver thought it prudent to fit snow chains to the tyres before proceeding any further; he only had two and, after travelling just a couple of kilometres, one of them snapped. Omar and the assistant to the bus driver, a thirteen-year-old boy with big, weathered, grandfather hands, trudged back to the nearest village to try to find more.

I was now officially freezing and, as we waited for our saviours to return, I lit a cigarette. I had unilaterally decided that smoking would be allowed inside the bus and the sound of lighters clicking to life around me signalled everyone's agreement.

It took the rescue crew an hour to return and, by that time, Nilu and I had made up nicknames for all the members of our team. The guy sitting behind us was 'Dragon's Breath' because his breath could strip paint off a wall . . . Omar was 'Box-Head Billy' because he had a noggin the size of a small TV set . . . the Fixer was 'The Camel' because his voice was strangely reminiscent of some camel cartoon character we both remembered from our childhood . . . and our handsome lead actor, who sat quietly by himself reading a book, became the mysterious 'Angel Face'. Okay, it was a tad juvenile, but much later I felt more comfortable about our silly little exercise when, after the shoot, I discovered that they had all been calling me 'Grandma' in Dari.

A huge cheer went up when Omar finally appeared beside the bus, victoriously holding aloft a single set of chains. However, our joy levelled out a little when we discovered that they didn't fit. There was another solid hour of tweaking, fiddling and fixing before the bus finally limped off into a twilight blizzard.

I was preoccupied with wondering whether my feet had perhaps turned blue when Nilu brought it to my attention that the windscreen wipers had completely stopped working. It was at this point that I discovered why the dear little bus assistant had old-man hands— squeezing himself in next to the driver, every minute or two he would reach out of the window and wipe the sleet and snow from the windscreen.

A line of traffic was now snaking its way slowly towards the Salang Tunnel. A truck travelling ahead of us skidded off the road; the shoulders of the highway were littered with abandoned cars. Our bus was full of cigarette smoke, but we were all shivering uncontrollably because of the draft from the open window being used by our brave little human-windscreen-wiper.

A couple of blankets were produced from somewhere and, as we entered the tunnel at a crawl, I was suddenly cosying up in a most un-Islamic manner with the closest available bodies. We were halfway through the tunnel when we stopped altogether. Omar (who actually seemed to be taking great delight in the relentless drama) wandered up ahead to find out what the delay was. He returned with an unnerving smile stretched across his big, wide dial and excitedly informed us that a truck had broken down, then he skipped off to go and help direct the traffic.

After two hours in the tunnel, I was convinced that my breath was getting shorter. Nilu and I were constantly in the grip of compulsive giggling—another sure sign that we were on the brink of carbon-monoxide poisoning.

To take our minds off our predicament, she and I talked. She told me stories about when she first arrived back in Afghanistan, just after the fall of the Taliban. She had been a member of a women's delegation that had come in a UN plane to Pakistan, from where they had driven across the border to Kabul (a life-threatening trip because the Taliban were still everywhere). Once they reached the capital, there were Afghans wanting to shake her hand on the street, women crying with joy at the sight of her. There was no running water, no reliable electricity, no guest houses, no supermarkets, but the exhilaration of being back in her birthplace, after close to thirty years away, made these deficiencies seem trifling.

She had been one of the first westerners to drive into Istalif, a small town north of Kabul. Her eyes filled with tears as she recounted seeing headless bodies hanging from the trees, rotting in the streets. So many incredible stories—all told with a modest, unaffected nonchalance that shamed me. My prideful notions of being a ballsy, brave woman for coming to Afghanistan quickly evaporated as I talked to this remarkable woman. I came here for work and adventure; Nilu returned because she was driven by an overwhelming desire to save her homeland.

After four hours we finally edged our way out of the tunnel and into a raging blizzard; then at midnight the sweet, uncomplaining boy who had kept our windscreen clean during our twelve-hour trip announced that he could no longer feel his hand. We stopped at the next town and decided to stay the night.

Aleem and Omar ventured out to find accommodation and arrived back twenty minutes later to say that they had found a guest house further down the road. The only drawback was that the manager wouldn't allow foreigners to stay. I wondered at this strange bias, but was too tired and deranged to question it. My glasses were removed; I was wrapped in a scarf, and I shuffled inside with my head bowed and my shoulders hunched. Unbelievably, I got through—and it was Nilu who proved to be the problem. Despite her perfect Dari and Persian good looks she was still clearly a 'foreigner'. It took some soothing, conciliatory words from Aleem and US$20 to get the manager to finally relent, but we were told that we had to be out by 5am, before the day staff turned up for work.

When Nilu and I were shown to the tiny room we were to share, fog streamed from our mouths and we were a touch disturbed by the cigarette butts and rodent poo that littered the floor. The large, curtain-less window didn't quite shut and our small, iron beds bore stained mattresses and filthy, dust-coated blankets.

The smell in the communal bathroom at the end of the corridor made us both gag and the steaming, fresh faeces that occupied the floor just shy of the squat toilet saw Nilu flee, determined to control her bladder for the next four hours. I, on the other hand, perched myself precariously above the stinking hole, juggling long-johns and under-pants with one hand as I covered my mouth and nose with the other.

We were finally settled in our beds, fully clothed, when the door handle slowly turned and the locked door started straining against the frame. We both jumped up and hurriedly pushed a desk and the end of my bed up against it. Of course, we stayed awake all night, buoying ourselves with mindless chatter and irrational chuckling, our eyes widening with horror each time an attempt was made to enter our room.

We made our escape at dawn. The bus lumbered into Mazar at 2pm—twenty-six hours after our journey began. When we came to unpack the bus, we realised that we had been smoking our cigarettes while there had been a generator and two cans of fuel sitting in the aisle. Aleem also sheepishly informed us that the town we had stayed in the previous night was Taliban country—the manager of the guest house hadn't wanted foreigners staying there because he couldn't guarantee our safety.

The three-day shoot was as smooth as our journey up had been rocky. The weather was warm and the people of Mazar were friendly and urbane. On our last day, we went to watch a Buzkashi game. Buzkashi is the national sport of Afghanistan and is a hard-core pastime involving two teams of men on horseback, competing to get hold of a headless goat carcass and carry it to their goal area. There is prize money and great prestige on offer to the winners, and apparently a fair amount of cash changes hands by way of betting on the match. It appears to be a bloody free-for-all, but at least there are a few official rules in place—riders can't intentionally whip other riders, deliberately knock them off their horses or trip their horses using a rope.

It was a stunning, cloudless day and there were easily a thousand men there to watch the game. As Omar led Nilu and me to a spot in the front row of the grandstand, it seemed that every one of them was suddenly looking at us. Phones appeared all over the place, held high to get photos of the two foreign, female Buzkashi fans, and it was an excruciatingly uncomfortable five minutes before focus once again returned to the game.

Later that afternoon, as we wandered through town, Omar happily allowed me to walk off ahead of him. I strode through the market-place, sailing through a sea of flowing white burqas, pretending I was some tourist on a lone-wolf adventure. It was the first time since arriving in Afghanistan that I had truly felt free.

That same morning we started receiving reports that conditions along the Salang Pass had deteriorated, so Nilu and I made the decision to fly the crew home. She called our production manager, Mehrab, back in Kabul to arrange it.

Mehrab was a diligent young fellow, but his miserliness led you to believe that he was bankrolling the entire company on his own pay packet. He refused outright even to entertain the notion of flying us, and Nilu took immense pleasure in reminding him how his penny-pinching on the bus hire had placed us all in great danger. He finally agreed to look into it and get back to us.

Just after lunch, he called us with a compromise—Nilu and I could fly home, but the rest of the team had to go by road. We refused his generous offer—if our Afghan crew was catching the bus, then so were we.

It was early evening when Nilu suggested that between the two of us, we could probably pay for all the flights back to Kabul. We went to our room and counted our money, determining that we could just cover the cost for the entire team. Nilu was on the phone trying to book tickets when Mehrab called me—he wanted to ensure that I knew that I could fly home, and strenuously encouraged me to do so. It was 8pm; I was angry and over it. I told him that I was well aware of the offer and had already declined it, before launching into a tremble-inducing rant about the value of human life, regardless of race. I also told him that I would be speaking with Jahid about our appalling treatment as soon as I returned, before signing off with some veiled threat to resign over the incident.

Ten minutes later Jahid was on the phone. Management had apparently approved flights for the entire crew that afternoon and he was at a loss to explain where the communication breakdown had occurred. I honestly had no interest in getting to the bottom of it and was simply grateful for the news that we could all fly home. The next afternoon our whole team was on a plane back to Kabul. Our bus driver and his darling assistant would travel back as soon as there was a break in the weather.

Five days later, one hundred and seventy Afghans died in avalanches along the Salang Pass. The bus had made it back into Kabul the day before the disaster.

We had very little time to dwell on our Mazar misadventure because, two days after arriving back in Kabul, we were scheduled to film our two remaining army spots. These shoots were based around showcasing the present-day military, so we needed not only approval from the Ministry of Defence but access to Afghan soldiers, tanks and helicopters. For this, we needed the involvement of our head of security, Ahmad, who was the middleman between ourselves and any government ministries or agencies that we needed to deal with.

Ahmad's job was to obtain all necessary filming permissions; he could be relied upon to round up police or army personnel as required. He called me 'sister', I called him 'captain', and we saluted each other every time we met. In his mid-forties, he was an old-school kind of Afghan and I sometimes had occasion to reproach him for censorious comments he made, for example to a female employee about the snugness of her top, or for making unfounded allegations about men and women at the company inappropriately fraternising. But he was a big-hearted bear of a man and every request I made was met with a 'No problem, sister'. To his supreme credit, he never failed to deliver.

You would imagine that the government would pounce on free airtime glorifying the military and that the ministry would pull out all stops to assist. But it was never quite that easy, and on this occasion poor Ahmad had to drink endless cups of tea with a whole bunch of bureaucrats to get them on board. He was saved the considerable effort of having to secure a military base as a filming location by virtue of our client offering to sort that out for us.

In our early meetings with the client, they had suggested that we shoot at a military base in Gardez, about two hours south of Kabul. They would organise everything. Our crew could all stay on the base and, due to the client's security concerns about us travelling down there by road, they offered to transport our team in a Chinook—a huge, twin-engine helicopter that they had at their disposal. It all sounded too good to be true. It was.

Our first attempt to reach Gardez, on the fourth of February, was thwarted when the Chinook was required for an actual military operation. The client assured us that we could travel down later in the week, perhaps the seventh, but I started to get jittery about the Gardez solution. Call me crazy, but it seemed highly probable that the blasted war might, once again, get in the way of us filming our little TV spots. Nilu and I met with Ahmad that same day and asked him if he could find a location closer to home. He recommended a military training centre in Kabul and put through a call to them while we were still in his office, before hurrying off on his motorcycle to seal the deal.

Mirwais and I inspected the location the next day and deemed it ideal. We made a tentative plan to shoot there on 9 February and Ahmad set off on another mission to the ministry to get the necessary approvals in place. We now had two locations at our disposal and I couldn't conceive how anything could go wrong. It could.

On 6 February, the client informed us that the Chinook would be unavailable to transport the team to Gardez the next day, and our back-up location in Kabul was looking incredibly iffy due to the fact that it had started snowing quite heavily and wasn't going to let up anytime soon. When I had inspected the dusty training base, I had noted that, even after the snows, the ground would be slushy then muddy for another few weeks.

We couldn't hold off shooting any longer. In a meeting with Ahmad on 7 February, he suggested to Nilu and me that we shoot in Jalalabad, where it was cool but sunny. On the morning of the eighth we instructed him to go, go, go. He explained that it would require a whole raft of new permissions, as the Jalalabad base had neither tanks nor choppers, and the ministry would have to approve it all being relocated from Kabul. We gave him a tentative date of 12 February and, with a salute and a 'No problem, sisters', off he went again.

Our fate firmly in the hands of Ahmad and his negotiating skills, we pushed on with pre-production. Mirwais and Aleem travelled to Jalalabad ahead of us and found a suitable location for filming and cast troops from the local base. The Kabul training centre dispatched two tanks on assurances from the ministry that the approval would go through, and also guaranteed Ahmad that the choppers were ready to roll. But when the rest of us set off in our bus the day before filming, the minister still hadn't issued the official approval.

We had planned an early start on our day of filming, but by 9am we were still waiting for Ahmad to phone through with the go-ahead. The call came at 10am. He had the necessary paperwork and the ministry had informed the commander at the Jalalabad base, via both email and phone, but the man was refusing to move until he had the signed, stamped document in his hand.

I'd like to say that the commander was a queer old fish and that his stance was some behavioural anomaly, but Afghans are fixated on stamped pieces of paper. After every production, my team would hound me for a stamped certificate attesting to their participation in the program; I offered email and phone references to ex-employees, but they were universally insistent that anything less than a printed, signed sheet of A4, bearing an inky impression of the company insignia, was simply unacceptable. I could put it down to some kind of technology time warp, but am more inclined to attribute it to the fact that Afghans just don't trust one another. So dear, dedicated Ahmad had to get on his motorcycle and ride the three hours to Jalalabad to hand-deliver the document.

He arrived just before 1pm and we got our hero shot—the troops, the tanks and the choppers all emerging over the hill simultane-ously—in the last of the afternoon light.

Ahmad, our stills photographer Wakil, and I took the thirty-minute ride back to Kabul on one of the choppers that afternoon. Nilu declined the offer, declaring the thing a 'death trap' and opting to travel back by road. The Afghan door gunner happily relinquished his spot so Wakil could take some photos of me holding the machine gun and looking out over the countryside below.

The gunner was at the back of the chopper, eating some food and talking with Ahmad, when I motioned for him to return to his station. With Wakil translating, and with a disturbingly straight face, he informed me that he was quite happy for me to stay where I was. Then he issued me with instructions to shoot anyone below who looked like the Taliban.

I turned to Ahmad and grimaced, but he just waved his hand at me: 'No problem, no problem, sister.' And, for the first time since knowing the man, I didn't quite believe him.

6.
A Luminous Shade of Grey

I have had my fair share of hangovers—huge, thumping, head-splitting affairs that have left me vowing lifelong sobriety—and a blinding monstrosity in March 2010 was up there with the best of them. The silver lining, if indeed there was one, was that it was a Friday (our 'weekend') and I was able to share my misery with my bed and Season Two of *Mad Men* on DVD.

This particular hangover came courtesy of a drinking session at The Den with a man I had only ever met once before—in fact, I initially failed to recognise him when he had wandered in the night before and caught me on one of my infrequent visits back to the bar. He was a security contractor who hadn't left the southern city of Kandahar in seven months and was on his way home to the

US to see his wife and meet his newborn baby. But our night's revels had had very little to do with his newfound fatherhood—rather, we had been celebrating the life of one of the most extraordinary men either of us had ever known.

After I'd finished up working at The Den the previous year, it became my local. For a time I still lived upstairs so, even on nights when I'd decided to stay in, I had the regulars hollering for me to come down and join them. I earned the nickname 'Rapunzel', and my appearances on the balcony to tell the boys to leave me alone were met with catcalls and jeers. I could say it annoyed me, but I actually relished being part of a community—I had grown up watching *Cheers* and its theme song suddenly resonated with me on a whole new level.

Al and his buddy Wayne continued to turn up every night. It took a bit of manoeuvring and the addition of a bar stool to accommodate the three of us at Al's preferred spot, but from our perch we'd caw and commentate on our fellow drinkers like a murder of merciless crows. There were workmates and buddies who regularly filled out our posse, but our tight little trio constituted the quorum.

In Wayne, Al had found a true brother and at times, when they were regaling me with stories of their outrageous antics or simply taking the piss out of each other, I could barely distinguish their voices. They had both been elite warriors, proudly serving their country in Iraq and Afghanistan, but had somehow completely lost it along the way. Neither of them ever really confided in me what had gone wrong, but the little detail they did offer hinted at drug and alcohol abuse. They both seemed to have made similar ignoble exits from the armed forces and in the aftermath suffered long bouts of depression. They'd messed up and been cut loose, and were then left all alone to battle their demons.

But to see them out together, you would never have guessed they were haunted souls. They were so large and hilarious, so loyal to one another and to their chosen tribe, that I felt honoured to be anointed as one of them. In truth, my two extreme, amazing friends made me feel safe in a place that could be dark and dangerous.

Although Al and Wayne lived and worked together, I never really saw them outside of The Den. Al and I kept in constant contact via Facebook and phone, but our after-work catch-ups were the only real times that our lives intersected. Their post-bar activities routinely entailed all-night drinking sessions back at their compound or trips to the local Chinese brothel, so I had to make do with hearing their shocking tales of drunkenness and debauchery the following day.

Soon after I started with Moby, the company opened a guest house for expat employees on the other side of town. Around eight of us—Paul, Jose and Tiggy included—all happily relocated to the double-storey, sprawling home, our only real house rule being that we didn't talk about work once we left the office. The move, combined with my increasing workload as we went into pre-production on *Salam,* meant my visits to The Den became less frequent. But I usually managed a couple of excursions each week, and my boys and my bar stool were always there waiting for me.

Then one day I turned up and Wayne was standing at the bar alone. His face looked drawn and pale, and he was sipping on a bottle of water. When I asked him if he was okay, he just shook his head; when I enquired where Al was, he looked positively shamefaced. 'Let's get you a drink, beautiful, and I'll tell you all about it.'

It seems that a few days prior they had scored a bag of coke and had hurried back to Al's room to sample their stash. After one line each, they knew they'd been shafted—the 'cocaine' was clearly heroin, and bad shit at that.

Al was hell-bent on tracking down the Afghan dealer and doing him some serious damage, but Wayne managed to talk him out of it, instructing him to instead flush the rest of the smack down the toilet and write it off as a bad buy. Then Wayne went to his room, but when he returned about an hour later, he found Al snorting more lines.

'Uggh! That stupid, stupid man!' I said. 'So what did you do?'

'I had more lines with him.' I thumped him hard on the arm. 'Yeah, yeah, yeah. But you know what we're like when we're together. Don't worry—we totally paid the price.'

They both eventually passed out and woke up a few hours later feeling violently ill. They then spent the next twenty-four hours constantly throwing up and wishing they were dead.

'Al's still not good,' Wayne told me. 'I only came here tonight to see you, beautiful, 'cause I'm headin' home on leave.' He promised that Al had finally flushed the rest of the heroin away and that they had sworn off any more dodgy drug deals. 'I think the big guy's gonna try and tone it down a bit. Look out for him while I'm gone,' he said as he hugged me goodbye.

I arranged to meet up with Al three days later and, when I walked into the bar, I was honestly astonished. He was clean-shaven, his hair had been freshly trimmed and his face, which of late had been quite red and bloated, glowed with good health.

'Hey, Trudi! Do you have any idea who this strange man is?' Tamim joked as I approached the bar.

'Well look at you!' I exclaimed as Al swallowed me up in his big-boy embrace.

He was having his first beer of the week and had indeed toned it down—laying off the steroids, working out more and sticking to his curfew. I still gave him a hefty punch in the arm for his starring role in the heroin debacle, but his clean-up campaign was impressive.

'Why did you do it?' I asked.

'I dunno. I just wanted to snort something.'

'You're going to end up killing yourself.'

'Gorgeous, I spent two days in hell. I swear I'm never going back there again.'

I had an early start the next day and Al walked me out to my driver. As we drove off, I watched him piggy-backing one of the kids along the footpath, a ragtag bunch of urchins excitedly chasing behind.

Al wanted to catch up with me the following Thursday night, but I had a work do. Paul thought I should attend and it wasn't a hard sell, as it was a party at the fabulous compound of one of our clients, with free booze and eats. I knew that Al was missing Wayne—he told me so—but he had plenty of other playmates, and I felt that I needed to start immersing myself in my new world of workmates and funders.

On Friday I answered Al's first call at noon—he was at The Den and insisted that I join him. I was feeling a little seedy and needed to work on scheduling the *Salam* shoot, which was imminent, so I begged off and promised to meet up with him later in the week.

He phoned me four more times that day. I could hear people laughing and yelling in the background, and Al was clearly wired on something. With each call he became more belligerent in his demands and after my final, late-afternoon refusal to get on board, he growled: 'You are dead to me.' Before abruptly hanging up.

I waited all day Saturday for his make-up text. This was standard practice for us and had been initiated back when I was managing The Den, when, full of beer, he'd storm off into the night over some perceived slight. But in the past he had always said sorry, always sent a message the next day telling me how much he loved me. This time I decided to break the impasse myself and tried phoning him, but my call simply rang out.

I headed to The Den straight after work, expecting to see Al propping up the bar, but there was no sign of him. I had barely made it through the door when Tamim hurried over and led me to a corner of the room.

'Trudi, have you heard from Al today?' he asked anxiously.

'No, why?'

'I think something has happened to him.'

'What do you mean?'

'I don't know, but something is wrong. Sue was in before and I heard Ernie talking with her about him. Ernie knows. Can you please ask him?'

I looked over to Ernie standing at the bar. He was an American guy, a recent arrival in Afghanistan. We'd been introduced and I'd say hi to him in passing, but I really didn't know him that well.

'Maybe he's been in a fight,' I suggested.

'Maybe. But can you ask him, Trudi? Please?'

As I approached Ernie, I was already formulating a plausible scenario. Al *had* been in a fight, with Ernie or one of his mates ...

Or perhaps he'd gone after the Afghan drug dealer. He was lying low or had been confined to his compound . . . I didn't even entertain the prospect that he might have been jailed or hospitalised. He was simply in trouble; I had it all figured out.

When I asked Ernie if he knew anything about Al, he frowned and told me that he'd rather talk outside. We headed into the garden and settled at a table in a corner of the yard.

We sat opposite each other for an age before he finally spoke. 'When was the last time you heard from him?'

'Yesterday. I tried calling him this afternoon but he didn't pick up.'

He twisted the neck of his beer bottle between his fingers for a moment and then met my eye. 'Look, I'm so sorry to be the one to tell you this . . . I know you two were close. But Al's dead.'

'No . . .'

'I got a call this afternoon from a buddy he works with. His body was found in a hotel room this morning.'

'No . . . Oh no . . . How?'

'I don't know for sure, but they're saying it was drugs.'

I think I tried to thank him then for letting me know, but instead I just cried—awful, heaving sobs that poured out of me with such force I could barely breathe. Ernie looked uncomfortable as he reached across and gently gripped my shoulder.

'Come on, Trudi, don't do this. You gotta pull yourself together.'

'I can't . . . I can't!'

'You have to. You gotta go back in there and break the news to Tamim.'

My heart splintered all over again. I took Tamim to the back room to tell him. I honestly don't remember what I said, but I guessed that by now he expected the worst. Afterwards we stood apart for a few minutes, both quietly crying. Then finally I turned to him and took him in my arms. We shook with despair, holding each other up against the weight of our shared grief. It was the first time I had hugged an Afghan man and it was only the arrival of Tamim's brother that finally separated us.

Paul and Jose came to collect me that night and I staggered out to meet them, drunk, distraught and utterly lost. There were tiny children everywhere: 'Al is dead! Al is dead!' rang in my ears as I stumbled into the car. They couldn't believe he was gone; none of us could, even though we had all really known he'd be the first to go.

Wayne and I were constantly in touch over the following weeks. We had so little to say, but the long silences over the phone somehow lessened the vast distance between us. While he attended Al's funeral in the States, we held a wake at The Den. Al's workmates had been in a company-ordered lockdown ever since his death and the gathering was the first time I'd seen any of them.

One of his good friends, Christian, sat with me at the bar, recounting the clean-up of Al's room. The steroids, the empty beer bottles, the sleeping pills and the drawer full of syringes were all to be expected, but his considerable book collection came as a surprise.

'Trudi, he had books on everything—religion, philosophy, huge novels . . . even poetry. He really was a complex guy,' Christian said. But I had known this all along—for me Al had always been a brilliant, luminous shade of grey.

Wayne came back to Kabul, but didn't last long; it was all too hard without his best friend. Other people left, new ones arrived, and in just a matter of months the impressive mark left by Al had begun to fade.

Then, one night in March I was sitting on the terrace at The Den when a man walked in. He was tall and broad, bushy-faced and wearing a baseball cap. When he stopped and looked straight at me, I thought my heart would stop. Of course it wasn't Al, but, as he approached me, his eyes still locked to mine, I wondered if some kind of mystical mischief-maker was toying with me.

He smiled when he reached me, and extended his hand. 'Trudi? It's Victor . . . I'm Victor, Al's buddy.'

'Victor . . .' It took me a moment to recollect.

Victor. He and Al had been in the military together, and I had met him one night when he was passing through town on the way to his job in Kandahar.

'Victor,' he repeated.

We embraced like old friends, and then I took him by the hand and led him to a table at the edge of the noisy crowd.

'I came here tonight to find you. Al talked about you all the time. I haven't left Kandahar since his death and I needed to be with someone who loved him as much as I did.'

We drank a lot of beers that night. Tamim kept them coming, while taking regular breaks from behind the bar to reminisce with us. We laughed and cried shamelessly as we remembered our friend. We were just winding up . . . or maybe we weren't . . . The timing, the moment really means nothing now, but Victor told me something that gave devastating meaning to Al's senseless death.

'You know, Al accidentally killed a kid in Iraq.'

In the silence that followed, it all fell into place. Victor continued. 'He told me when we were drunk one night. He was stationed in a village, his regiment was helping to rebuild it, and then . . . I don't know . . . he shot the kid dead.'

'How?'

'It was an accident, that's all he told me. I asked him the same question and he just said: "It's done, I'm done. It's over." He never spoke to me about it again.'

I wonder now if Al ever really spoke to anyone else about it . . . I'm no psychiatrist, but I'm guessing he simply manned up and carried on, paying his own personal penance for a tragedy he would never be able to forget or forgive himself for.

And I will never forget my wonderful, generous friend—a man who, I suspect, ultimately paid for his mistake with his life.

7.
Helmut's Secrets

I had never really been a boss before. Sure, I'd had various stints at being 'top dog'—I was once a supervisor at a VIP domestic cleaning service. But with only one person to supervise, and my supervision consisting of ensuring that there were no crusty spots left in the toilet bowl or dust remaining on the skirting boards, I figured that didn't really count for much.

During my four years of lawyering, I had personal assistants and the odd legal clerk under my direct authority.

After giving up the solicitor game to explore my creative bent, I landed a plum job as a cook at a public hospital, where I had three kitchen hands working for me. But we were a fairly egalitarian little bunch. Having fluked my way into the position (I actually thought that I was interviewing for the job of dish pig too), it turned out that Guillermo, Li Wei and Salim knew as much about serving up meals for two hundred people as I did.

I guess the most responsibility I ever had before my time in Afghanistan was when I was a tour leader on the Sydney Harbour Bridge. But I wasn't terribly comfortable with that scene—I'd be strolling up the arch, taking in the breathtaking views of Sydney, only to have some bothersome tourist ask me whether they could expect to see kangaroos hopping across the bridge anytime soon. That would snap me out of my reverie and forcefully remind me of the disheartening fact that I had twelve people to babysit for the next two hours.

So my appointment as head of drama at Moby was an exciting and bracing first. My stint as boss-woman on the *Salam* shoot had given me a tiny taste of what it entailed to be in charge, but the buck there had always stopped with Paul. Now, however, I was to have an actual department all to myself—a team of around twenty writers, producers and directors who had all been beavering away for the past few years, quite happily making drama serials and TV spots without me. Initially the prospect of managing them was a mite unnerving.

Following the successful delivery of the army TV spots, I was directed by management to focus on improving our weekly soap opera—*Secrets of this House.* It was externally funded and based around an extended Afghan family, all of whom lived together in the one home. In 2009, in only its second season, the client pulled the show, with five episodes of the series still to air, and refused to fund a third season until major changes were made.

In fairness to the funder, their action was completely justified. For most of the first two years, the show had been shot in a building at work. A few walls were knocked down to make a living room; a couple of tiny offices were continually being reset to represent the various bedrooms of the family members; and a noisy alleyway outside the 'set' (home to a hideous grey stucco fountain) was the backyard.

Then, in November 2009, management decided to convert the *Secrets* set to offices for our HR Department and, without any reference to it in the script, the on-screen family magically relocated to the big swanky house on the other side of town that had previously been my home.

Our wholesale pullout from the big swanky house (which occurred about six months after the Moby expats mob had initially moved in) had been somewhat of a mutual decision between both landlord and tenants. For our part, we weren't overly comfortable with having staff who could potentially report all our personal ins and outs back to our employer and work colleagues. As it was, Paul and Jose had to pretend to sleep in separate rooms.

We had a sheet that everyone entering or leaving the house— ourselves included—had to sign, but I had my doubts about the validity or effectiveness of the exercise. One Friday we had a rooftop barbecue and three Russian mates variously signed themselves in as Adolf Hitler, Osama bin Laden and George Bush. Our security guard made a note of their arrival time next to the audacious monikers and didn't so much as flinch.

The house manager (whose father worked at Moby) was a rather interesting little fellow who was constantly trying to give me gifts.

His first present was a box of chocolates, which I made a big show of sharing around with everyone. When he attempted to present me with a necklace I immediately declined the offer, questioning the appropriateness of the gesture, considering he was married with two children. He insisted it was all legit, as his wife had actually made the pendant herself. I had good cause to doubt the claim because I'd seen the silver-plated peacock with lapis stones embedded in its wings at a half a dozen jewellery shops on Chicken Street, the main tourist market in Kabul.

Our communal issue with this man was our suspicion that his 'managing' extended to matters that didn't entirely fit that job description. One of my housemates, Martin, arrived home one day to find that someone had been trying to track down 'porrne' on his laptop. On other occasions, I'd enter my room to find my two pillows propped up against the bed head, a clear dent in my mattress and the TV switched to the Hindi movie channel. But what ultimately ended his career with us was the day we arrived home, after a long and exhausting week in Jalalabad, to find him fast asleep on Jose's pretend bed.

For Moby's part, we were a demanding lot and I suspect they had no real concept of what they were taking on. There were calls for pot plants, furniture for the rooftop, a microwave oven that actually worked, air conditioners and reliable internet connection. My only real request was for screen doors to keep out insects. During summer, the heat in the house was insufferable and it was impossible to sleep with the doors closed. But our home was inopportunely located two hundred metres away from a communal rubbish dump and the resulting fly plague was sickening and immense. After weeks of asking nicely, I finally lost the plot. During the course of one evening, I massacred thirty-seven flies in my room with my trusty swatter and threatened to dump them on the desk of our HR manager if screen doors weren't installed. They were fitted the following day.

I imagine the company finally tired of playing landlord to a mob of unruly, insistent expats, and wisely decided to stick to the media game and leave the inn-keeping gig to the experts. However, the house, with its many levels and multiple rooms, would prove perfect as a film set. It would also be easy enough to concoct a storyline for season three of *Secrets* that would explain the change of location. Unfortunately, though, the client had other complaints too. They wanted to see more 'traditional' Afghan characters, more outdoor scenes, more rural scenes . . . more scenes full stop. The actors had to 'act better', the production values needed an almighty upgrade . . . in short, there was general all-round dissatisfaction with the way we were delivering our client's propaganda requirements.

The show was being entirely produced by a small Afghan team, most of whom I didn't really know. *Salam* had consumed all of my time and energy, and I had spent most of my initial stint in Afghanistan living in Jalalabad.

Thankfully I knew the senior producer, Merzad, a softly spoken nineteen-year-old, who had helped us out in Kabul on the *Salam* shoot. He had little to offer in our initial meeting and was obviously sensitive to the criticism being levelled at his show. His defensiveness was entirely understandable—he had no production team at all to assist him and I quickly realised that my experience on *Salam* had been a walk in the park compared with Merzad's lot.

I had no doubt that the *Secrets* kids had heard stories of the demanding she-wolf who railed about boom mikes being in shot and ranted at crew members who turned up late to the set. At my first meet-and-greet with the entire team, I was anxious not to be seen as an invading force. But I was playing to a hostile crowd, who scowled in response to my encouraging smiles and shrugged their shoulders when I asked them how we could improve the show. It could have been bloody, except for the fact that they resented the client more than they resented me.

The client's representative was a German man called Helmut. I had met him once during my early days with the company and he had seemed thoroughly nice—expansive, enthusiastic and openly declaring that he was quite in love with Afghanistan and its people. Unfortunately, this 'love' was flagrantly paternalistic and the *Secrets* kids—all intelligent, forthright individuals—weren't buying it.

The head writer, Hamid, was particularly vocal. He had left Afghanistan for Pakistan with his family in 1992 after the Mujahideen came to power and, at five years old, he had been working as a carpet weaver by night while attending school during the day. When he returned to the country in 2001, he sold water and toys on the street while continuing his education. Over the years, he had developed a love of filmmaking and was already writing feature scripts when he was selected by our company to attend a film workshop.

When *Secrets* was commissioned, Hamid was asked to take on the job of overseeing the writing team. He was a proud, uncompromising Afghan and resented being told what was important and relevant to his people by foreigners. But his real peeve was Helmut's fondness for quoting the Koran. 'Who is he to talk to me about Islam? Fucking idiot foreigner!'

We had a get-together with the 'fucking idiot foreigner' scheduled for the very next day. By the end of the first meeting with my team, I had at least elicited promises that they would be polite and would feign interest in Helmut's opinions, so as to ensure that they would all keep their jobs for another year.

Merzad didn't say much during this meeting. In fact he deliberately looked away if I made any attempt to engage him in the lively discussion. I took this as a very bad sign. Perhaps I was an overbearing foreigner as well; I was quite certain that he wasn't happy with the obvious usurpation of his authority that was now taking place.

But after it was over, as I was hoovering back a cigarette and wondering what to do with my taciturn team, he approached me. 'Don't worry, Trudi *Jan*. We will fix everything. I will make sure it's all fine.' Before smiling and walking away.

The meeting with Helmut was an edgy affair. When he began by welcoming me to the team and assuring everyone else that the show would be so much better with a 'foreigner' on board, I wanted to punch him in the throat. And, despite the fact that he was just the cash cow and we were the creatives, he had an abundance of story ideas that he imagined would be ideal!

We had a couple of characters in the show who had recently become engaged and he wanted a storyline where the girl, Soraya, became the boss of her fiancé, Kabir. I nodded enthusiastically and agreed it would make for great soap opera fodder, willing the others to play along. It was when he suggested that our female writers script the scenes that it all turned ugly.

Merzad was translating and he looked at me for a panicked second before reluctantly passing on this brainwave to the girls. One of the women, Alka, let forth with a spray that was obviously hostile. Through Merzad, we discovered that she thought the storyline implausible and the suggestion that she write it positively patronising.

Helmut was surprised, nay aghast, by her reluctance to take on his idea and began quoting passages from the Koran in support of women's rights. I immediately looked at Hamid. His face glowed crimson and he groaned loudly enough for Helmut to turn and address him. 'You like my idea. Yes?'

Despite being competently conversant in English, Hamid growled out a response in Dari that was even and low, before picking up his notebook and calmly walking out the door. The client turned to Merzad for an explanation and I just grinned like an idiot as I envisaged our contract floating away in the wake of Hamid's passive fury.

Merzad cleared his throat and looked Helmut squarely in the eye. 'He says that this is a very interesting storyline and he will take some time to think about it. But now he must leave to drive his sick mother to the hospital.'

He threw me the briefest of smiles before turning his attention back to our client.

'Oh this is very sad, no?' responded Helmut. 'What is the matter with her? Is it high blood pressure? Her heart, yes? You know this is a very serious problem in your country. It's because of the food you eat. So much oil, always too much oil. You must all, all of you, stop using this oil. And not so much meat. Stop eating the meat. Eat vegetables, fresh vegetables; this would be much better for you. And you must exercise. Yes? . . . Yes! I have a great idea! You know what we should do in the show? One of the characters should decide to become healthy and try to teach the rest of the family about diet and exercise, yes? This would be good for all of your people. Everyone in this country needs to learn about this. Yes?'

'Yes!' I offered a little too quickly. Helmut, of course, was right, but his appreciation of your average Afghan diet failed to factor in the scarcity of good, fresh vegetables and domestic budgetary constraints that meant that most families were fortunate if they could afford beans, rice and bread once a day.

I desperately wanted to avoid any further confrontation, so I quickly looked at my watch and politely informed Helmut that the team really had to get back to work—scripts to write, actors to cast and all that. He glanced at his phone and agreed that we should wrap things up; then he declared the meeting an enormous success and took his leave.

Straight after the meeting, Merzad translated for me what Hamid had said in Dari before he left. Apart from the memorable declaration that Helmut was a 'donkey fucker', I can't exactly recall what other words Hamid uttered, but I know I was able to add around five new expletives to my Dari vocabulary.

While Helmut was happy to approve the storyline that justified our change of location, he still wasn't entirely sold on the house we were moving to. He demanded its complete refurbishment. The chintzy lounges and 'modern' tables and chairs all had to go, making way for Persian rugs, throw cushions and charpoys—a traditional cot consisting of a wooden frame and a base of tightly woven rope. He also wanted to see the sky and surrounding landscape through the windows, but this request wasn't going to be so easy to accommodate.

On either side of the house, two-metre-high sheets of corrugated iron had been erected atop the three-metre-high cement fences. This had happened during the expat occupation of the compound as a courtesy to our Afghan neighbours. At that time, because the two-storey house had no real yard, its rooftop had become our favourite hangout. With wonderful views across Kabul and the chance of an evening breeze, it was our preferred place for sitting and decompressing after a long day at work. For Paul and me (both early risers) it was also the ideal location to start the morning—over coffee, cereal and cigarettes we could catch up on all the chitchat we wouldn't get time to cover at the office.

Then one evening, we had arrived home to discover that the roof area had been enclosed on all sides by huge tarpaulins and our stunning city vista had been reduced to a lousy rectangle of sky. Allie, one of our project managers, was straight on the phone to HR, demanding to know what the deal was. She was informed that the neighbours had made complaints about the foreigners on the roof—particularly the bareheaded women—and so the company had respectfully agreed to cover us up.

Allie was livid and the next afternoon took to the tarpaulins with a pair of scissors, cutting huge squares out of each section. On days when she was feeling particularly oppressed, she'd stick her uncovered head through one of her DIY windows and brazenly shake her hair about.

A few weeks later, the ruined canvas was replaced with sheets of grass matting, but they too were quickly demolished. Despairing at ever being able to keep us hidden, the company had opted instead to block our neighbours' view with the super-high fencing solution. Which our people now wanted to remove.

Ahmad was dispatched to begin negotiations, his most compelling argument being that the infidels no longer inhabited the house. The people on the left were happy for certain sections of the iron to be removed, affording us a decent glimpse of sky and surrounding homes through the main living-room windows. However the neighbours on the other side refused to budge, concerned that our cast and crew might take advantage of the unfettered sightlines from the rooftop to look at their women when they were out in the yard.

Ahmad's assurances that nobody would be permitted onto the roof failed to sway them. Thankfully, Helmut sympathised with our dilemma and was satisfied that, with what we had already achieved, we would show enough outdoors to fulfil his edict.

I was anxious anticipating our first day together on set, so I was absolutely delighted to discover that two of my boys from *Salam*—Massood the sound man and Javid the lighting technician—were on crew. I didn't want to appear pushy and had decided I would just hang back and watch how they worked. But then I found I was compelled to intervene in the first shot of the day.

We were actually shooting in the basement of The Diana, the guest house where I was now living. The scene featured two of the show's resident bad guys having a conversation about kidnapping one of our main characters. I sat at the back of the room and watched as the actors rehearsed their dialogue, while Merzad and the director, Farrukh, moved furniture around.

I thought that their decision to place a television set smack-bang in between the two actors, its screen facing the camera, was interesting, but I let it slide without mention. Once we were ready to roll, I moved up to sit next to Farrukh so I could watch the action on the monitor. I allowed him to tape one take before calling a halt to filming.

Using Merzad as my translator, I asked Farrukh to carefully look at the monitor and to tell me whether he could see any problems with the shot. He confessed that he couldn't. Merzad and the two cameramen were similarly convinced that the set-up looked just fine. In desperation, I called in Massood and Javid to offer their opinions and I must admit to having experienced a moment of self-satisfied, motherly pride when Massood correctly pointed out that you could see all of our reflections in the TV screen. The inevitable post-pride fall cameth about two hours later when, at another location, Massood failed to detect that a groaning air conditioner was completely ruining his sound.

We spent seven days filming episode one—virtually an eternity in terms of making Afghan television, but we all knew that the future of the show and indeed our jobs depended on our first offering to Helmut being tip-top.

One of the last set-ups we filmed was in the mountains on the outskirts of Kabul. It was a brilliantly clear day, but bitterly cold and windy, and one of our two actors kept fluffing his lines. We were racing against the light and launching into our tenth take when a distant but thunderous explosion rolled up from the city below. We all froze and, as one, turned to scan the valley for signs of smoke, expecting to hear the faraway pop of gunfire in the sinister silence that followed.

We stayed like that for some time, but the truth was that our schedule simply didn't allow us the luxury of standing and pondering whether another terrorist attack was taking place somewhere in our town.

'Sound ready?' I finally called to Massood.

He looked at me for a long moment before replacing his head-phones and lifting his boom microphone above his head. 'Sound ready,' he replied. Farrukh turned to me and nodded.

'Camera ready?' he yelled as the actors hurried back to their starting positions.

I would like to say that it was all slightly surreal but, after ten months in Afghanistan, it was just another day at the office.

Helmut's critique of episode one was typically effusive. In an email that Helmut requested I forward to the entire team he waxed enthusiastic about the '200% improvement in production values', the 'excellent, awesome' job we had done, and his feelings that the offering was 'very, very, very close to European standards'. And in a subsequent meeting he presented us with a huge, cream-covered cake to thank us for all our hard work. Even Hamid had to admit that for a 'fucking idiot foreigner', Helmut wasn't such a bad bloke after all.

8.
Rumblings
Around
Ramadan

We had just completed sixty shooting days on a new series called *Eagle Four*, working six-day weeks. Thirty of those days fell during Ramadan and all of them in the height of summer, and we still had twelve days of filming left to go. We were shooting at fifty-three different locations and the scripts included seventy-eight main characters.

It was September 2010 and we were in the final stretch. Then, with just two weeks to go until we presented episode one of the thirteen-part series to our client (a foreign embassy), the machine it was being edited on crashed. And after five days of tinkering, IT finally admitted to me that they had no idea how to fix it.

Some consultants from Dubai were flying in that very day to sort out the problem but I could barely rally a smile let alone the 'Rah!

Rah! Rah!' that the head of the IT department felt this announcement so justly deserved. Exhaustion had rendered me quite numb, while months of overcoming constant obstacles to get the show made had blessed me with an air of equanimity that was apparently a little unnerving.

Eagle Four was the biggest television drama production ever mounted in Afghanistan. The client was funding us to create a series that portrayed the Afghan National Police as professional, hard-working and honest. It was an incredible stretch—the ANP were regarded by most of the population as corrupt drug-taking thugs—but we would be paid well for this particular piece of propaganda (at least by Afghan standards) so we had been instructed to pull out all stops to impress.

Our original brief was to make an Afghan *24*, at the time the most popular series in the country—a dubbed version of the American show was the highest rating program on our Dari-language channel. But I knew that we couldn't do it alone. We had stumbled our way through our first action series, *Salam,* which had become the most successful show ever aired on our Pashto-language channel, but this was taking it to a whole new level. I would still have most of my *Salam* crew; regrettably Sidique had moved to sales and marketing, but the wonderful, reliable Aleem was still with me. However, Paul and Jose had finished up at the company in late 2009 with Tiggy following them out just a few months later, so, in terms of expats, I was now it.

On assurances from both my CEO and head of business development that money wasn't an issue, I decided to ask two mates from Australia to come across and help mentor the team. Muffy, my business partner in Australia, was producing corporate videos and music clips while continuing to pitch show ideas for our production company. Lynchy had just finished directing a comedy series for an Australian broadcaster and was looking for his next gig.

But, despite both of them sending me off to Afghanistan with love and excitement and their confidence that it would all be okay, they were strangely reluctant to take the leap themselves. However, after they had received my confirmation that, yes, there was alcohol in Afghanistan and absorbed the fact that I was indisputably still alive and kicking after almost a year in a war zone, they both decided to get on board.

They turned up just as my energy levels and enthusiasm were beginning to wane. The responsibility of producing *Salam* had been enormous, and the complexities and complications inherent in making television in Afghanistan had sobered me considerably. The long, difficult shoot had also taken a toll on my health and I had welcomed in 2010 languishing in my bed for two weeks, recovering from a mild bout of typhoid, a chest infection and six different stomach bacterias. After delivering her diagnosis, the doctor glibly added that I was merely suffering from ailments that most Afghans are commonly forced to endure.

I'd flown out to Dubai to meet them in mid-February and the reunion was bliss. As we sat around in an upmarket bar on our first night together, drinking fine wine and smoking shisha, Lynchy exclaimed that this wasn't as bad as he'd imagined. I was tempted to let him live with the illusion that this was Afghanistan all over but, instead, gently reminded him that we weren't quite there yet and that he might notice a couple of minor differences between Kabul and Dubai.

The subsequent flight into the Ghan had been a bumpy affair; as the glorious, snow-capped mountains gave way to the muddy, brown cloak of the city, Muffy and Lynchy tightly gripped each other's hands. It was interesting to watch the shock set in: as they took in the spectacle of Kabul International Airport (a big tin shed), palmed off the persistent, pushy baggage handlers, and later gaped from the car windows at the sandal-shod Afghans standing ankle-deep in snow, I started to feel a little guilty.

Their arrival at our guest house did nothing to dispel their bewilderment. At the time I was living at The Diana or, as it was commonly known without a trace of affection, The Dirty Diana. It was a rundown, drab hovel and newcomers had been known to arrive and check out again within the space of twenty minutes.

Despite meals being part of the package, I never ate there. I had a personal policy of not eating meat if I couldn't tell what it actually was, so dinner was definitely off limits. Catching the chef one day picking a winner from his nose and wiping it on his apron just reaffirmed my stance on that particular matter. Even breakfast—a couple of hunks of bread and a pot of jam—ultimately made my personal black list. It was delivered each day by a sweet, meek chap who refused to knock before entering my room and had a continuously weeping eye. Everyone at the guest house had chipped in at one stage to send him to a proper doctor, but his eye never seemed to improve and the thought that he might be handling my food each day somewhat turned me off my morning meal.

Women could never venture out of their rooms unless completely covered for fear of offending the mostly male, Muslim staff. The only upside was that it made me cut back on smoking because having to fully dress every time I stepped out into the garden for a fag became a tiresome exercise.

In the end we finally convinced our company to allow us to relocate after around ten grand's worth of gear—phones, cameras and iPods—mysteriously vanished from our rooms over the course of a fortnight. It took us a while to twig to the fact that our stuff had actually been stolen because everyone individually struggled to recall whether they *had* taken their camera out at that bar, or used *their* phone to call a car at that particular party. When the realisation collectively hit us, made definite by the fact that I had been on leave and couldn't have possibly left my Afghan phone anywhere else but in my room, I stormed up to the owner of the guest house and threatened to call the police.

He simply smirked and nodded his head, before offering to call them for me. I realised then that he had us. Our rooms were stacked with duty-free booze and the attending police officer would no doubt turn out to be the guest-house owner's cousin anyway.

But all that was in the future at the time Muffy and Lynchy settled into their rooms at The Dirty Diana early in 2010. After taking in their new home, they were close to catatonic, so I quickly steered them down the ice-slicked road towards The Den, imagining that a night at my local, surrounded by my friends, would lift their flagging spirits. However, Lynchy stepped into the sewage trench outside The Den just as we were entering and instantly gagged at the toxic mix coating his lower leg. And, despite it being winter and dreadfully cold, he was forced to hobble around all night with one bare foot while his boot and sock dried near the gas heater.

When we finally hit the office the following day, all the shock had been shaken out of them and they were only mildly perturbed by the prospect of four people sharing an office the size of your average toilet cubicle. There was talk at one stage of the three of us moving into the office next door but, when Raouf began insisting that we cut a hole in the wall so we could continue to include him in our conversations, I thought it best that we all pile in together.

Raouf was happy to have some new friends to practise his English on, and was particularly taken with Muffy. 'Muffy very nice girl. She very good girl. Muffy very beautiful girl,' he purred.

I should have counselled him to cool his jets but, instead, I tantalised him by joking that she was on the hunt for a husband and that I was certain she wouldn't mind sharing that special someone with another wife. When, a week later, he presented her with a lapis ring, I was forced to do a fair bit of backpedalling; while crushed by the news that she was neither on the market nor willing to convert to Islam, he was content enough to sit and breathe the same air as this bewitching, nubile westerner.

By that stage, my long-distance relationship with Nick was starting to crumble and, having only just welcomed Muffy and Lynchy into the fold, I was forced to abandon them soon afterwards while I flew home to Sydney for an emergency patch-up job.

There was a bomb attack the morning after I left, followed by an earthquake two days later. By the time I returned in mid-March, Muffy and Lynchy had experienced being in a lockdown (from which they had snuck out, to go party); they had foolishly sampled the food at The Diana, ensuring a good few days of diarrhoea; and handled a gun (courtesy of a drunk security contractor they met at The Den);

and Muffy had taken a stack on the ice. All of that, together with Lynchy's sewage-trench slip-up, had effectively ticked every box on Kabul's initiation to-do list.

Pre-production was now in full swing. While Lynchy worked with Hamid plotting out the scripts, Muffy despaired at our lack of resources and skilled crew for a show that we were told needed to be up to 'western standards'. Our client wanted to see as much bang for their buck as possible and, if the show proved as popular as we hoped, it would be reaching an audience of anywhere up to thirteen million people. Muffy was endlessly on Skype, consulting with contacts back home regarding lights and cameras and sound gear, and finally presented management with a modest wish list that made their collective heads spin.

It took weeks of negotiating before a compromise was reached. We could maybe lose a light, but not the radio mikes . . . The cheap sound mixer from China would probably suffice . . . If we had to choose between lenses, we'd take the long over the wide. It was with a great sense of relief that we finally handed over the order to Jalal, the Afghan–American head of technical services.

Finding a location for the whiz-bang headquarters of our imaginary elite commando unit was equally challenging. There were no sound studios in Kabul, so we had to find ourselves a suitable house in a relatively quiet spot that would accommodate a set with multiple locations, plus a make-up room, kitchen, wardrobe department and living quarters for our actual guards and one of our lead actors.

All up, thirty-eight houses were inspected and most of them were deemed unworthy at a cursory glance. One home, however, seemed ideal and Aleem and Muffy excitedly called me in to give it the final nod. We sent the procurement officer around the next day to negotiate a contract, but he returned empty handed, informing us that the owner didn't want westerners anywhere near his place. We finally settled on a sprawling, two-storey house that was fortuitously close to the office.

Meanwhile, Lynchy was having problems of his own. He and Sayed, the Afghan co-director, had begun casting for the show, searching for the three men and two women who would play the leads. It was the usual routine of running an ad on TV and radio calling for actors, but the resultant pickings were decidedly slim. Sifting through a huge pile of CVs, I wondered aloud whether being proficient in Excel bore any real relevance to the job at hand until some wit suggested that they could perhaps create their own call sheets.

Around two hundred and fifty actors mugged, aped and hammed their way through their auditions, and Lynchy and Sayed were made to witness some appalling crimes against acting before they finally selected three outstanding male leads. Only five women auditioned to be on the show. One was a seasoned film actor and would prove perfect to play the older 'Sumayah'. Three of them thought they were applying for a job in dubbing; one girl didn't really know why she was there, but her cousin worked in the graphics department. The hunt for a young, competent, female actor, whose family would allow her to appear on television, grew typically desperate.

Salvation came in the form of a sassy, twenty-something thespian who had grown up in Germany but had recently returned to Afghanistan to try her luck on local TV. She was comely and didn't make a complete meal of her audition piece, but she wanted accommodation in an upmarket hotel, a personal driver and $30,000. Thirty grand was just under half our entire budget, and our counter-offer of a room in a lovely little place called The Diana, a taxi allowance and $400 per episode wasn't well received. Once again Muffy had to don her negotiating cap to push it through.

It also became apparent around this time that we needed an experienced director of photography. The cameras we had ordered would give us great pictures, but only if they were operated by people who actually knew how to use them. Our crew didn't. And Lynchy wanted to adopt a fast-paced, fly-on-the-wall shooting style that was beyond our team's experience. Muffy once again took to Skype, following up leads and interviewing potential candidates before we settled on an Australian guy, Damien, who had the CV, the skills and, most importantly, the laid-back demeanour required to work in our world.

The hiring of a Hungarian sound engineer and an Indian assistant director completed the line-up, but, even with our expats, we still only had a production crew of seventeen people, who would have to work day and night for seventy-two days to make the thirteen-part series.

There were still gaping holes in our team that we just didn't have the money to fill. We had no set designer, wardrobe consultant, props buyer, continuity, runners . . . the list went on and on. Lynchy spent his nights assembling bombs and suicide vests, spray-painting plastic guns, and making up bottles of 'blood'—a sticky concoction comprising strawberry syrup, caramel topping and red food colouring—while I was dispatched to Dubai to purchase furnishings for our set. Blinds, lamps and light fittings were all bubble-wrapped in my hotel room late at night before being lugged back to Kabul as overweight luggage.

Our need for a first-rate make-up artist on the shoot brought to us Shakila, a high-spirited, fabulous Hazara woman. She had been with the company for years and could certainly do exceptional face and hair, but had no experience at all in special-effects make-up, so Muffy ordered in a kit from London and then downloaded how-to YouTube clips for Shakila to study. In the lead-up to the shoot, we all walked around the office looking like trauma victims, carrying evidence of bullet holes, burns and knife wounds as this talented and industrious young woman practised her craft.

We were still waiting for the arrival of our equipment and beginning to get antsy. Our constant enquiries to Jalal about its whereabouts were always met with evasion: 'You should check with finance' . . . 'Perhaps it is in Dubai' . . . 'There are always hold-ups in customs.' It all seemed so very strange that finally Muffy and I strode into his office one day, determined not to leave without a definitive answer. The answer we got wasn't pleasing; in fact, it made me choke back a smidgen of vomit. He hadn't yet ordered the equipment as he was apparently waiting for approval from management.

By this stage, the Dubai office had effectively morphed into the decision-making hub of Moby. In the early part of the year a whole host of expats had been hired; they had colonised finance, human resources and business development, from where they were now running the show, housed in a high-rise building in the UAE. With their focus firmly on new territories and ventures, they seldom drifted from the mother ship to make the trek to Kaboom Land and, if any of them did deign to pay us a visit, it was more often than not a single-day stay—literally, a first-plane-in, last-plane-out affair.

For the Afghanistan mob, the Dubai factor had simply created a whole range of extra approval processes, covering everything from new hires to buying props, and at first we were a little unsure of our footing. 'Passing the buck' (already an entrenched practice in the company, if not the whole country) had now become a compulsion and we all initially spent an inordinate amount of time and energy simply covering arse. So, getting to the bottom of the equipment debacle was never going to be an easy task.

Muffy and I spent the rest of that day stalking from office to office, trying to sort out the unspeakable mess, but ultimately we failed to discover where the process had gone pear-shaped or why Jalal had never bothered to chase it up. There were even suggestions that Muffy and I should have been chasing it up ourselves . . . who knows? However, by close of business, we at least had the go-ahead from Dubai to order in the gear. The best guesstimate we could squeeze out of Jalal was that it would be a five-week wait.

We were due to begin shooting in three. Even though our funding came with a strict timeline, we were now left with no option other than to delay the shoot by a month. And, even with this delay, we still filmed the first three episodes in virtual darkness as we waited for the delivery of our lights.

A week away from the new start date, our Indian assistant director called to tell Muffy that he had broken his leg in a bike accident and couldn't make the shoot. He had found a replacement locally but, being fully across the prolonged visa process, we knew that his substitute was a good four weeks out from arriving. I would have to step into the role.

I had been on enough sets to know my way around the job. You basically had to keep things running smoothly and to time, and needed to be able to scare the willies out of your cast and crew when necessary. Having perfected the 'big eyes and red face' routine on *Salam,* I was sure I was up to it. Muffy had already taken on the task of breaking the scripts down and making schedules because, due to budget constraints, our assistant director was always going to be a last-minute starter. And, with that settled, we were kind of, sort of, ready to go.

And then we made the show, and everything ran smoothly, and we had the best time of our lives! Well, unfortunately, that's a sentence from another story—it's about another show, one that was made far, far away from Afghanistan.

By the time we were nearing the end of the shoot, I could boldly claim that, although not necessarily the 'best time of my life', it had been a rollicking, hilarious, incessantly frustrating adventure that I wouldn't have missed for the world. And I felt so blessed to have my wonderful Aussie friends along for the ride.

Being a police action drama, we were shooting most of it on the streets of Kabul. The good thing about shooting in Afghanistan was that, most of the time, there were no permits and permissions required: we simply rocked up to the location and, with the help of our two-man security detail and a couple of local police, we shut down the road for an hour or two.

The bad thing about shooting there was that you were guaranteed an audience wherever you went. As soon as we got the cameras out, children appeared from everywhere, shouting excitedly about the · television show being made in their hood. The sight of a bunch of westerners running around like headless chooks only fuelled their delirium. There was simply no containing them and, on more than one occasion, I was forced to stomp into the fray and clamp my hand over a chatty child's mouth.

Now and then, there would be some unsuspecting tiny tot who didn't know that it was all pretend. One day we were shooting a scene where our two male heroes shot and killed a suicide bomber who was threatening to detonate outside a mosque. Two dear little innocents wandered in holding hands, to see what all the excitement was about, and shrieked with horror before racing back down the road. I quickly dispatched Aleem to calm them, but unfortunately his pursuit only added to their terror and it took him a two-block chase, complete with screaming and hysterical crying, before he finally caught up with them to explain it was a game.

As we were making a series that showcased the police, the Ministry of Interior guaranteed us its full backing. They promised us officers to beef up our security, and people and jeeps to appear in scenes where a police presence was needed. But the officers invariably turned up late, typically thoroughly disinterested, and attempted to scarper as soon as they'd been fed. They were constantly demanding 'compensation' for petrol or time spent on set beyond their shift; they snoozed on traffic duty, talked loudly on their phones during takes, and left their guns lying around the set. At that time the average wage for an officer was around one hundred dollars a month so I'm fairly sure that babysitting a team of pedantic television types didn't rate highly on their list of priorities.

Still, it was almost laughable that we were attempting to glorify these men on-screen. Even the child onlookers thought they were a joke—whenever an officer waved his baton around, threatening to silence the crowd with a savage beating (something I had to firmly shut down every time a new officer came on board), the kids simply laughed and ran away, throwing taunts behind them as they made good their escape.

Our relations with the police hit an all-time low on the day we needed them the most. The scene involved our on-screen heroes trying, yet again, to foil a bomb-toting terrorist; we required the officers to race into shot in their jeep and provide back-up for our crack commando team. Muffy had spent weeks sourcing a location where we could accommodate all the action—thirty extras would stroll along a street, with our insurgent wandering amongst them and our two lead actors in close, but covert, pursuit. Then there would be an initial showdown, at which people would scatter, before the arrival of the police, hurtling along the road and stopping just short of the stand-off, before jumping down and making an arrest. The Ministry of Agriculture had reluctantly agreed to let us shoot outside its building, but it needed to happen on a Friday when they were closed for business.

It was the middle of summer; we were already sizzling when we turned up to the location at 7am. By 9am you could see waves of heat rising from the road. Our team wasn't happy with having to work on what should have been their one day off, but they toiled like troupers to cover the ridiculous number of shots we had scheduled for that day.

The police, predictably, turned up late with a communal attitude worthy of a diva. They sniffed and scowled and sneered in Dari about the plausibility of the scenario; we had to undertake some serious bum-licking to get into their good books. By the time we got around to shooting their cameo—the last scene of the day—I was ready to shank the lot of them. Still, we all smiled and bowed as we gave them a detailed briefing on what we wanted, making sure to thank the commander for the zillionth time for being so very obliging.

The sun was getting low and we had no time to rehearse, and I admit to being a tad nervous as the police jeep made its way to its first position. Our initial set-up was a wide shot, taking in the entire showdown; on the call of 'Action!', the villain raised his hands in surrender as the car rounded the corner and roared down the street. It screeched to a halt within metres of our cast and you could actually hear Lynchy scream 'Fuck!' on the footage. Our prima donna police then dismounted like professionals and lined up before the bad guy, their guns raised. It was fortunate for us that they did so because it was the only shot we got of them.

Feeling cocky after his thrilling performance, the driver of the jeep took it upon himself to speed down to the end of the street; as he went to make a U-turn there, he sent the cast and crew scattering in all directions. Our armourer on the set, a British police trainer, immediately approached the car, banged on its bonnet and gave the driver an expletive-riddled serve about his reckless actions. The commander was utterly outraged by our armourer's impertinence, and all the bum-licking in the world couldn't save us. Within minutes, they were all back in the jeep and disappearing into the distance.

We had some officers providing security that day and we quickly shuffled them into the scene to get what close shots we could. As we were shooting the last of it, Ahmad hurried towards us, a jibbering jabbering mess. He had just taken a call from the Minister of Agriculture. It seems that we had shamed the police, and a representative from the ministry would be arriving on set within the next ten minutes to delete everything we had shot that day. I immediately called 'Wrap!' and Muffy and I screamed at everyone to grab the gear and get into the vans.

The bump-out was a shambles, with cameras and sound gear all slung willy-nilly into our idling vans, people piled in on top of one another and those who couldn't fit simply clinging onto the sides of the vehicles as we sped away. We ended the day with a smashed monitor and a missing mike, but it was worth it to keep our hard-earned footage.

The drama wasn't only confined to the set; back at the office, Muffy was also engaged in daily battles. Despite the fact that she had budgeted the entire show with complete accuracy, the finance department (a mix of expats and Afghans) was all over us—they studiously pored over every receipt, hoping to unveil some outrageous discrepancy to proudly report back to the mother ship.

One day Muffy was hauled in by our Afghan manager and accused of including her personal receipts in the mix. The anomaly in question concerned money spent on a can of shaving cream and a packet of cigarettes. Through gritted teeth, she calmly explained that they were props used in episode three and that, on her handsome wage, she had no need to buy her toiletries and fags on the company dime. Besides, she waxed.

Another time, when she sent our kids to collect water for the day, they arrived back with twelve bottles, informing her that the head cleaner (who was apparently also responsible for beverage distribution) refused to hand over the fifty bottles she had quite rightly requested for a full-day shooting in the fierce summer sun. She stormed off to the supply room, brushing past the king of the cleaners on her way in and, without even consulting the man, lugged out the extra stock herself. Over beers that night she marvelled at how she was able to take a half-dozen unloaded AK-47s to the set as props, no sweat, but that adequate water supplies were a genuine concern.

Afternoon snacks and cans of Red Bull, despite being budgeted for, became another whopping bone of contention. The studio crews didn't require them, so why did we? Muffy's argument—that the studio crews spent their days in air-conditioned comfort, typically propped up against the walls, while our crew lugged their gear around the streets of Kabul from morning to night—made little headway. No, it was clear that we were having a 'party' and the company would no longer be paying for our festivities. I received news of this as we were shooting in the rain on Russian Swimming Pool Hill (home to a disused, thirty-year-old Olympic-sized pool built by the Soviets) and immediately shot a text to our manager:

> I am currently standing ankle deep in stinking mud on the side of a mountain and am soaking wet from being rained on for the past three hours. Come up here and see what kind of 'party' we're having!!!!!!!! You're always welcome. Trudi.

We ended up paying for the 'party favours' ourselves; it wasn't worth the hassle and the scandal became insignificant once Ramadan hit us, because from sunrise to sunset our Muslim crew couldn't eat, drink or smoke. Out of respect for our team and because we were constantly out in public, we all refrained from indulging or found a hiding place where we could sneak a cigarette or sip on some water. Most Afghans work shorter hours during the month-long fast, but our rigid production schedule didn't allow us that luxury. Instead, we simply adjusted our times—beginning our day at 6am and winding up at 2pm. Our darling crew never complained, but there were tension-filled days when I prayed we'd wrap before they finally unravelled.

One of our final episodes featured a street kid who was unwittingly used to deposit a bomb outside the gates of the Ministry of Defence. He ended up on the run from both the police and the insurgents, and returned to his hidey-hole to wait it out. We found the perfect hidey-hole early into pre-production—it was an old, Russian army tank, parked in a deserted lot at the end of our street. There was a bit of rubbish strewn around it, but nothing that we couldn't easily clear. So, with that location sorted, we shunted it from our minds and didn't bother to inspect it again before the shoot.

We turned up on the day to discover that the entire area had been converted into a communal garbage dump; even at 7am the fetid stench was already overwhelming. The tank had not been spared and, together with a mound of refuse, it was also home to a nest of angry wasps. We couldn't relocate, we just didn't have the time, so I dashed off to the supermarket to buy insect spray, garbage bags, rubber gloves and face masks.

Damien took on the wasps, bravely drenching the tank's bowels with insecticide before he fled the scene. We all screamed and ran for cover as the peeved insects vacated their premises. After a suitable wait, we began clearing the tank. I swear there were things moving in there; I had visions of huge rats leaping out and latching onto my filthy face. There was obstinate, gooey stuff growing on the floor that we just couldn't remove, so I raced off again, this time to retrieve a blanket from our guest house to cover the putrid muck.

The location backed onto a busy road, close to an even busier intersection. Our traffic cop that day was of the dozy variety and, despite working out hand signals with him and practising them until I was sleeping with my eyes open, he continually let cars through in the middle of takes. I spent my day dashing up and down the road, trying to hold back the traffic myself.

At 3pm we were still shooting; we were already an hour over and still had one more to go. All of us were dirty, hot and dispirited, compulsively smacking our dry chops like frenzied Labradors. As I squatted on the ground, waiting for the cameras to reset, raised voices roused me from my languid funk. There was some kerfuffle between our cameraman and sound guy—Mustafa and Massood were always at each other—and for a red-hot second I considered just letting it go. But when I saw fists flying around, I thought better of it.

It took four of us to break up the fight, and a lot of agitated to-ing and fro-ing to discover the cause of the fuss. It seemed that Massood had hit the wall, and had slipped behind a van to rinse his raging Ramadan mouth with water. Mustafa had caught him. Despite his protestations that he hadn't actually swallowed, Massood then copped a couple of punches to the head for being the worst kind of Muslim.

On that September day, the two IT experts from Dubai had been fiddling with the editing machine for the entire afternoon and were grateful for our invitation to join us for a bevvy at our local after work. They finally arrived at the bar at 7pm and reluctantly informed Muffy, Lynchy, Damien and me that they still hadn't figured out the problem but were certain that they'd get to the bottom of it the following day. Our various responses included shoulder shrugs, assurances that they shouldn't worry, and a call from Lynchy for another round of drinks. They were truly confounded by our obvious composure. Hey, we all knew it was a huge issue—just one more hump on an endless, bumpy road—but if we'd allowed ourselves to be shaken by every production pothole on *Eagle Four*, we'd have all been committed long ago.

9.
The Great Bar War of Kabul

In the time I lived in Afghanistan, I became accustomed to saying goodbye. People constantly floated in and out of the Ka-bubble and friendships, often transient and brief, were endowed with an intensity that belied the brevity of the relationship. Some farewells were splendid, protracted affairs spanning a month full of dinners and drinks—an excess of constant, if perhaps slightly desperate, catch-ups. Other people disappeared in the time it took to catch your breath . . . But my dear friend Dick Willy's leaving was the most inglorious departure I was a party to.

Dick made his debut on the Kabul scene when he opened a bar called Rahimi's in my neighbourhood. Bars in Kabul are in short supply and are under constant threat of closure. It could be a vengeful government crackdown, in retaliation for some perceived western slight, or a bid to placate the religious Right. Or a surprise raid by the local police because the owner refused to up the baksheesh. So if a new establishment opened, it was always worth a look-in.

My first excursion to Rahimi's was a memorable event. I had wandered down there in March with Muffy and Lynchy, and two more mates fresh off the boat—Rick, an Australian producer and friend of mine, and Giusi, an Italian producer. They had both recently joined Moby to revamp *The Morning Show*. We headed to the bar to sample the deep-fried chicken we had heard so much about.

Dick greeted us at the door, and was expansive and loud and welcoming; the stub of a cigar was clenched firmly between his teeth. We placed our orders and were ushered to the bar, where Dick fetched us drinks. Then, in his earthy Texan drawl, he ran through the outstanding features of his fine establishment, proclaiming with open arms: 'We have the best drinks and the best food in town.' He handed us all business cards, before excusing himself and heading towards the kitchen.

We settled for a minute, taking in the place . . . when a thunderous explosion rocked the room. I instantly raced to the other side of the bar, certain I'd be seeing bearded men brandishing AK-47s storming the joint at any moment. Muffy, Rick and Giusi remained frozen on the spot, while Lynchy, inexplicably, raced towards the direction of the noise. You could tell by our various responses which of us had been in the country the longest.

Dick hurried in a heartbeat later, assuring us that it was all okay. The pressure cooker had exploded in the kitchen. Everyone was fine, but there would be no dinner service that night. Sorry. He held up a twisted metal bracket to reinforce his claim. We sucked back our drinks and said our goodbyes, promising to return the following evening.

We didn't go back for a good two months. Kitchen mishap or not, the explosion had cast an ominous pall over dining at Dick's place.

We finally ventured back midway through summer. Some of our good mates had started frequenting Rahimi's and had christened it their new local, abandoning the bar I once managed just up the road.

The Den had been taken over by Gary, a private security contractor who had some very punchy, surly friends regularly propping up the bar; it no longer had that friendly, easy-going ambience we had initially fallen for. So Rahimi's soon became our haunt and most evenings, after shooting on the hot, dusty streets of Kabul all day, we'd stagger in there to hang with our buddies and unwind.

Business seemed to be going very well and Dicky was the queen of the castle. He had endeared himself to his patrons by being open pretty much all the time. Living out the back, and with most of his local staff living upstairs, Dick would answer his phone at any time of the night or day and let you in. He never seemed to sleep, with the exception of passing out behind the bar for a quick kip during full service, and you sensed that your 6am intrusion was almost a relief.

It quickly became apparent that Dick was quite a complex character. For starters, he was a gay Republican. Go figure. And his time in Afghanistan had left him undeniably damaged. He had been run out of Kandahar with a price on his head during his stint in defence communications, and had survived the suicide attack on the Safi Landmark Hotel just a month before opening the bar. His retelling of this event was disturbingly surreal . . . Asleep in his room when the five bombers detonated, he made his way to the roof, smoked a cigar, and marvelled at the rainbow array of birds escaping from the damaged aviary next door, as the bloody drama unfolded below. I got the feeling that reigning over a bar full of booze wasn't exactly aiding his recovery.

Generally the smartest person in the room, Dick could contribute to almost any conversation, even when he was barking mad, but he seemed lacking in basic common sense. He was clearly a tough nut because running a bar in Kabul is not for a lightweight. Dealing with corrupt police, dodgy government officials, angry drunks who carry guns and crazy chicks who take on angry drunks who carry guns requires a solid pair of balls. But he was also incredibly sensitive, not afraid of a good cry, and naive to the point where you wanted to shake him. And it was this open-hearted ingenuousness that ultimately undid him.

From the start, Dick had tried to nurture a good relationship with Gary. He didn't want to see The Den go out of business and initially suggested that they keep in touch to ensure they weren't planning events on the same night—that one bar's karaoke gig didn't clash with the other's monthly poker tournament.

Gary was amiable enough, but simply not buying it. 'No offence, mate, but we're in competition. No thanks.'

Dick reluctantly let it go and continued to effortlessly pilfer Gary's customers.

One night, after around eighty-seven bourbons, Dick decided to pay a neighbourly visit to The Den. It was a sad affair and in distinct contrast to the rocking party that was going down at Rahimi's. A couple of drunken birds sat at the bar; a smattering of security contractors stood out on the terrace. Dick started chatting with the female bar flies, who mentioned that they missed really good ice cream, so Dick told them they could get it at Rahimi's. Having just shipped in an ice-cream machine, he could guarantee them the best cones in Kabul; and then he raced down the road to bring them back a sample.

I can only assume that, when Gary heard about this encounter, he was less than impressed; he turned up at Rahimi's a few days later with a couple of his thug mates, locked Dick in a room and beat the living shit out of him. It was a shocking retaliation that left Dick battered and bewildered. He showed me the X-rays revealing his four broken ribs and wept at the senselessness of it all.

But while Dick was grieving over this 'betrayal', his friends were fired up and furious. And a few days later, two of them arranged for some local police to stage a raid on The Den. Everyone thought it a brilliant revenge, until we learnt that two of the Afghan staff and Shane, the mouthy American bar manager, who'd been privy to Gary's plans to beat up Dick, had been arrested during the sting and thrown into jail. They stayed there for three days, while Gary made no attempt to secure their release.

You would never want to wear the blame for sending someone to jail in Afghanistan. I'm told prisoners don't eat unless someone brings them in food. They don't wash; they don't sleep, for fear they'll be beaten at best, or raped or murdered. When the three finally returned to The Den, they found it deserted. The cash box was empty and Gary was gone. Shane was on a plane home the very next day and, when one of the Afghan boys, Khairy, turned up at our office a few weeks later, enquiring about work, he couldn't speak about the ordeal without tearing up and trembling.

For Dick's part, he felt burdened with guilt. Already traumatised by the brutal attack, the knowledge that he was inadvertently responsible for the suffering of the two Afghan boys saw him spiral into depression.

With The Den closed, we all assumed it was over—that the Great Bar War of Kabul had run its course. Still, it came as no surprise when Dick phoned me a few weeks later to say that there was a local TV crew out the front of his place. The reporter spoke English and, through the door, was demanding an interview with Dick. He had 'discovered' that Rahimi's was, in fact, a Chinese brothel and wanted to talk to him about it. As I worked in media, Dick asked my opinion on how to handle it.

I strongly advised him to stay inside; if he didn't make a statement, they didn't really have a story. He argued that he wanted to defend himself and firmly refute the scurrilous allegations.

'Darling, you're being so naive,' I countered. 'They can edit the piece however they like and still make you look guilty. And what are you going to do then? Huh? Take them to court for defaming you? Good luck with that.'

He seemed to accept my reasoning . . . but called me back about a half-hour later to say that he had completely ignored it. He had gone outside to deliver a curt 'No comment' and couldn't see how they could possibly use that against him.

The story aired the next day. On high rotation. They had crafted his clever 'No comment' into a thirty-minute piece. The kids at work talked me through it.

It began with the reporter speaking straight to camera, claiming to have uncovered a brothel in Kabul. He then went into a lengthy, impassioned rant about prostitution being against Islam and Allah, before vowing to track the owner down. They brought up a snapshot of the Rahimi's website as proof of his claim. Dick's catchphrase had been doctored to read: 'We have the best drinks and the best Chinese girls in town.' The location of the bar and his email address were displayed for all to see. The bulk of the story saw the reporter driving through the city streets looking for Rahimi's, which was a bit strange, considering he actually had the address. It was shameless padding for an incredibly flimsy piece of 'investigative journalism'.

But it was Dick's defiant cameo that truly stole the show. It was just as he'd described it to me: he ventured outside, delivered his lines, and then stepped back in and closed the door. A fleeting, five-second walk-on. But when they repeated the shot again, straight afterwards, the action was rather more protracted—it was shown this time in slow motion with a huge white circle around Dick's head. The third go saw the picture enlarged, again with the slow mo, but now the white circle had been replaced with a blazing red arrow that moved up and down the screen as it pointed at Dick. The final version was also close and slow, but this time Dick shared a split screen with the shot of Rahimi's crudely doctored website.

I casually asked my colleagues whether anyone really watched the channel on which the story had run. They quickly assured me that everybody did—Merzad's father had brought his attention to the brothel piece just that morning. Merzad asked me who this godless western man with his Chinese prostitutes was. I said I didn't know.

By the time I called Dick, he was already receiving emails. He forwarded me one to give me a taste of their tone:

From: silsilall
Date: 2010/11/11
Subject: hello MR . . .

MR PIMP, how are you . . . bring your wife so that we can fuck you and her also in double system that you haven't seen in America also . . . .

IF WE SEE YOU IN KABUL WE WILL FUCK YOU 1ST THEN ALL THE CHANIES LADIES . . . .AND THEN WE KILL YOU!!! !!

BRING YOUR AMERICANS TO HERE AND WE CAN FUCK THEM IN BOTH SIDE . . . ..

WAITING FOR YOUR CONFIRMATION MAIL BACK WHEN YOU CAN GIVE US YOUR FAMILY NUMBER?????

Not surprisingly, Dick didn't reply and, despite being quietly fascinated by the 'double system', he was truly freaked. I talked him down, advised him to stay inside and promised to check in again after work.

By the end of the day, he had received over two hundred emails. A mixed bag—some were seemingly genuine enquiries about rates, but others were threats of violence and guarantees of death by people claiming to be the Taliban, and clearly these weren't hateful cyber-trolls, simply having a go. I finally got him to agree that he might just be in danger.

But his greatest concern wasn't for himself. His Afghan staff were now being contacted by their families—some in Kabul, some in faraway provinces where the story had filtered through—demanding to know why their sons were working in a brothel. His bar manager, who had briefly appeared in the story when the camera crew first arrived, had been on the phone with his father all day. He was due to marry in the coming months—his fiancée, a cousin, was no longer keen and his family was threatening to disown him.

Dick loved those boys like brothers and despaired at what he had done to them. He felt he had to fix things. He had spoken to the local police chief, who was on his payroll but who regretted he could do nothing to protect him. He did, however, suggest that Dick do a follow-up piece, with the police in attendance, to prove that there were no Chinese sex-workers on site. The chief had his own reputation to protect and needed to prove that his precinct was clean.

Dick imagined that this would be the answer to everyone's problems and argued that he really had no other choice. I pleaded with him to let it go—to cut his losses and move on. But he was beyond reason by this stage—he was calming his nerves with alcohol and hash, and had gone to a place that I couldn't reach.

The production crew and police turned up the following morning. Dick hadn't slept all night. He was angry and wild-eyed—the epitome of the lunatic running the asylum. The tour of the premises they filmed simply didn't make the cut and the story solely focused on an interview with Dick, where he ranted and raved and chomped compulsively on his cigar, accusing the reporter of having evil eyes and repeatedly telling him he was a shame to his mother.

Just to compound the damage he had already inflicted on himself, at the very end of the piece two female Japanese NGO workers innocently wandered in, looking for lunch. The final shot had Dick, in slow motion, launching himself at them and yelling 'NOOOOOOO . . .', before chasing them out the door.

It went to air that same afternoon, and there was no sense in trying to negotiate further with a crazy man. I ordered him to pack his stuff. For good. He needed to hide at my guest house until we could get him out of the country. A car would be picking him up in thirty minutes, and I wanted him ready to leave. He sobbed like a child, but I stood my ground—playing tough mum to his frightened boy.

Fortunately the owner of our guest house, Glen, a stocky, ruddy Aussie bloke who ran a de-mining company, was out of town. I called his business partner, Mack, and casually conveyed the news that I had an American friend in need of short-term accommodation. He was on his way out and just required a room for a couple of days. Room 7 was free, wasn't it? I would personally cover the cost.

Mack thought that all sounded okay. Sure thing—my mate could stay. He'd let Glen know the next time he called.

And so my mission to save Dick Willy went into full swing. Muffy and Lynchy were both home that day, felled by a stomach bug that was doing the rounds. I called them up, filled them in and tasked them with minding Dick until I got home. Muffy immediately called the emergency hotline at the US Embassy. She got an answering machine. She left a message saying that one of their citizens was in serious trouble and was being threatened by the Taliban, and requested that they call her back.

By all accounts, the babysitting detail was a harrowing affair. Dick was as mad as a meat axe by then, constantly crying and pleading to be allowed to return to the bar to check on his staff. Lynchy distracted him by reciting lines from their favourite films.

Dick became stuck on a quote from *Apocalypse Now.* As he repeated this monologue over and over, Muffy kept trying to contact the embassy. They never did get back to her.

By the time I got home, Dick had settled considerably, thanks in part to a Valium or two, but he still wasn't accepting that he had to go. Besides, he threw in as an innocuous aside, his passport was currently in the possession of the Ministry of Interior because his visa was being renewed.

This 'insignificant' detail sent us all into a spin. We had very real fears at that point that it wasn't just the Taliban who were out to get him, but perhaps the authorities as well. Over beers and endless cigarettes we grappled with the situation we now found ourselves in.

We weren't the only people staying at the guest house, and it also doubled as an office for Glen's business. People came and went all afternoon and, in the evening, Glen's Afghan fixer, Rameen, arrived to drive a New Zealand employee, Des, to a bar across town. It was a Thursday night, but our posse was staying in—we couldn't leave Dick for fear he'd escape.

After days without sleep, he finally collapsed; meantime Muffy, Lynchy and I drank ourselves sober. We were navigating territory beyond our imagination. We made soapies in Kabul, we were simple Aussie folk, but now we were harbouring an unhinged American fugitive, accused of being a pimp in the Islamic Republic of Afghanistan.

Breakfast the next morning was a sombre affair, until Des turned up after a thirteen-hour binge. At first he was charming and jovial, insisting we share with him his stone-cold pizza and offering us up shots of his prized tequila. We all declined, quite politely I thought, too distracted by our dilemma to want to party with Des. It was then that he turned like a whirling dervish. He knew who the guy was in Room 7—Rameen had recognised him from the TV reports.

'You're placin' the whole fucken house in danger. Who the fuck do youse think youse are?' Des slurred. 'That guy's gotta go, no question about it. Mack is on his way over now to show him the door.' He then staggered to his feet. 'No, fuck that! I'm gonna throw him out meself, right now!'

I confess to having been too shocked and exhausted to respond adequately to Des's drunken declaration. But Muffy found her voice. She had never liked Des (primarily because he was always hitting on her) and I suspect she was happy to have an excuse to finally take him on.

'No, I'm sorry but you'll do no such thing! Yes, okay maybe we messed up—we admit that. But the guy was in real trouble. So why don't you just sit back down, eat your rotten pizza and SHUT UP?'

It was a sterling performance that saw a stunned Des immediately collapse back into his chair. Then we all sat in miserable silence, waiting for Mack.

Mack arrived about ten minutes later with Rameen in tow, and was more disappointed than angry. Everyone in Kabul was looking for this bloke—why the hell did we bring him here? Then, turning to me: 'Why the hell did you lie to me, love?'

The jig was up and I was almost relieved. I apologised to Mack, and explained that we were just helping our mate and had had no idea what we were taking on. I boldly claimed that we'd do it all again if we had our time over and, appealing to the Australian mindset of 'Never leave a digger behind', questioned whether Mack wouldn't do the same.

Mack shook his head like a dad we'd let down, but when he spoke again he was decisive and definite. 'Righto. Don't you lot worry. Me and Rameen will sort this mess out. But I'm tellin' you right now—if that bloke so much as steps a foot outside this door, he's straight outta here. You got that? And you're not to tell *anyone* that he's stayin' here with us.'

I think I teared up a little at that stage—the release was divine. Our rock-steady Papa Mack and the unassuming, well-connected Rameen were going to save the day.

Dick had his passport back the following day; the exit visa needed to get him out of the country had cost fifteen hundred bucks. We all praised Allah for the rampant corruption in Afghanistan and finally relaxed because we were almost there.

We farewelled Dick before work—he was flying to Dubai in the afternoon. Rameen had 'contacts' at the airport and he would person-ally see him on to the plane.

When we caught up with Rameen at the guest house that night, he could only laugh at the 'covert escape'. Despite being advised to keep a low profile, Dick had wept and wailed all the way through the airport. And when they got to Immigration, the officer looked at the passport and then at Dick and asked Rameen in Dari whether this was the pimp from the Chinese brothel.

A nudge and a wink and a lightly greased palm saw Dick safely on the plane. The flight was running two hours late, but Rameen didn't leave until the plane had rumbled down the runway and lifted off into the evening sky.

10.
Hakim's Word of the Day

It was a Thursday afternoon. That meant my twenty-two-year-old translator, Hakim, was preparing to dispense 'Word-of-the-Day' cards to Muffy, Merzad and me.

Word-of-the-Day was one of Muffy's initiatives. She received the tiny deck of cards in a care package from her aunty and excitedly explained to Hakim and Merzad how it all worked. You took a card from the deck each morning, read the word printed on it, and that was to be your guiding principle for the day. The first word Merzad picked was AUTHENTICITY, but the fact that he had no idea what that meant kind of put a downer on his enthusiasm for the game. Possessing a slightly superior command of the English language, Hakim thought it was inspired and happily added Word-of-the-Day Dispenser to his extensive job description.

Each morning, after Muffy and I were settled at our desks, he would prance over holding the cup that contained the cards and offer it around. If we were hungover or he sensed we were gearing up for a particularly horrendous day, he would take out all the boring words like DETAIL, DISCIPLINE and EFFICIENCY and hide them, leaving us with a slim selection along the lines of FREEDOM, JOY and PLEASURE. On Thursday afternoons, he would allow us to pick a second card so that we had a word for Friday, our one day off, and he was always extra careful to ensure that we all came out Word-of-the-Day winners.

Hakim already had three very important tasks to perform. His primary role was translator and he initially came on board to work on *Eagle Four*. During the writing phase of the show, we quickly realised that our original tiny office just wasn't going to suffice for such a huge production so, bidding a sad farewell to our good buddy Raouf, we relocated across Main Street to a more spacious locale. Needing to work closely with Hakim on translating the scripts for client approval, he was eventually installed in our office for easy reference.

Hakim's initial contract had ended months ago, but by then I had fallen in love with this hard-working, good-natured boy and managed to convince the newly appointed general manager of our production company, a German man named Christof, that I couldn't possibly exist without him. So by November 2010 he was working on all of our drama productions, and spent his days translating Dari scripts to English and back again. I acted as script editor and, at times, sole writer on projects, so Hakim was kept very busy in his dual-language world. I always had to do final checks on his English translations before they were delivered to our clients and sometimes I had moments of utter bewilderment.

'Hakim, darling, what is a *very hooey man?*'

He sat bolt upright in an attempt to appear alert because inevitably he was checking the cricket scores online.

'Where?' he asked.

'*Secrets of this House.* Episode twenty-five. Scene four. "Kabir knew that the landlord was a very hooey man."'

Intense concentration as he clicked on to the script and scrambled to find the word: 'It's a man who is very hooey.'

'But sweetheart, that means nothing to me. Describe what the landlord is like.'

'He's hooey.'

'Yes, so you keep telling me. But what is your understanding of this man? What do you mean?'

More furious clicking and pointing at his screen 'It's in the translation dictionary. It's here and it says —'

'I don't care what's there, darling. Back away from the computer and look at me. Now. You tell me, in your own words, what the landlord is like.'

He thought very hard because he didn't want to get it wrong and disappoint me. 'He's very silly.'

'Thank you. "Kabir knew that the landlord was a very silly man."'

There was a long beat of silence as I went about replacing the word.

'What's wrong with saying he's a *hooey man?*'

'Well, darling, it's just not something that we'd say. Believe me, in all my years of speaking English—and I've had a few—I have never heard anyone throw into *any* conversation that somebody is *hooey.*'

He nodded sagely and made a note of it on his pad, but I don't think he ever really bought any of my revisions. He was studying English at university, with the aim of becoming a professor, and couldn't comprehend how a woman, who didn't know a 'subordinating conjunction' from an 'indefinite pronoun', could possibly hold herself up as an authority on the language.

Hakim's second job was toilet watchman. Occupying the desk closest to the glass-panelled door, it was his job to alert Muffy or myself as to when the toilet next to our office was free. With forty people sharing just one bathroom, it was an intense and nerve-racking task.

'Hakim! How's the toilet looking?'

He'd crane his neck to get a better view before casting me an earnest and sorrowful look. 'Not good . . .'

'Well, I'm busting. So you're on toilet watch.'

Toilet watch filled Hakim with incredible anxiety because there was always someone lurking in another office or lingering in the stairwell, waiting to pounce as soon as they heard the door being opened.

'Now! Now! Now!' he would cry.

I would jump out of my chair and dash across the room, only to have him groan and throw his hands up just as I reached the door. 'No, you missed out again.'

'Bugger. Who is it?'

'Ahmed from IT.'

'Oh Lord. He always takes forever.'

Hakim nodded in agreement. 'Last time he took thirteen minutes,' he confirmed.

Toilet timer was part of the watchman role and we both knew that Ahmed was one of the staff who routinely and inexplicably went into double-figure minutes on his visits to the loo. Muffy and I had our theories around this—virile young men, sharing a room each night with five siblings, the toilet at home nothing more than a mud brick outhouse *sans* a door . . .

'Right darling, you're still on watch. Rattle the handle in five minutes.'

Rattling the handle was a risky business, because there was always the chance that you'd be caught doing it just as the person was exiting the toilet. Hakim hated these embarrassing encounters and, more often than not, I'd end up doing the rattle—quite happy to endure the shame of intrusion for the sake of my aching bladder.

The period just before call to prayer was a traffic jam—everyone rushing to get their obligatory ablutions in before praying. The ritual requires the careful washing of the face, arms and feet, and very early on I quickly learnt that it was hopeless trying to get a look-in at certain times of the day. But my initial ignorance about the practice caused Hakim untold grief.

Hakim was a devout Muslim—he wouldn't even wear aftershave that contained alcohol. So while he was trying to find a gap in the traffic for me, he would also be anxiously awaiting his turn to ablute before dashing off to the mosque next door to pray. I'd like to say that I possessed the profound awareness to figure this out all by myself, but it took a quiet word from Merzad to alert me to Hakim's unspeakable dilemma.

Hakim's third job was strictly a summer gig. He was the fly killer. The task was much less taxing than toilet watchman and he grew to enjoy the thrill of the chase. He was called up for duty soon after joining us, when we were still sizing each other up.

For me at that time, Hakim was an enigma. He had none of the bling and brashness that the other boys in the department had. He was quiet and sensitive; he continually smiled and had no concept of personal space—he'd stand so close when talking to me that I could hear his heartbeat. To be honest, and to my great shame, I initially had him pegged as the 'Most Likely to Arrive at the Office One Day and Mow Me Down with an AK-47'.

I can't really say what Hakim thought of me at that time, but I'm guessing that 'wanton heathen' was up there in his assessment as I was constantly exposing him to depravity. The corruption of poor Hakim's mind wasn't a conscious act. In fact, being mindful of his conservatism, Muffy and I were initially very careful to mind our Ps and Qs—or rather, our 'bastards and shits'—and we saved our discussion of after-hours activities for our coffee and ciggy breaks, or bantered in some lame and rather obvious code that Hakim never twigged to.

'Oh! Did you talk to Kim last night?'

'Just briefly. Why?'

'You know she's playing tennis with Neil.'

'No! Stop it now! I thought she was playing tennis with Steve?'

'She is.'

'Does Steve know she's playing doubles?'

'I doubt it.'

No, the subversion was quite unintentional. For starters, there was our unfortunate weakness for *So You Think You Can Dance*, which aired on Indian cable every afternoon. While the boys were allowed to watch sport or dreadful Hindi movies most of the time on the sole television set in our office, *The Dancing Show* (as we referred to it) was our one viewing indulgence, and Muffy and I usually insisted on watching it. I might as well have been making Hakim watch hard-core porn.

At first he tried not to look, but the sight of all those apparently super-fit women—wearing nothing more than sequined tea towels and filling the screen with their leg splits, shoulder-high kicks and heaving bosoms—proved irresistible. I often caught him, his head lowered and fingers hovering over his keyboard, but his eyes clearly focused on the TV. If he caught me catching him peeping at the girls, he'd grin his unnerving grin, and blush and gush about the wonderful dancing.

Once, during the audition stage of the show, an overweight, strung-out stripper performed a particularly poor pole-dancing routine. Hakim couldn't take his eyes off her. When I asked him what he thought of the dancing, he opined that it wasn't very good and wondered why the woman had bothered to try out.

'Oh darling, she's just some poor delusional stripper on drugs,' Muffy offered by way of explanation.

'What's a stripper?' came his innocent reply.

'Well, sweetie, it's a woman who takes her clothes off for money.'

'Who gives her the money?'

'Men. Men pay to watch her take her clothes off.'

Hakim was genuinely astonished and clearly horrified. 'Why would anyone want to see her take off her clothes?'

I also have to take responsibility for making him look at dirty pictures on the internet. One day Shakila came to me wanting to buy cosmetic latex for her make-up kit. Because there were no suppliers of it in Afghanistan, we would have to order it online, so I asked Hakim to look it up for her. I then returned to the script I was editing.

Shakila's giggling made me look up. Hakim's ashen face alerted me to the fact that the search had perhaps gone slightly haywire. When I walked over to take a look at his screen, I was confronted with images of women in black latex cat suits, men dressed as gimps and young girls cavorting in sexy nurse gear.

I also had a plastic, yellow baseball bat parked behind my desk— my whacking bat. I originally had a whacking stick, a decorative piece of wood that I found amongst the rubbish one day, but it mysteriously disappeared when the kids moved all my gear into our new office. If any of the boys were in 'trouble', I'd beat it menacingly against my hand or, at worst, demand that they bend over and cop a whacking. It was all in good fun—the whacks were no more than taps, and it gave us a giggle when the day was dragging. But at first, Hakim would just look at me, wide-eyed and expressionless, when I administered my 'punishments'.

So when the first of the summer's blowflies buzzed into the office and I delivered the sombre news to Hakim, bat in hand, that if it wasn't dead in five minutes he'd be fired, he just sat in his chair and stared at me for a good thirty seconds.

I looked at my watch. 'You've only got four-and-a-half minutes now before you're out of a job, Hakim.'

He instantly leapt up and threw himself around the room searching for the fly swatter, and then frantically hunted his prey as I delivered regular time updates. As Muffy, Merzad and I counted down the final ten seconds, he became positively manic. And the

'Time's up!' call saw him slump against the wall and lower his head with a look of real anguish. I turned to Merzad, who just shrugged his shoulders and raised his eyebrows. Muffy bit her lip before mouthing a concerned 'Ooh-ah!' in my direction.

I got out of my chair and slowly walked towards him. It was too early in our relationship to give him a hug, so I just gently touched his shoulder. 'Hakim darling, I'd never fire you. At least not for being unable to kill a fly . . .'

He lifted his face to look at me . . . and smirked for a brief moment before dissolving into giggles. He then jigged around the office on his toes, tittering and pointing at me and loving himself sick. Hakim received his first whacking that day, squealing with delight at every blow, for having tricked the infidel tricker.

So, as we tidied our desks and closed down our laptops that particular Thursday afternoon in November, Hakim approached each of us, fanning out the cards like a seasoned magician. The good-news ones were extended out of the pack just a little; his winks and nods, meant to alert us to their positive portents, were really not necessary.

Hakim was the last to choose and, as seemed to be his constant good fortune, he once again got LOVE. His delight at this remarkable turn of events was only marginally tempered by Merzad's assertion that he had cheated. As we headed down the stairs, another week spent, I predicted that his parents would spring a surprise betrothal to some distant cousin on him over the course of the weekend. The idea made him positively giddy.

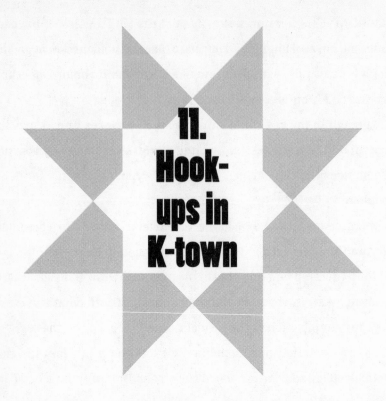

11.
Hook-ups in K-town

A group of my female friends and I gathered one night in March 2011 at Gandamak, a big British bar in the centre of town, to eat pizza, guzzle white wine and dissect Marg's recently failed relationship. There wasn't a great deal to pick over, really, common consensus being that Marg's ex-boyfriend was an absolute nutter.

Muffy, Marg and I had all met him on the same evening about a month before at Gandamak. He seemed friendly and sweet, and he and Marg had soon cocooned themselves away from the rest of our party, engaging in hours of animated and flirtatious chatter. As they wandered off together, hand in hand in the early hours of the morning, Muffy and I cooed like contented parents.

It all moved rather quickly from there, propelled along by the nut-job, and at her birthday dinner just three weeks into their coupling, he stood before all her best friends in Kabul declaring that he was madly in love with her and was so excited about their future together. This enthusiastic assertion caused Marg's eyes to pop just a little, while the rest of us stole sideways glances at one another, confounded and a little embarrassed by this seemingly premature pronouncement.

Apparently, at 5am the next day, Marg awoke to find her beloved sobbing next to her in bed—he regretted that he had to end the relationship as he was, in fact, in love with Muffy.

Muffy herself was totally in the clear. She was truly astonished to learn that a five-minute chat with this man in the loo line at the birthday bash could have elicited such intense feelings—that a casual conversation, comparing her penne chicken to his spinach ravioli, had been endowed with so much subtext and meaning.

A lot of people hook up in Kabul—it's kind of like a hobby. I could try to propound some worthy excuses for this—how the stresses of living in a war zone compelled us to embark upon reckless sexual encounters, how our constant craving for intimacy in the midst of the chaos and madness drove us onwards to *la petite mort,* and all that. But I imagine it had more to do with the fact that we were forced to spend so much time indoors—once the drinking, karaoke, TV viewing and video games had lost their charm, copulating seemed like just another appealing diversion.

Of course the romantic in me is right now cursing my deceitful pragmatism and I fully concede that there are certain physical attachments that you hope will lead to true love. After Nick and I had broken up during a teary phone conversation on an afternoon in May, soon after I'd returned from the patch-up job, I initially dipped my freshly manicured toes into the hook-up slipstream with the somewhat desperate intention of finding the next 'one'. But whether it is in the pursuit of love or leisure-time activity, the hook-up is an entrenched part of expat life in Kabul.

At one time there was a chlamydia scare that had half my posse racing to the clinic to be tested; for months afterwards expat conversations were riddled with scandalous assumptions as to who was 'ground zero' for the outbreak. A friend of mine was a prime suspect and, when his test results came out clean, he posted them on Facebook to proclaim his innocence.

The Kabul hook-up was fraught with complications. It's a small town, so you went into the hook-up fully expecting everybody to know about it before it was even over. And gossip being the most valuable form of currency, intimate details that you'd shared with your housemates over a friendly drinking session could end up as table talk at an embassy function that very same week.

As a woman, you had to keep your guard up for men who were 'Kabul single'—hiding away a wife, partner, maybe kids back home while on the prowl in the Ghan. Vague excuses as to why they couldn't be contacted while on leave were a giveaway, as could be the absence of a Facebook account. And if they did have a Facebook account, comfortable photos of that 'special divorcee' with his children in a nice domestic setting were another clue. As my mate Andy said: 'If there are photos with the kids, you have to ask yourself: who's holding the camera?'

Men in Kabul are just lucky to get a look-in. With the ratio of males to females standing at a steady nine to one, chicks could afford to be choosy and the same guys seemed to be on high rotation. In conversations with members of this elite group of Lotharios, I was told that their only real issues were with 'stalkers' (a rather odious and exaggerated term for sexual partners who found it hard to accept that a 'one-night stand' was simply just that) and women looking for baby makers. I did know that the phantom-pregnancy card had been played on more than one male acquaintance who had foolishly entered into the hook-up *sans* protection.

One Thursday night a group of twenty-something male friends were invited to a party at an embassy where the women, all a considerably few years older, rarely got out. The men had headed off in good spirits, certain of scoring, all carrying condoms. As my Italian mate explained in his irresistible, lilting tones: 'These women are of that certain age where they will view getting pregnant as fate, or God's will, or some nonsense like that. I am taking no chances.' I was tempted to put up the misogyny call, but being on the downhill side of forty, and living a lifestyle that was certainly not conducive to conceiving a child, I myself could possibly have been tempted to view a surprise pregnancy as some miraculous sign from the Almighty.

Hook-ups could last a mere matter of hours, or a couple of weeks, or for the duration of the respective parties' Kabul internment. And a small number managed to survive outside the theatre of war. When Lynchy left the year before, he walked away with not only a terrific TV show to add to his CV but a stunning wife in tow—a beautiful American woman, Joni, who had worked in business development.

My appointment as best man for their happy nuptials was nominal at best, as women aren't actually allowed to witness official documents in Afghanistan. So, as we wandered from court house to court house with two male Afghan colleagues obtaining all the necessary approvals for their betrothal, I simply took photographs—only to have my camera stolen at the Thai restaurant where we held the hastily arranged reception.

My dear mates Dave and Sienna were the most unlikely hook-up I had ever witnessed. I think it had something to do with the fact that, when they first met, Dave was faithfully married with four grown children back in the States and Sienna, a Kiwi and twelve years Dave's junior, was engaged to Dean, a British security contractor living in Kabul.

Dave was one of my longest-standing friends in Afghanistan. He was a regular at The Den when I worked there during my early days in Kabul, sneaking out of his compound every night with his two mates to arrive bang on my doorstep at 5pm. They were a funny trio, welcoming and warm when I was first finding my feet, and inevitably arguing over the bar tab as I attempted to shove them out at the end of the night.

For me, Dave epitomised mid-west America. He was an ex-army captain... A Republican... And he shared his Facebook account with his wife because his local church frowned on personal usage. He also carried around a photo of him and his missus wearing matching, hand-knitted, reindeer jumpers on Christmas Day. He dutifully sent home his entire pay packet to his wife each month, existing on a meagre $400 allowance that he dwindled away on drinking and a Thursday-night feast at the local Chinese. But, despite all this show, their union had obvious cracks, and Dave returned after more than one leave break troubled and distressed that his wife had dabbled in talk of a trial separation.

Dave was also one of the nicest people I knew. He chatted to anyone that everyone else was studiously ignoring—the strange fellow in the corner of the bar who had some Tourette's-like syndrome that compelled him to snort compulsively like a pig; the edgy contractor just back from Kandahar, enjoying his first taste of alcohol in six months and loudly declaring that he only lived to 'Drink, fuck and fight'; the drunk NGO girl who was crying because she lost her shoes (and a fair bit of dignity) as she staggered to the bathroom. You rarely saw Dave without a smile; he seldom swore . . . He was so sweet he was positively gooey.

Sienna arrived on the scene after Gary took over The Den. She was engaged to Gary's best mate and soon became a fixture. The fact that I had moved on to Rahimi's by then meant that I didn't get to meet her for a while but Dave constantly referenced her whenever he could.

'I was talking to Sienna last night and . . .' (insert—white noise . . .)

'I texted Sienna yesterday and . . .' (insert—white noise . . .)

'I sent a funny email to Sienna the other day and . . .' (insert—white noise . . .)

Nothing he ever said about Sienna bore any relevance to the discussion at hand. He just liked saying her name, a lot, and was soon being universally taunted for having a crush on this mysterious woman from the Land of the Long White Cloud.

When I finally met Sienna, I was thoroughly impressed. She was funny, friendly, smart and not afraid of a drink. I admit to having been slightly suspicious of her ability to look immaculately groomed at all times, and her predilection for wearing two-inch heels on the dusty Kabul streets disturbed me a little. But perhaps that was just straight-out envy, as I commonly looked like a bag of hammers in my oversized shirts and bulky headgear.

Dave quickly gave in to our teasing; I suspected he secretly enjoyed any stated association with Sienna. He finally confided to Marg and me via a meandering email, sent one morning at 3am, that he was indeed smitten.

From that point on, Dave discussed every exchange between himself and Sienna at great length—text messages were dissected for meaning; emails or conversations were probed for signs of reciprocated affection. After a month or two of this, Marg and I both gently ventured that it was all in his mind. Sienna was *engaged*, and had a rock on her finger the size of Uluru; he should just stop torturing himself and let it go.

So I was genuinely shocked when he turned up at brunch one Friday to announce that the hook-up had happened. I was with our mutual mate Ernie at the time and Dave bounced into the restaurant, positively beaming. He had partied with Sienna the previous night, but the white noise that typically followed that tired old opener took on a twist of Agatha Christie proportions.

Our last sighting of our hero on that particular evening had been at around 11pm. When both Ernie and I left the bar, he had been deep in conversation with his crush. Apparently, soon afterwards, an impromptu drinking session had been called at Sienna's house and Dave had gone back with the pack.

He had crashed out in a spare room at some stage, with Sienna rightfully ensconced in bed next to her comatose fiancé. Some post-beddy-bye texting had ensued, with innocuous chatter about Dave being cold and Sienna having a spare blanket. But after the bedding had been duly delivered, with Sienna apparently tucking him in tight with a loving and lingering touch, Dave had taken the plunge and they had made out for twenty-two minutes!

This news sent Ernie straight to the bar for a sobering beer, while I sat trying to digest the information. I was intrigued on two levels: the obvious one was that Dave had actually scored, but of equal fascination was the fact that he had timed its duration so accurately.

My assumption that the hook-up was a one-off encounter was dispelled a week later when they organised a secret rendezvous in Dubai—Sienna was heading back from a business trip and Dave was flying home on leave. Sienna confessed that she, too, was terribly unhappy in her current relationship and the tryst was an undeniable success, as both of them departed the UAE determined to break up with their respective partners.

Dave copped a mobile phone to the head and a dressing down that went on for the duration of his time at home, but there was worse waiting for him when he returned to K-town. Dean was deeply disturbed by the cuckoldry, particularly as he had always ignorantly assumed, and outwardly proclaimed, that Dave was, in fact, gay. And, as opposed to Dave's wife, he had more sinister resources at hand to mete out his revenge.

The lovely Gary acted as go-between. He phoned Dave up late one night, outlining three options for repairing the damage he had done. It was like Dante's take on *Who Wants to be a Millionaire?*

A: He could take a solid beating, and end up dying in a ditch.

B: He could be set up for being a drug dealer, and rot in an Afghan jail.

OR (drum roll, please) . . .

C: He could pay Dean $10,000 for the inconvenience of having to find a new missus.

Dave's glib suggestion that a 'D: None of the above' option should be included masked the fact that he was truly rattled. The beating of Dick Willy had only just occurred, and we all knew that Gary had both the means and the psychotic demeanour to carry out his threats. Still, loved up and truly happy for the first time in forever, Dave proudly stepped out with Sienna the following Thursday to see a live band.

Gary and Dean were also there. When the former cornered Dave, pushing him up against a wall and drunkenly insisting that he make a choice from Dean's appealing list of demands, Dave's personal security guard, a hulking, ex-Navy SEAL, stepped in to save him. Soon security contractors from both camps had entered the fray, resulting in some serious scuffling. While this ruckus was going on, Romeo and Juliet were unceremoniously dragged into an armoured vehicle and quickly spirited away.

A security-contractor blood feud is not in anyone's interest—egos, guns and alcohol make for a volatile mix. And when Dave's boss found out about the Thursday-night fiasco, he immediately shut the conflict down. Dave had only recently joined the company and had to bear the shameful responsibility for him and all his colleagues being confined to their compound for the next four weeks.

By the time Dave emerged from hiding, things had settled considerably. The bad blood continued to bubble for a while, but Sienna being called a 'nerd fucker' by her drunken ex-fiancé across the bar was vastly superior to having her current squeeze killed or thrown into jail.

After dissecting Marg's break-up with her nut-job hook-up, we ended our night's girly congress at Gandamak with lingering hugs, sloppy kisses and slurred mantras along the rather hackneyed lines of 'All men are bastards', before parting ways. But each of us knew that, come the next Thursday night, one of those bastards might just prove to be exactly the distraction needed for another chilly Friday-at-home in Kabul. Or perhaps even the bastard of our dreams.

12.
Extras
and Ali
Hitchcock

Muffy and I had just spent the day in Jalalabad, working on what was undoubtedly the wildest shoot we had ever been on. We arrived back in Kabul hoarse, wind-blown, sunburnt, and exceedingly grateful for the copious wine and scrummy, home-baked dinner we were treated to at the home of some of our journo mates. Our dinner hosts had actually asked Moby whether they could do a story on the shoot. The bureau chief—the Big Juice—thought it would make a great feel-good story about Afghanistan, but our current CEO in Kabul, Saad (who had taken over from Jahid), wisely declined her request, correctly guessing that the day could just possibly go arse-end up.

The scene was for Season Two of *Salam*. Our team had been down in Jalalabad since February running the shoot themselves because

Ahmad had prohibited Muffy and me from accompanying them due to security concerns. They had done a wonderful job to date but, knowing how potentially chaotic this day could get, Ahmad personally escorted us down there to assist them.

The script called for an uprising against the provincial governor and his mob of thugs. The local police were to arrive to quell the uprising; but they were unsuccessful until two helicopters, carrying counter-narcotics commandos, landed on a hilltop to save the day. Apart from our actors, the police, and the commandos, we had eighty extras—local lads who had never been on a set before.

Rounding up extras to appear on Afghan TV wasn't very hard. It was not so much the lure of being on the small screen—a lot of locals didn't even own televisions—but ten dollars for a day's work was a good deal, and the guarantee of a free lunch proved a sweet incentive. But getting them to actually hang around on set and do their job could be a world of pain.

Sure, there was always a handful of boys who viewed it as a stepping-stone to stardom. They'd arrive on set with bouffant hair, shiny shirts and dazzling jeans for a funeral scene—and serve up more ham than a Christmas dinner. But, for most of them, it was just another job and, like most non-industry people across the world, they had no real concept of how tedious making TV could be. Into the fourth take of walking into the same shop, or strolling down the street *again*, they were routinely demanding their money and wanting to go.

With large groups of extras it was like keeping frogs in a box. They would concoct more and more elaborate excuses for nicking off. 'I have to go to my sister's wedding/My mother got hit by a car/ My goat fell in the river.'

Or, deciding to simply blow off the big bucks, they'd try to quietly slip away. 'Aleem!' I cried in dismay. 'Where is that man going? The guy in the blue. Chase him! Quickly! We're losing him!'

Holding them prisoner on set didn't foster a great deal of enthusiasm for the job, so attempts to make them laugh at the lead actor's joke, or to look genuinely happy during any type of celebration, were almost pointless.

'Okay, guys!' I enthused. 'We're going to do that again. Because you need to look excited! Salam has saved the day. Laugh! Smile! Cheer! Okay?'

'When's lunch?' asked one of them plaintively.

Post-lunch was always the worst time on set because, having been fed their beans and rice and been granted the luxury of a can of Coke or Fanta, the extras were often content to forgo their cash payment and escape, happy to have eaten at least one meal that day. Early on we learnt to hold off feeding them for as long as possible.

During the filming of *Eagle Four* we'd had a particularly big scene. The storyline involved the attempted assassination of the British ambassador and his wife (yours truly) during a stately reception attended by the bigwigs of Afghan society. We had booked out for the day an upmarket local restaurant that normally catered to rich Afghans and westerners. The entire main cast was on set, and we had placed an order with Nangali, our extras wrangler, for thirty people.

As the first of the extras began dribbling in, I almost had a seizure. They were a bedraggled, raggedy, moth-eaten bunch and my guess was that Nangali had dragged most of them in from the shantytown under the Kabul River bridge. We raced around, trying to find decent clothes for them and then arranging them into groups where those facing away from camera were the poor sods who had no teeth or looked as though they might possibly be going through drug withdrawal. We'd pulled in a few expat mates to play foreign dignitaries; one of our leads had brought along a bunch of his university friends who, in their suits and ties and fashionable eyewear, we featured prominently at the front of the throng.

It was the middle of summer and the scene was rather complicated. The smoke machine made everybody cough, the lights made us sweat and after two hours, the extras had uniformly had enough. The promise of lunch after 'one more take' was empty and meaningless. There was no way we were going to feed them before two and, when they finally sat down for their lunchtime 'feast' just before three, they devoured it like men on the verge of starvation. Which I'm guessing most of them were.

I didn't eat that day; I was acting as well as working on set, so I spent the break discussing the next set-up with the directors. Mid-discussion, I sensed something was amiss. I turned to notice that a couple of the long dining tables were completely empty and my heart lurched.

I raced to the foyer to find a horde of extras attempting a breakout. I threw myself against the door, demanding that the security guard lock it immediately, before bellowing loudly for back-up. Aleem arrived and tried to quell the uprising with promises of cake and biscuits in a few more hours. As he attempted to calm them and usher them all back to the set, the university posse pulled me aside and pleaded for mercy. One of them explained that he had an exam that afternoon and, after a rigorous interrogation, I agreed that he could go.

He was one of our key featured people-props, and our continuity would be shot, but I couldn't let the poor kid fail his course for the sake of our show. I decided to sneak him out the back through the kitchen, fearing a stampede if I unlocked the main door. But, as I led him away, his friends suddenly started calling after me, declaring that they too had exams they'd forgotten to mention.

I returned to the group, dragging Exam Guy back with me. 'All right. I believe that your mate actually does have to attend uni for an exam. I don't believe the rest of you. You're all friends, right?' They nodded. 'So here's the deal. If your friend here really does have an exam, you'll let him go quietly. If you're going to keep insisting that you all have exams, then the lot of you stay—including him. He misses his exam, he's facing a problem and it will all be down to you—his *friends*. Now tell me again: which of you genuinely has an exam today?'

Exam Guy readily raised his hand. The others murmured amongst themselves in Dari for a moment before shaking their heads: No.

Cranky, Bad Arse Western Woman: 1

Bored, Antsy Arts Undergrads: 0

The shoot the previous day in Jalalabad had been ambitious, and had been months in the making; Muffy and our client had attended endless meetings with government officials just to lock in the choppers and get the commandos on board. And because we were shooting in a potentially dangerous area, with the Taliban apparently lurking in the nearby hills, we needed a hundred and thirty Afghan soldiers to secure the location's perimeter. To add to the enormity of the event, the choppers would only be landing three times, so we had to be on our game.

We'd decided to use six cameras. Truth be told, that's all we had; one of them would be mounted on a six-metre crane. In the week leading up to the big day our camera trainer, a crusty old German called Luther, held numerous meetings with the crew to go over the shooting plan. We had clashed with Luther on a number of occasions since his arrival at Moby six months before. He had never worked in Afghanistan before and had no real concept of the difficulties involved in making television there. He would blithely pass judgement on our work with no regard for the lack of resources and experience that we had to contend with, and his supreme arrogance as he delivered his various verdicts made me want to slap him.

I had also come to question Luther's teaching techniques. While we simply wanted him to equip our untrained kids with the basic skills to be able to point the camera in the right direction, focus it, and make the thing go, he was intent on gearing them up to make art-house films worthy of Fellini. Our team often came away from his sessions with more questions than answers.

'Trudi, Luther asked us what the difference is between fashion and style. What does that mean?'

'Trudi *Jan*, what's a *genre*?'

'Trudi *Jan*, who is *Ali Hitchcock*?'

His game plan for the Jalalabad shoot was elaborate and compli-cated and, being the only person on the crew to have ever actually shot at the site, I had serious doubts we could pull it off. The fact that he refused to use his translator during meetings only added to my concern.

He wanted a camera mounted onto a flatbed truck, which was something we didn't have the budget for and which I was certain would become bogged in the sandy soil. He devised the ingenious plan of wrapping a camera in plastic and burying it in the ground, to capture the feet of the commandos as they ran down the hill— another artistic initiative that I had to firmly nip in the bud. We were short on cameras as it was and, to lose one under a misplaced boot or as a result of dirt getting into the casing, would prove to be an immense loss to our department. We finally settled on some kind of compromise that I still wasn't entirely sold on. At our final briefing, as I tried to make sense of his detailed diagrams, he proffered me a patronising pat on the back and reassured me it would all be okay because he would be personally supervising the team.

Luther pulled out at 10pm on the night before the shoot. The German embassy had advised him that it was unsafe to travel to Jalalabad, and he felt he had no choice but to stay put in Kabul. The fact that his fellow countryman, Willy, the wonderful, laid-back lighting trainer, was coming along, for shits and giggles, failed to convince him otherwise.

It's fair to say that Jalalabad had turned decidedly nasty in the time since Tiggy, Jose and I first worked there, and the road to the city—a narrow affair that wound its way precariously along the side of a mountain and was regularly targeted by the Taliban—had been voted the most dangerous road in the world. But my feeling was that, when you chose to work in a war zone, you sometimes had to just suck it up, monkey, whatever your misgivings. Particularly when that 'monkey' had devised a shooting schedule that involved seventy-two different shots that nobody else could decipher.

We left at dawn to make the three-hour road trip and liaise with our crew. The drive down was breathtaking, although slightly uncomfortable. Due to the fact that we had to take an extra make-up artist with us, I was relegated to the doggy-box in the back of the jeep, and the Afghan security guard stationed beside me kept casually laying his arm across the back of the seat in a bid to cop a feel of my infidel shoulder. If I'd allowed that to happen, it would have been the western equivalent of performing oral sex on the man.

I'm guessing he thought I was easy game as just the week before he'd witnessed me being felt up. The public grope came courtesy of a lovely little man we all knew as 'Wheelie'. The poor guy had no legs and made his way around town on a wooden board with wheels, using his hands to paddle along the road. Whenever we came across him in our car, the drivers would speed up and veer towards him. He would simply laugh and wave and call out, 'Darling! Darling!' (which I gather he assumed was my name) while we pulled over, and then he'd scuttle up to collect a couple of bucks through the car window.

Then, just on the previous Wednesday, we arrived home to find Wheelie parked outside the gate to my guest house—I was guessing the begging business had hit a bit of a slump that day and he wanted to be certain of a windfall. After I slipped him some cash, he thanked his 'darling' and held his arms out for a hug. I thought that was kind of sweet and leant down to embrace him. The clinch was just getting to that stage where it had become a little lengthy and awkward when he suddenly released his grip on me, quickly reached around and gave my breasts two short sharp tweaks.

Even now, I'm not quite sure how I should have reacted. In the immediate aftermath, all I could think of was that the unfortunate fellow probably hadn't copped a handful of bosom in quite some time and I'm not a miserly person by nature. I was also uneasy about publicly berating a legless beggar for chancing a bit of grab and tickle with a shameless foreigner. So I just smiled as I backed away towards the gate, keenly conscious of my grinning security guard, who was now sporting a rather disconcertingly lascivious glint in his eye.

I decided to let slide the attempts at hanky-panky in the back of the jeep on the way to Jalalabad. Hey, after the 'make out' session with Wheelie he'd seen the week before, he no doubt thought he was in with a shot. So, rather than make a fuss and risk getting the security guard sacked, I leaned forward awkwardly for the entire trip, 'captivated' by the conversations happening in front.

We stopped along the way to take the obligatory 'war junk' photos—we perched on abandoned tanks, with the security guards' guns slung casually across us—and arrived at the location in high spirits. The euphoria lasted approximately eight minutes. I immediately consulted with our director and head cameraman, who both confessed to having no idea what Luther's shooting plan meant, so, with the assistance of Willy, we hastily simplified it to ensure basic coverage. Essential to the scene was getting a shot where everything was in frame—the fighting in the valley, the choppers descending on the hill and the commandos running down it. If we didn't have that, then we might as well have been shooting it all separately.

We were stationed about twenty minutes from town, so our eighty extras all had to be ferried to the site by bus. Muffy and I initially considered this a blessing because it meant they couldn't possibly run away from the set, but we had cause to reconsider this when, during its very first run, the bus became bogged, smack-bang in the middle of the location. It took us an hour to get the bus moving again and, by the time we had bussed in all the extras, we were running hopelessly behind schedule. The choppers were arriving at 3pm, an arrangement that was non-negotiable, and by noon it became a manic race to get the cast fed, rehearsed and ready for action before the first landing took place.

The scenario was a bloody battle, so we had to find a handful of extras to cop imaginary bullets and take a fall. We had come with our fancy-pants, special-effects make-up—water bottles full of home-made blood together with the last of our professional latex for shaping bullet holes. We just needed to find a few suitable bodies for close-ups.

My experience had taught me that Afghan actors don't do 'dying' well, and this bunch did nothing to dispel that notion. Muffy and Aleem lined up extra after extra in front of me to take a 'bullet' from my upraised finger. They either folded to the ground like dying swans, or clutched their chests (despite being shot in the head) and staggered around for an inordinate amount of time, or just stood stock-still and stared at me.

I'd smile and thank them in their native Pashto before hissing, 'Rubbish—be gone!' to Aleem in English. In Kabul I would have shown them how to take a hit myself, but my security guards were particularly twitchy, to the point where they would sternly shake their heads if I dared to roll back a centimetre of sleeve. So I called in our assistant director to give them a demo. He wasn't brilliant, but it gave them the gist of it; with just two hours to go, we had found our men.

The next thirty minutes saw our director explaining to the extras and the recently arrived police officers (running approximately two hours late) exactly what they had to do. First the villagers had to get ready for battle. Then the bad guys would turn up and a big fight would ensue. The police would then arrive and find themselves outnumbered, before the choppers descended just in the nick of time.

The final hour was spent scrabbling around for close shots of the villagers preparing to fight—sharpening axes, loading fake guns and praying to Allah—and getting footage of the bad guys and police arriving in their cars. By the time we received the call from our co-director on the flight to say that they were well and truly on their way, we had simply run out of time to rehearse the battle. So, as the first of the choppers appeared on the bend of the river, we just shoved the extras into position and told them to fight.

It was mind-blowingly terrifying. Axes and sticks and fists went flying. Muffy and I simply clung to each other; both of us having literally lost our voices by that stage from yelling so much, we barked out croaky exclamations of alarm. They may not have been so hot at dying, but these men could really scrap.

The crane and wide shots were totally unusable as the diligent Ahmad was in frame. He had raced up to the top of the hill, on his own initiative, to wave the choppers down (despite there being huge red crosses marked out on the summit). It also didn't help that somehow the commandos failed to disgorge.

As the choppers ascended into the sky and circled us for a second landing, we all scrambled on to the battlefield to inspect the damage.

One guy, smiling, held up a thumb that looked freakishly out of kilter with the rest of his hand. Another man proudly showed me the plum-coloured egg already forming on his forehead. I instructed Aleem to gather up the wounded and take them off set. He was to apologise to them profusely and guarantee that they would still get paid. But none of them wanted to leave—they were having too much 'fun'.

The second take saw our hardy extras fight with even greater ferocity. I looked away as an axe came precariously close to one man's head . . . and groaned as the commandos alighted from the choppers and ran in perfect formation down the wrong side of the hill.

Our props were in pretty bad shape by this stage and, as the choppers circled for their final descent, we foraged about for sticks and stones to replace our broken plastic guns. The final take was a triumph. The extras fought like firebrands, the cops arrived on cue and the commandos disembarked and followed the game plan.

Muffy and I were too focused on the action and the order of events to notice where the cameramen had positioned themselves for the final enactment. On reviewing the footage the next day, we realised that all of them, with the exception of the crane operator, were on top of the hill, mercifully hidden from view but exclusively trained on the choppers. We came away from the shoot with just one lonely wide shot that took in the entire scene, courtesy of our crane operator (who I suspect would have also raced up to film the impressive-looking helicopters if he could have got there in time).

Luther's appraisal of our work the next morning was typically pleasant, constructive and supportive:

Guten Morgen,

I saw the material in the editing with the editor together. Sorry, but there are so many mistakes, I can't believe it. There is one point I don't understand. The director inform the cameramen before shooting to ignore my camera script. Please let me know why, now we have the chaos.

Cheers Luther

'Cheers'—really? Muffy composed a brilliantly abrasive reply but, on assurances from Christof that he was totally on our side and would deal with Luther himself, it was never sent.

That afternoon, when I visited the suite to check on our editor's progress, he enthusiastically and correctly pointed out that you could actually see the director's head jutting above a sand dune. He had only just spotted it, so we agreed to keep the information to ourselves. And, as far as we were both concerned, said head was just a big, brown rock. Which happened to move now and then.

13.
The
Eagle
Soars

As Muffy and I pulled into work, Aleem and Sayed were waiting at the end of the driveway. I was greeted with hugs and delighted smiles and, as news of my arrival filtered through the ranks, I had most of the drama department trailing me upstairs to my office to view the contents of the blue velvet box I had in my possession. I felt like a mother arriving home from hospital after just giving birth, but the 'baby' belonged to all of us, as I had just returned from Korea where I attended the Seoul International Drama Awards to accept the Special Jury Prize for *Eagle Four*.

It was an amazing three days of five-star accommodation, fine dining, business-class flights (a personal first!), and red-carpet strolling. But the real boat-floater for me was watching my team this particular August morning, proudly passing around the heavy marble trophy, a very public acknowledgement of the excellent efforts they had all put into making the show.

Saad directed us to enter the competition earlier in 2011 and we dutifully did so, not really expecting a result. Back in May, Muffy sent off our little bundle of DVDs, complete with their neatly hand-written labels. Then, in July, we received news that we had won an award.

We were initially sceptical about the significance of the 'Special Jury Prize', and Muffy and I secretly harboured suspicions that it could very well be the 'Good on You for Trying' trophy. But, after conferring with the organisers, we learnt that, out of two hundred and four entries from thirty-seven countries, our show had made it through the initial cull. The jury ultimately didn't deem us worthy of first prize in our category, but they had all agreed that we deserved recognition for our outstanding work.

Our success had the tang of honey, particularly as the show had initially been so badly maligned by our own people.

We'd just been winding down production on *Eagle Four* when Christof was appointed general manager of our company, and the mother ship in Dubai instructed him to approve episode one of the series before we showed it to the client.

Christof confessed to knowing very little about drama production, so he called in his octogenarian compatriot, Luther (who was in town directing the telecast of a music concert) to evaluate our work. We hadn't met Luther at that stage; he wasn't yet working for our company and he'd been in Afghanistan for approximately five days.

To say that Luther savaged us would be an enormous understatement. He tut-tutted and tch-ed his way through the thirty-minute show, continually pausing the program to patronise us.

'Where is your depth of field?'

'Why is the light so bad?'

'Is that all the coverage you have?! Ha!'

We were genuinely floored by his assessment and, for each ignorant contention he raised, we felt we had a perfectly valid comeback. We tried to tactfully explain that we were under-resourced, understaffed and time poor, and that we believed our crew had done an exceptional job considering what we had to work with. We finished off the session by gently urging him to cast aside his exacting, western artistic sensibilities, because this show *was* the best drama serial he was ever going to see in Afghanistan, if not the entire region.

Despite not ever having seen any other Afghan drama serials, he highly doubted our claim. All our reasoning and assurances seemed to be falling on deaf ears—in this case, on his extremely hairy deaf ears. I think it was at about this point in the discussion that Lynchy offered up the most cogent comment of the day. 'You're just a bloody dickhead, mate.'

Unsurprisingly, Lynchy's verdict didn't hold much sway. Luther's final verdict, that the show was not fit for broadcast, delivered to management in Dubai with the full backing of Christof (who himself had only been with the company a month), came as a huge blow to us. Worse still, it was an incredible insult to our young local team, who had worked so hard to pull it off; our Afghan director, Sayed, who had been in the meeting with us, walked away from the encounter a shattered man.

By close of business that day both Lynchy and Damien were ready to resign, and I certainly wouldn't have blamed either of them if they'd done just that. We headed back to our guest house and unwound by indulging in a horrifically bigoted display of goose-stepping and barking at one another in varying degrees of dodgy German; our collective mood became as shambolic as our accents as we drifted from rage to disbelief to indifference.

After sucking back our combined body weight in beers, we managed to calm down a little. What finally saw us all off to bed that night with dopey, sleepy grins and inebriated giggles was Muffy's Facebook status update: *Who the fuck is Luther????*

I received a 'What the hell is going on with *E4*, Trudi?' phone call from Saad the following day. It took a fair bit of arguing, as well as persuading him to actually come to Kabul to view the 'unworthy' episode, before we convinced him that Luther was mistaken.

Needless to say, the client was delighted with our presentation and the series attracted a huge audience. There is no ratings system in Afghanistan, but it was easy to gauge when a show was a success. Having around one thousand Afghan colleagues, who were unashamedly vocal about what they and their families did and did not like, we quickly got a sense as to whether a program was working or not.

With *Eagle Four*, I would often enter the edit suite to find groups of people huddled around the monitor, catching their first glimpse of the upcoming episode. Our actors reported that they were constantly being stopped on the street by members of the general public wanting to snap selfies with a 'star'. Actual police officers would also pull them up, either calling them 'brother' and congratulating them on their work, or joking that they were showing up the ANP by setting the policing bar way too high.

When the kids living in our street found out we were responsible for making the show, we became celebrities as well. One day, when I brought home caps and T-shirts bearing the *Eagle Four* logo to distribute amongst them, I was literally mobbed and had to be hauled inside the guest house by my security guard.

The show also attracted quite a bit of international press and Maria Abi-Habib, a journalist for the *Wall Street Journal*, quoted a twelve-year-old boy as saying: 'The police on the show are great. They care for the people and defuse bombs. The show makes me want to be a policeman.' She further reported that, when she asked the boy whether real-life Afghan policemen made him want to join up, he paused for a moment before replying 'No.'

And now we had a prestigious award to reaffirm our unwavering faith in the program.

I was in a meeting with Saad, discussing a new project, when he told me about our success in Seoul; he invited me to go and accept the award on behalf of the company. The day on which he broke this news to me was 31 July, my birthday, and the celebrations that night relegated the personal passing of another year to a mere footnote. We headed to the Gandamak bar where Muffy and I spent most of the evening crowing about our win.

I think I mentioned that I would be flying business class about 487 times that night, but, alas, I was playing to a jaded audience.

My friends—a mix of journalists, security contractors and various consultants for major companies—frequently fly business, and they thought my excitement about turning left on the plane rather cute, if not a little pathetic. For the women in our group, however, it was all about the dress, the shoes and the hair, and I would most certainly need a few days in Dubai to get my styling sorted before heading to Korea.

Once Gandamak closed its doors for the night, a group of us headed back to the home of one of my journo mates, Hamish, so as to prolong the party. By 3am we were all shedding pants, tops and undergarment whatnots, and plunging into his pool. I'm not sure how long I was in there, but I know I was the first one out; as I stepped up onto the ledge, I promptly slipped over on the water-slicked tiles, slithering over the side of the pool and landing on my back on a concrete path below it.

I didn't pass out (a question I was asked at least five times by my worried-looking friends, who now hovered over me), and I wiggled my arms and legs to prove that I hadn't broken anything. I knew what day it was—it was the day after my birthday! Duh!

But the routine where they held up fingers for me to count was a serious cause for concern. 'Four!' I incorrectly answered. 'Two!' was my erroneous second attempt. It was then that I realised I didn't have my glasses on—the truth was I couldn't really see a thing.

They finally agreed that I could sit up. But it was then that they noticed the puddle of blood staining the cement where my head had been—I had split it clean open.

Darling Fred, who ran security at the house, gently sterilised the wound and bandaged my head. Afterwards, all the pool party guests took turns signing the bandage, adding witty and endearing little comments like: 'I'm a loser', 'Don't try this at home' and 'It's my party and I'll die if I want to'. We then all sat around and devised a plausible story as to how I had come to injure myself. My suggested scenario, that I fell getting out of the pool, was immediately howled down.

'You're just lucky that the Big Juice is on leave. Otherwise we'd be in all sorts of bother,' Hamish exclaimed.

I adored the Big Juice—she was one of my best friends in Kabul—but, being bureau chief, the buck always stopped with her. If she ever found out the truth about my misadventure, she'd fret about any possible liability issues and agonise over whether she should report the incident to her superiors in the motherland. Hamish's only concern was that they might fill in his lovely new pool.

I can't remember now why I wasn't allowed to have simply slipped over in the shower (I suspect that scenario was rejected in order to inflict maximum humiliation on me for my predicament). With the thoroughness of a *CSI* unit, they decided that the location of my accident should be at the most obvious scene of the crime—I must have fallen down the stairs when I was leaving Gandamak.

Now I had actually seen people fall down the stairs leaving Gandamak. They were typically inebriated to the point where they were unable to talk and certainly had no business walking. Great.

The next day being a public holiday, there were no medical centres open. I could have risked a public hospital, but Fred reasoned that I might very well emerge from there in worse shape than when I went in. So the blessed man spent the morning putting out feelers all over town, even trying to get me on to the International Security Assistance Force base to see a doctor, but it was a no-go. He made do with sterilising the wound, re-dressing it and assuring me that it was already healing nicely.

When I finally did get to see a doctor, about thirty-two hours after the initial fall, she admired Fred's handiwork before admitting that, apart from giving me a tetanus injection, there was really nothing more she could do. It was certainly a big gash but, because I had scraped away most of the skin around it, she couldn't stitch it closed. She simply shaved off a section of hair, patched me up and prescribed antiseptic lotion, gauze pads and bandages, with instructions to change the dressing every morning. She then advised me that I would have to keep the wound completely covered for the next month—I couldn't expose it to the putrid Kabul air or even wash my hair, for fear of infection.

'Oh no! Are you sure?' I wailed.

She gently smiled, patted my hand and promised me that it would all be okay. She was certain that, given a month . . . or maybe a little longer . . . the cut would be nicely healed. I wasn't to worry—I was actually lucky that it hadn't been worse.

In vain I pleaded with her to come up with an alternative treatment. I claimed that I would be happy to live with a hole in my head for the next *year*, if only I could get my hair dyed and done for the fabulous television awards ceremony I was attending at the end of August!! This probably wasn't the most appropriate response to give to a doctor in Afghanistan, who had undoubtedly seen her share of horrors. She didn't look overly impressed.

Muffy then spent the next month playing nursie—coming to my room each day just after breakfast to apply the yellow sticky solution to the cut, followed by the gauze, then wrapping a bandage around my head. It was the only time since arriving in the country that I had really appreciated the headscarf; I took to wearing it tied in a knot at the base of my skull *à la* 'funky gypsy'.

And *I* spent the month trying to convince people that I wasn't thoroughly smashed when I descended the steps of Kabul's most popular bar.

A week before leaving for Seoul the wound, although having sealed, was still rather jelly-like and watery; the hair around it was a matted, amber mess. Muffy thought that the cut needed to get out a bit more, so at night she'd release it from its crepey bondage and I'd sit alone in my room, hoping that the air I was exposing it to was simply drying it out and not turning it septic.

These evening outings seemed to do the trick and, the day before I left for Dubai, I returned to the doctor for her prognosis. She probed the wound for a while before finally deadpanning that she was sure the crusty dent in my head could withstand a little bleach, as long as my hairdresser was careful.

I purchased three tops, two skirts and a dress in Dubai but in the end opted to wear a floor-length gown that Tiggy had left behind, together with a silver Afghan necklace Muffy had picked out for me in Chicken Street. The young Korean make-up artists styled my newly dyed hair to perfection; however, the bronze glitter they liberally brushed all over my dial left me looking like the over-tanned old bird from *There's Something About Mary*. I raced back to my room and spent a good half-hour, pressed up to the bathroom mirror, frantically trying to wipe it off before the limousine arrived to ferry me to the ceremony.

I had learnt my thirty-second acceptance speech off by heart, but still my voice trembled as I delivered it. It wasn't nerves kicking in—it was pure, raw emotion. I was so indescribably proud of our tough little team and I could barely find my way off the stage because of the tears welling in my eyes.

The ceremony was followed by a salubrious after-party, which ended quite early, so a group of us headed back to the bar in our hotel. A British producer, a Brazilian director, an executive producer from New Zealand, a Chinese actor . . . all of them as excited as me about the success of their respective shows. And I wandered off to my room in the wee hours of the following day, shoes in hand and promising to stay in touch with my new-found global posse.

I awoke around noon. I knew in an instant that I didn't have the trophy. I remembered bringing it back with me—my darling interpreter had carefully placed it in my hands before we boarded our bus to the hotel—but a manic forage around my room confirmed that it was no longer in my possession.

I raced to the bar and explained my distressing problem to the manager. He understood completely and led me to a table. Here there were four blue velvet boxes laid out; each was waiting to be claimed. It seems I wasn't the only reveller who had become careless in my euphoria! I quickly found my baby and briefly considered adopting another foundling, just in case I lapsed into negligent mothering again somewhere between Korea and Kabul.

And so, arriving back to work that August day with Muffy after my trip to Korea, I gave my camera and the trophy to Merzad, informing my crew that they had two hours to have their photo taken with the award before it was relegated to the display cabinet outside the office of the CEO. There were dozens and dozens of photos taken—kids posed for the camera, some holding the trophy high, some of them people who weren't even working for the company when the series was made. But nobody seemed to care. In a country where there is usually so little to celebrate, this recognition of our show was something we were all happy to share.

14.
Plan Bs and Whisky Shots

I lost count of the number of bombings I went through in Kabul. The Indian Embassy, the Safi Landmark Hotel, a UN guest house, ISAF headquarters... Soft targets, hard targets; but inevitably the results were always the same—overwhelmingly it was innocent Afghans who were killed in these attacks.

More often than not, it was a distant *boom* that alerted you to the danger. If you were with other people, it would be followed by a collective intake of breath, a palpable silence and a quiet 'I don't like the sound of that' from someone in the group. The subsequent wail of sirens confirmed the worst.

If the attack happened across town, it would be a text message, or a tweet or an email from another expat that put you in the loop.

When a suicide bomber detonated outside the Heetal Hotel three blocks away from work, the noise was thunderous. My office shook, a window cracked and I initially thought that a new studio being constructed next to our building had collapsed.

But there was no mistaking the attack on the US Embassy on 13 September 2011. It felt like it was happening all around me, and seemed like it would never end.

There had been intel for days of an imminent strike. UN security had issued a 'confidential' email to their staff that had found its way into the inboxes of every expat in Kabul; it warned of attacks on, amongst other targets, western guest houses in Wazir Akbar Khan. *I* lived in a western guest house in Wazir Akbar Khan. The security consisted of Afghan guards who were typically either stoned or sleeping, backed up by a low metal fence trimmed with a feeble brush of barbed wire, and a rusting iron gate that was constantly left unlocked. And my first-floor room with its glass frontage offered a clear target for any sniper who may have wanted to take a pot-shot at a foreigner. Muffy was in the US making a documentary and my journo mates were so concerned about my security (or lack thereof) that they insisted I stay at their compound for a few nights.

That morning I'd woken early at their home and, realising I had run out of clean work clothes, decided to head back to my guest house. Not wanting to wake my mates' driver, who was on call 24/7, and knowing that I couldn't spring a random 6.30am pickup on my guys, I wrapped myself up tightly, lowered my head and bustled the two blocks back to my house. I trailed behind a garbage collector, with his cart and donkey and his rhythmic cries of 'Rubbish!', which I imagined would afford me some anonymity.

Soon after showering, I made the decision to work from home. I had a deadline on some script outlines looming and the circus atmosphere of my office afforded me little headspace for writing. I called Merzad, to let him know my plan; he assured me not to worry—the department was safe in his trustworthy hands.

At 1.30pm I heard an explosion nearby. Some gunfire. I was drawn to my balcony by the sounds of yelling and cars tearing along the street. I stood and watched as people raced up my road, and vehicles vied with one another to turn into the side lane opposite.

I texted my journo friends—even in the midst of gathering intelligence and filing reports, they never failed to respond. Their reply was dark: 'Get to a safe room. Gunmen at the end of your street.' With no safe room and gunfire hammering all around, I made my way out into the corridor where Bela, the Croatian manager of our guest house (a feisty, salty woman, who could love and hate you in the space of thirty seconds) was herding all the residents to the ground-floor restaurant.

I tried calling Merzad on my way downstairs, but there was no network coverage; our office was only three blocks away, so I knew they were close to it as well. In the restaurant, Croats, Russians, Afghans, a Frenchman and I all sat and watched the local news. My heart raced as I saw police officers running along the route I had taken home earlier that day.

The restaurant refugees had no common language—all we could do was look at one another and shake our heads in disbelief. Then one of the Russians reached into his backpack and produced two huge bottles of scotch. He looked around the group and asked 'Whisky?' A universal 'Yes!' in four different languages was the reply.

By that stage I had managed to contact Merzad and all our people were accounted for. But, because there were no safe rooms at work either, they were simply sitting at their desks or huddled together in basements. To my utter astonishment, he and some of the other boys were in the outdoor cafeteria drinking tea! I could hear guns popping down the phone as he excitedly described watching a mortar hit the rooftop of our radio station.

I ordered him to get everyone inside. He coolly countered that Ali had an upset stomach and needed fresh air, so he and the others would be staying outside to keep him company. I replied that I didn't care if Ali vomited all over the office floor for the next four hours, they were to immediately get indoors. He laughed. I yelled—something I rarely do. He clearly sensed that Mum was going off, and I didn't need to tell him that he'd be facing more than the whacking bat if I found out he'd defied me.

We stayed in the restaurant for the next six hours. At some point, on the pretext of going to the toilet, I conducted a quick recce of the guest house, looking for a hiding spot. Despite the whisky-fuelled camaraderie, I knew that if things got serious, I would be on my own. I finally found a space underneath the stairwell where I could conceal myself behind some storage boxes and an old mattress.

I had lived in seven different houses in Kabul and, apart from The Den, none of them had safe rooms. So with each move a new escape plan had to be formulated. I had been told by various security mates that most of my creative little survival schemes were ludicrous, dangerous and, quite frankly, useless. No doubt, but inventing them gave me *some* sense of control over my personal safety.

In most of the houses I'd lived in, I'd been lodged on upper floors, which presented a whole unique set of problems. Could I really make the leap from my balcony to the kitchen roof? Would I seriously have the presence of mind to grab my doona for the climb over the neighbours' barbed-wire fence? And would their horse of a guard dog, which I was compelled to watch humping a deck chair as I smoked my morning cigarette each day, eat me if I actually made it over? Or try to mount me at the very least? Edging along a narrow ledge to a tree I could climb down sounded good in theory, but would I be able to do it after a few drinks?

My Plan Bs in such situations involved hiding. Actually my personal all-time favourite amongst these was where I would secrete myself away on the top shelf of my cupboard, cover myself with a large garbage bag and then use a wire coat-hanger to pull the cupboard door closed behind me.

It was a decidedly better plan than my housemate Rick's, who, at six foot two, couldn't even entertain the cupboard option. His elaborate strategy entailed placing a chair marked with a grubby footprint below his open bathroom window and then hiding behind his lounge. He thought it was ingenious, until I broke it to him that you could clearly see the top of his head as soon as you entered the room and that the Taliban would no doubt blow it off before they ever got to see the clever decoy chair.

They evacuated the office that day at 3pm and I finally went back to my room at 7.30pm. The fourteen shots of whisky had calmed me considerably and I figured that an open-plan restaurant without a door, a gate or an iron grille offered up little more protection than my first-floor abode. But by then the battle was clearly raging elsewhere. Any gunmen who may have been lurking nearby earlier in the day had long since been dealt with and it was a small group of insurgents, bunkered down in a half-built high-rise, that were keeping up the fight.

I called home as soon as I closed the door. It was early morning back in Australia, but insurgent attacks still managed to make head-lines and I wanted my family to know I was safe. My sister-in-law, Lisa, answered the phone and the mere sound of her voice burst the levee banks of an emotional flood that I had sandbagged all day with alcohol and bravado. The firmness—which had seen me be so stern with Merzad, which had compelled me to conduct a thorough reconnaissance of the guest house and to make breezy assurances to the frightened young Russian girls in the restaurant that we'd all be okay—instantly dissolved in a rush of fragile tears.

The crackle of war and a generous half-Valium lulled me to sleep, but I awoke the next morning with the thumping of choppers and distant gunfire still audible. Twenty hours after the attack began, Afghan and coalition forces shot and killed the last of the insurgents.

I had rancid whisky breath that day—a harsh, heavy taste that all the mouthwash on the planet couldn't possibly disguise. I had never really been a fan of whisky, but I was thinking that, going forward, it would most certainly be my preferred tipple in times of crisis.

15.
Scarfgate

During my time in Afghanistan, my job presented me with problems and situations that I never imagined having to contend with. I comforted hysterical young women who were being forced to marry some distant cousin—my hugs and kisses were all I could offer because the marriage was inevitable. I broke up fistfights between angry men; I intervened in heated squabbles between spirited, headstrong girls and confused boys who were unaccustomed to this new-fangled 'female empowerment' thing. I tactfully sucked up to difficult actresses who weren't happy about having to hug their on-screen husbands; I even roared at an actor who held a gun to Aleem's head.

I once had to issue a formal warning to one of my lovely writers because Hamid had reported that she was continually late delivering her scripts and that the work she usually handed over to him was typically riddled with mistakes. About an hour later I found her downstairs, crying on the phone. I waited for her to finish the call before approaching her and giving her a hug. I told her that I was sorry I had upset her, but she wasn't to worry—she was an excellent writer and I was certain that, with a little more effort, her work would improve. She just stared at me for a moment before revealing the true source of her grief—her brother had just been kidnapped and his detainees were asking US$30,000 for his release. The police rescued him the following day and it turned out that her uncle had masterminded the abduction.

But nothing could have prepared me for Scarfgate.

Khalid was hired as a make-up artist on our soap *Secrets of this House.* I was initially resistant to taking him on—having a man in such close contact with women was a definite no-no and I doubted that our female actresses would tolerate it. But Shakila and Merzad assured me that it wouldn't be a problem, because Khalid was a *boy–girl.* It took a fair bit of back-and-forth, and a considerable amount of wrist flapping from Merzad (clearly the universal gesture to denote homosexuality), to convey to me that they meant *gay.* And, after meeting Khalid, I was thoroughly convinced that this assessment of his sexuality was spot-on.

He literally minced into my office, greeting me in his limited English with a pronounced lisp. He was blinged to the hilt and, in a country where shiny pastel satin shirts, bejewelled jeans and chunky silver bracelets are normal male attire, that's quite a claim. Khalid was hired on the spot and everyone was happy. Shakila was the only make-up artist on our all-female team whose parents allowed her to do night shoots, and she now had someone to share the load.

I loved Khalid from the get-go and I so admired his courage and daring. I had been told by numerous expats that most Afghan men have their first sexual encounter with another male; I had witnessed police officers standing at their checkpoints holding hands. When Hamish did a report on the Afghan army, he stumbled into their barracks to discover a hash-fuelled orgy taking place. And yet being openly gay in Afghanistan is a dangerous proposition. It is against Islam; it is a sickness. It's up there with a woman being out in public with her arms and legs exposed—it can get you killed. Yet a giggling Khalid assured me that he had no shortage of boyfriends.

It took Khalid only two weeks before he was back in my office with a problem. Using Merzad as his translator, he explained that the production team and the crew were teasing him. The sound man was impersonating him on set; the assistant director referred to him as a 'girl'; everyone was generally taunting him because of his sexual orientation.

Muffy immediately pulled the production team together and told them that this type of behaviour would not be tolerated in our department. They were to leave their personal feelings regarding homosexuality at home and anyone caught persecuting Khalid would be disciplined. The boys promised that they would no longer tease him, and Muffy and I walked away from the episode feeling particularly proud of our superior management skills.

Khalid continued to be the butt of a variety of jokes and pranks, but they were based on his limited English skills rather than his sexuality. He appeared in my office one day asking for a tablet, because he had a little 'poo-poo'. It didn't take me long to figure out that his 'poo-poo' was, in fact, a 'headache' and that Ali had coached him on what to say. When he turned up to work sporting a stringy hairpiece glued to his prematurely balding pate, he proudly stroked it and asked Muffy whether she liked his new 'balls'—again a translation kindly provided by one of the producers. We could only laugh at their cheek—after all, by instructing them to respect Khalid's sexuality, we had taught them an important life lesson in tolerance that went way beyond harmless shenanigans.

But a few weeks later, two of the producers, Wassi and Farhad, were back in my office looking grim-faced and serious. Farhad, a gorgeous young boy with jade-green eyes, did the talking. They had been shooting at a hospital that day and something terrible had happened. The cleaner who had witnessed this 'very bad thing' had told the director of the hospital, and my team was told never to return. Wassi had eventually managed to sort it out, but the situation was far from good.

I quickly established that the issue concerned Khalid, but getting to the core of the problem took some digging. It centred on a toilet ... Khalid ... a male extra ... and 'connecting'. My continual queries about the 'connecting' part were met with an abundance of head shaking and constant repetition of the term in question. Muffy and AK (an American director who was working with us at the time) snorted back giggles as I soberly enquired whether the connecting involved a penis ... or perhaps two. Apparently it did.

Khalid was summonsed to the office and Farhad did the translating. Khalid tried to convince me that he was only hugging the extra—a friend he hadn't seen in months—but I confidently replied that, in a country where men habitually hug, kiss one another on the lips and massage each other's shoulders, I doubted very much that a little bit of cuddling in a cubicle would have caused such a scandal.

Khalid knew he was nailed. I explained to him the seriousness of the offence, the damage it could cause to the company's reputation and my fears for his own personal safety. He lowered his eyes and nodded his head. It was Farhad who asked that I spare Khalid his job—he came from a poor family and, on his $400 per month wage, was the only breadwinner in his home. We all agreed to keep it under wraps and not inform Christof, but Khalid was to be on probation for the next month and, if I got wind of any more 'connecting' at work, I'd have to take the matter further.

They were all back in my office two weeks later. Khalid was the first to arrive, with another tale of persecution—Farhad's scarf was wet and everyone was blaming him. I was busy and distracted; I sent him on his way with the kind of sensible advice my mother administered when, from the ages of ten to twelve, I sported a wart on the end of my nose and was nicknamed 'Witchypoo'. If you just ignore them, my mother counselled me, they will get sick of teasing you and leave you alone.

Wassi and Farhad were the next to arrive, and now the water-on-the-scarf story took a sinister turn. Most of the team had been out on a shoot all morning, with Wassi and Khalid the only ones remaining in the producers' room. Wassi claimed that Khalid had been looking at some 'very bad photos' on the internet at the time. Wassi then left to go to the editing suite, leaving Khalid alone in the room for a good twenty minutes; when Farhad returned with the team, he found his scarf shoved at the back of his desk drawer and mysteriously wet. It seems that Khalid had connected again, this time with the beautiful Farhad's scarf.

In fairness to Khalid, I did thoroughly investigate the matter and all parties were questioned. IT tracked down the 'very bad photos'—Facebook pictures of some of Khalid's friends. A shirt-less German chap, kneeling on the grass, his frayed, denim shorts revealing well-toned thighs; a UK bartender wearing an outrageously tiny thong on a Goa beach; a blue-eyed Dutch fellow, reclining in a chair and looking seductively at the camera. At AK's suggestion, the vital piece of evidence (which had since been thrown in the garbage bin) was produced. The fact that the scarf peeled apart when Khalid unfolded it said it all, really.

Khalid was dispatched to double-bag the scarf and throw it into the outside bin and Farhad was called back to see me. I apologised for what had happened, while Muffy's offer to buy him a new scarf was met with a grunt of disgust. I explained to him that I would be taking the matter up with Christof and that Khalid would probably lose his job.

Farhad sadly shook his head. He reminded me of Khalid's precarious financial position, but finally conceded it was probably for the best as Khalid had been sexually harassing him for weeks—sending him dirty text messages, brushing up against him on set, and calling him late at night to lisp obscenities down the phone. Wassi was called in to back up Farhad's claims that he had been harassing other members of staff as well. Our male actors were all refusing to work with him and one crew member had threatened to shoot him when Khalid admired his belt buckle and allowed his hands to wander.

I was astounded by their admissions and wanted to know why they hadn't told me any of this. They were equally perplexed—they explained that we had told them to tolerate Khalid's sexuality and thought that they couldn't complain. Needless to say, there were meetings to follow—discussions on acceptance versus abuse as Muffy and I attempted to shore up the gaping rents in our cloak of 'superior management'.

16.
Yule
Tired

Happy Christmas to me. I was spending it in a public hospital in Sydney, where one of the non-nursing staff, wearing a facemask, gloves and gown, together with a decidedly limp Santa hat, had just delivered my Christmas lunch. It consisted of a piece of processed ham plonked on a plate, plus a slice of round white meat, which was some poor facsimile of either turkey or pork, and a sticky ball of mashed potato and some colourless string beans.

I took a photo on my phone and cried for only the second time since arriving there four days ago. I had no right to feel sorry for myself—the pneumonia that I'd been diagnosed with had been creeping up on me for weeks now, but I deliberately dismissed the persistent cough, the rattling chest and the aching back as trifling so I could celebrate the festive season with my friends.

I first felt a tad off when I attended an early Christmas soiree at a friend's house at the start of December. The fumes from her bukhari (a traditional Afghan wood-burning heater) made my chest feel tight; I actually went home quite early for a change, and for the next few days struggled to draw in deep breaths.

I hauled myself off to the Christmas markets at the British Embassy a week before I left Kabul. It's an annual event where Afghan stallholders sell clothes, jewellery and various crafty knick-knacks that are guaranteed to impress family and friends when presented as Christmas gifts. I sat outside in the cold that afternoon chatting with my mates, eating barbecued bratwurst and drinking spiced wine, dissolving into unpleasant fits of coughing every time I laughed.

I seriously considered attending the yuletide carols at Gandamak the night before I flew out, but, having left work early and taken to my bed for the entire afternoon, I wisely decided against it. Muffy rubbed my aching back before leaving for the festivities, while my friend Eugene (a work colleague and a lovely new buddy) went to collect an asthma inhaler from one of our housemates. I spent the night shivering uncontrollably, freezing under my heavy doona despite my room being more than adequately heated.

If I hadn't flown when I did—a sweating, pain-ridden, phlegm-filled mess (benevolently upgraded to business class for the seventeen-hour flight)—I don't think I would have had the strength to get out of there.

I spent my first night in Sydney bent over on my knees in the middle of the lounge-room floor, two pillows supporting my tummy, trying to find some relief from the pain in my back. When my dear friend and housemate, Maree, came down in the morning to find me struggling to breathe she ordered me to go straight to a doctor.

I didn't, chiefly because I'm an idiot. Instead, I dragged myself off to a meeting with a production company to discuss their possible interest in a show idea that Muffy and I had been floating for years. The man I met with spent most of the twenty minutes he had so generously allocated to me taking phone calls, and was far more interested in discussing his own projects than talking about ours.

As I stood hunched over in the street trying to hail a taxi back to my house, I finally gave in. I called my brother and asked him to please come and collect me, as I feared I was quite ill. I was admitted into hospital within a matter of hours and the first hit of morphine administered to me in the emergency department was an exquisite release that I doubt I will ever forget.

And so there I was, receiving top-rate medical treatment for free. I even had a private room, because there were fears that I may have contracted tuberculosis. While back in Kabul, twenty-two street kids had died so far that winter. No, any self-pity would be an extravagance and one that I most certainly did not deserve to indulge in.

I had had other health scares during my time in Afghanistan. The regular bouts of diarrhoea are nothing more than annoying—everyone gets it and discussions around stool consistency are commonplace. The typhoid was a bit of a worry, particularly as I had been vaccinated against it. The intestinal parasites, chest infections and asthma were inevitable by-products of living in Kabul, considered to be one of the most polluted cities in the world. Open sewers line the streets. Diesel-powered generators, old cars running on dirty fuel and the dust from unpaved roads all conspire to strangle the life out of the air.

My specialist was a gentle, softly spoken man with a kind, round face like a kewpie doll. In my mind I had taken to calling him Doctor Baby Head. He had already examined me that morning, accompanied by a team of young interns, all of them genuinely fascinated by the weird old chick in Room 9 who earned her crust making soapies in Kabul.

On his return visit, he sat down in the chair beside my bed and told me that so far they'd been unable to identify the specific cause of my pneumonia. Apparently that wasn't unusual and I had nothing to be worried about. It seemed I was still not in the clear with the TB and would need to stay in hospital for a few more days, coughing up sputum into little plastic cups for further testing, before they could rule that out.

He then told me that he had been doing some research into Kabul. He had been alarmed by the levels of air pollution and had noted that the winter was particularly harsh. The bottom line was that he didn't want me to go back there until I had returned to full health. Even if the TB was nothing more than a scare, I could be stranded in Australia for anywhere up to six weeks.

I initially took the news surprisingly well. After he left, wishing me a Merry Christmas as he headed out the door, I settled down into my bed, quite shocked by my sense of relief. On previous occasions when I had been back in Australia, my feet had grown itchy within a week or two of touching the ground, and I had begun counting down the days until I could return to my friends, my workmates, my job . . . my 'home'.

I reasoned that being unwell had a lot to do with my mood that Christmas Eve, but it wasn't just that. I honestly felt tired and old. I realised that my six-day working week was taking its toll, and that my 'leisure time'—almost exclusively confined to house parties, bars or hanging out in my room watching DVDs—was seldom rejuvenating or restful.

There was the lack of good food; the constant moving house; the need to have a security guard trail me around the supermarket as I searched for sanitary products. Then I remembered the incredible friends I had made, and who had now left me behind. The mud, the snow, the dust, the heat . . . I was suddenly so angry and under-whelmed by my life that I burst into tears. The rage ebbed away after a minute or two, but I continued to cry for a very long time as I considered whether my love affair with Afghanistan was finally starting to wane.

But all that was on Christmas Eve. I woke up on Christmas morning and shooed those thoughts away. I looked at the big, beautiful flower arrangements sent to me by Eugene and the Mohseni family. I recalled the phone call from Muffy, with all the work kids in the background screaming out their well wishes. I re-read the text message from Aleem, where he told his 'second mother' how much he loved me and was praying for me to get better.

And by the time my Christmas lunch arrived, I knew with certainty that my time in Kabul was far from done.

I replaced the cover on my untouched Chrissie feast, knowing that very soon my wonderful friend Natasha would be there. She was bringing my mum, along with a Christmas tree, presents and leftovers from lunch. Then more friends and family were expected throughout the afternoon.

I was surrounded by love; I had a life in Australia that offered me comfort, safety and freedom. And, unlike my cherished Kabul kids, I could leave Afghanistan whenever I wanted.

'But not yet,' I thought. 'Not just yet.'

17.
Four in the Bed

I woke up in bed one February morning with three men, all of us spooning one another against the raging blizzard outdoors. It's tempting to spin this as some tantalising tale of Expats-Gone-Wild, but two of the men, Hamish and Bruce (who was in Kabul short-term consulting at an embassy), were gay. And Eugene was like a little brother to me. The unconventional sleeping arrangement was purely convenient.

We had spent the previous evening doing the expat party circuit and, when the last venue had shuffled us out, we drifted back here to raid my healthy stash of duty-free alcohol recently smuggled in from Dubai following my five-week convalescence in Australia. Despite my best intentions, the brush with pneumonia had done little to curb my lifestyle. When the weather turned woolly around 4am (with Eugene returning from a quick inspection of the snowstorm announcing that, according to his iPhone app, the temperature outside had dropped to minus thirteen degrees Celsius), my cohorts decided that finding their way home was simply beyond them. So we all bunked down in my king-sized bed to snatch some sleep.

I was grateful for their companionship; it had been a god-awful week, due to Aleem being forced to resign from the company. The circumstances that led to his sudden departure were convoluted, but essentially he had been accused of siphoning off company funds while working on *Salam 2*. He was facing not only the axe but also, according to Christof, possible criminal charges. Despite suggestions from certain expat mates that I was perhaps being naive and blinded by 'motherly' love, I simply refused to believe it was true.

Corruption is so commonplace in Afghanistan as to be an accepted part of everyday life. Teachers take bribes to pass students; patients pay doctors on the sly for preferential treatment; public servants think nothing of topping up their salaries with a little extra compensation. It isn't something confined to the high end of town or urban areas—right across the country, billions of dollars by way of bribes change hands every year.

I paid my first 'bribe' to a police officer on Season One of *Salam*; he was one of three men tasked with ensuring our security in Jalalabad. We had been shooting all day and had scheduled a shot of our hero striding along a mountain ridge as the last set-up.

I wanted to film it during 'magic hour'—the last hour of daylight, when the sun sits low on the horizon before disappearing behind it. At this time, the light is warm and soft and the colours are magnificent.

We were running a little behind, so it was going to be a mad dash to pack up in the village, race across the river and get to the top of the mountain in time. Just as we were about to drive off, Sidique hurried over to inform me that the police weren't coming with us—it was 4.30 and they had decided to knock off for the day.

I got out of the car, marched over to the officers and, through Sidique, demanded to know what was going on—the mountains could be dangerous, particularly after dark, and besides, their commander had assured me that they would stay with us until we wrapped. Two of them turned their backs on me while the third man simply shrugged his shoulders and grinned.

'Tell him I'll call his commander,' I barked. But my threat merely elicited the same blasé response.

It was getting late and I was desperate to get moving. 'Sidique, what do we do?' I asked.

He led me away from the infuriating little man and lowered his voice. 'I think he wants money.'

'What?'

'I think, if you give him some money, they will come with us.'

'This is absolute bullshit!'

'This is the way it is done.'

The sun was truly sinking now and I didn't have time to argue. 'How much?' I enquired, before running to the car to grab my wallet.

By the time I'd returned, they'd agreed on ten dollars. I only had a twenty, and literally threw it in the guy's face before screaming at him to get into his jeep and follow us to the location.

On Muffy and Aleem's first props-buying expedition for *Eagle Four*, the shopkeeper angrily haggled with Aleem over the price of a clock for a good five minutes. After they left the store, Aleem translated the gist of the debate. 'He kept saying to me, "She's just a foreigner, brother! Why are you arguing with me? Let me just charge her three times the price and I'll cut you in on the profit."'

From then on, the two of them would stroll into stores separately and then, using some weird facial tic and a roll of her eyes, Muffy would indicate to Aleem what she wanted to buy. She'd then saunter out again, with Aleem finishing off the transaction in order to secure us a reasonable price.

Corruption was also a major workplace problem that management had worked hard to tackle. A few years ago the banker on one of our game shows arranged for his best friend to be a contestant and the guy rather fortuitously won the grand prize. My Australian producer mate, Rick, was mentoring on the project and he quickly uncovered the feeble deception. The contestant never got his money, the program never went to air and, lacking any solid evidence that the 'win' was actually a scam, the employee kept his job but was severely reprimanded. Rick was truly shocked by the outrageous brazenness of it all.

Nepotism had also been an issue. Over time, a whole host of cousins, brothers and in-laws had managed to gain positions in the company due to their family connections.

A few years back, when we'd interviewed for two new writers, I oversaw the process, but I let Hamid make the final decision. It was only six months later that I learnt that one of the writers he'd hired was, in fact, his brother. He was a gifted young scribe and nobody else in the team had a problem with it—it was just another cultural norm that I had to struggle to get my head around.

However, the latest HR policy decreed that siblings were no longer allowed to work in the same department. In the past, logistics officers had been caught trying to hand out lucrative contracts to unworthy relatives, and employees had been investigated for doing jobs on the side using company equipment.

But still, I struggled to believe that Aleem—the kid who had been with me from the start, the boy who called me 'Mum'—could be capable of such deceit.

Christof initially presented me with scant evidence to back his claim—it seemed entirely based on some unnamed colleagues accusing Aleem of the theft. And he couldn't seem to explain to me why the production manager on *Salam 2*, Najim, who was actually the person on the shoot accountable to Finance (and who coincidentally was related to one of our senior managers), was not being investigated as well. Aleem was not at all well connected, but he had worked incredibly hard to distinguish himself, moving rapidly through the ranks. I suspected that there could be a bit of jealousy and resentment at play.

Christof finished off our meeting by assuring me that Muffy and I would be kept in the clear. I honestly had no idea what he was on about so he had to explain to me that, because Muffy and I had done the final sign-off on all the finances, the company and the police would be entitled to pursue us as well.

Yeah, right. I was quietly confident that the command at the mother ship would merely scoff at any suggestion that I was ripping off the company. Certainly, if management did inexplicably decide to pursue me, they'd be doing it along the runway of Kabul Airport as I hightailed it out of town on the first available flight.

For the past six months, Aleem had been working on a crime re-enactment series with Tahir, a talented Canadian–Afghan director. So I met with Tahir soon after these allegations surfaced to get his take on the whole thing. He was adamant that Aleem was innocent but added that, regardless of the final outcome, Aleem's name had now been blackened and the shame over the incident would be something he would never live down.

When I finally got to speak to Aleem about it, he simply screwed up his face in disgust. 'Mum, you know that I'm a good and honest boy.' He then went on to describe his fantasy of revenge on Christof—a chilling scenario that saw our general manager being arrested by a police chief Aleem knew and thrown into jail. It seemed my 'good and honest boy' could be a vengeful one too.

On the next Wednesday afternoon, in order to ease our doubts about the lack of due process and transparency around the matter, Christof called Muffy and me into his office and presented us with some irregularity over the payment of a driver that he had uncovered, to which he added assurances that he had finance searching for more.

Muffy had been subjected to a similar style witch-hunt over *Eagle Four*, so we both knew that finance sometimes could and *did* get it wrong, but we ended the meeting in tears. Our distress had nothing to do with us doubting Aleem, but we now realised that Christof wasn't going to let this go. He honestly believed that he was on to something, the recent crackdown on corruption and workplace theft no doubt fuelling his crusade. And as Muffy and I sniffled outside his office and calmed ourselves with nicotine, we both agreed that the best thing would be for Aleem to leave.

I was truly heartbroken, but managed to find him a position with another production company that same day. The company's CEO was an Aussie mate, Peter, who used to work for Moby.

'Well, what do you make of it all?' he asked me.

'I honestly don't know. It all seems so strange. That shoot wrapped almost a year ago; HR here knows nothing about the investigation, so I doubt Dubai does either. Right now, I just want him to go on his own terms while he still can.'

Peter, who was busy tackling corruption and nepotism in his own organisation, seemed unfazed by the whole affair. 'Sure. I really like Aleem. He's a great worker. Happy to take him on.'

And so, the next morning, Tahir and I convinced our dear young friend to resign. He was initially determined to fight it out, but in the end, he angrily conceded that he'd had enough. He emailed his resignation to Christof and HR later that day:

> I don't have anyone in this company to back me up and don't have any groups I belong to. I only have the work as my friend. This is why I think it was easy to blame me for corruption in the company.
>
> I feel that I am not guilty of anything. I feel tired of all this and now am leaving the company.
>
> I want to say thank you for all the years of work. I learned many things. It was like a big school. It has made me proud to work here.

And so it was, at sunrise on a cold February morning, as my bed buddies and I floated off into a Valium-induced sleep, I had a sudden little cry about losing my favourite boy. Hamish wrapped his arms around my waist and comforted me. 'Sweetheart, you did everything you could for him. You even found him another job. Hey, you're not going to be around forever to look out for him . . . for any of them. Trust me, he'll make it on his own.'

We were still all asleep when a mobile phone started ringing from somewhere in the bed. Bruce groped under the sheets for it and, after looking at the screen, let out an almighty 'Fuck!' It was his private security detail—he operated under a strict curfew, which he had broken by a good twelve hours.

There was a bit of chatter down the other end of the line and we listened as Bruce told the caller that he was in his room. The man calmly informed him that he was, in fact, standing in Bruce's room and that he was nowhere to be seen. The caller demanded to know where Bruce was so they could pick him up.

Aleem was momentarily forgotten as we waited for Bruce's ride. He was agonising over whether or not he would be placed in lockdown for the remainder of his stay. 'I just wanted to get laid!' he moaned. Which, sadly, hadn't happened.

Unfortunately, in his fragile state Bruce repeated this phrase to the PSD dudes who picked him up; it featured in the official security report that was subsequently written up about his night on the town.

When he called that night to tell me this, I laughed—the biggest and best belly-laugh I'd had all week. It almost felt improper considering the sadness I was still carrying over Aleem. But that was how we learnt to roll; our ups and downs were often spaced so closely that we barely felt the shift, and Bruce's shameful predicament was just what I needed to pull me out of my funk. Besides, Hamish was right. My cherished Aleem would indeed survive, while poor old Bruce had to wait two more days to learn his fate.

18.
Purple Caterpillars and Kuchi Queens

Nilu was leaving soon. The excited, hopeful woman who first returned to Afghanistan a decade ago was planning to exit her homeland, disillusioned, exhausted and angry. My spirited friend, who had talked to me on the Mazar bus ride two years ago about her dreams for rebuilding a glorious new Afghanistan, had given up the fight.

It had been a long time coming, even if she didn't realise it herself. As an Afghan–American woman, she had seen a side to this country that I had never really been exposed to.

Quite early on, Sue told me that western chicks are like purple caterpillars—so strange and foreign to the Afghan men that they don't even try to understand us. An Irish mate in security, who had been in Afghanistan for seven years, put it more bluntly. 'You're all wanton infidels. You're going to hell anyway, so they don't really give a fuck what you do.'

But as a Muslim woman, Nilu had needed protecting. When she was still working with our company, certain drivers would lecture her on the clothes she wore or the way she spoke. There were a couple of security guards who would gossip about her if she went to a bar or a night club or met a man for dinner. She was one of theirs and they felt that they had every right to try and keep her on the straight and narrow.

I remembered one day about a year before, shortly before she left to work for a rival TV network, when she arrived at the office shaken and distressed. On the drive in, she had seen a woman in a burqa trip over and drop her tiny baby on the footpath as she fell. Men all around her just watched it happen, and not one of them tried to help the distraught young mother or check on her child. Nilu screamed for the driver to stop but, with the traffic in Kabul moving for a change, there was no opportunity for him to pull over.

As she looked back through the rear window, watching the woman kneeling on the footpath consoling her crying child, Nilu demanded to know why none of the men had bothered to assist. The driver explained that it was against Islam for a man to touch a woman who wasn't his wife, mother or daughter (this was delivered as a lecture, the implication being that she should have known better).

Nilu ranted and raged at him for the remainder of the trip. She arrived at work sick at heart. Through tears she told me that she was just so tired of Afghans who used Islam to justify bigotry, a lack of humanity and hate.

I, too, had moments of despair, but the stakes weren't as high for me. I was just a purple caterpillar watching sadly from the sidelines. I still had hope that this country could right itself. There were progressive men trying to lead the way, but I believed, and still believe, that the future of Afghanistan lies in its women.

It floored me that, during my three years as a 'propaganda merchant', female empowerment had never been a primary concern for our clients. At times, and after prompting, it had sometimes been included as secondary messaging—behind counter-narcotics, anti-insurgency and transition. At a meeting with one of our clients late in 2011, where my new female head writer, Alka, and I outlined storylines for the upcoming season of one of our shows, we were quite bluntly told by an American major that they weren't really interested in women's rights. Then he asked us to cut back a bit on 'the ladies stuff'.

But I just had to look around my company, at all the amazing young women fighting for change, to know that they were the way forward. The next day a group of women were heading to India. Shakila had had a short film, which she wrote, produced and directed, accepted into an international film festival there and they were all going for the screening. They had been planning the trip for weeks—all five of the women were fortunate to come from liberal families, who were happy to allow their single young daughters to travel alone outside their homeland.

Young girls like these demonstrated on the streets against public harassment, and had founded organisations for women's rights. They took on the boys in the office with terrifying boldness and had inevitably been labelled as lesbians for their refusal to marry the first cousin who came along.

Unfortunately they were in the minority, as unique and strange to most Afghans as purple caterpillars. In Kabul, there are still women forbidden to leave their homes unless decked out in the blue burqa and escorted by a male relative. Shakila had turned up at work just the previous week feeling frustrated and angry over an incident that happened on her way to the office. An outraged woman in a burqa stopped her as she made her way along a road she travelled every morning.

'She was yelling at me. You know what she say to me, Trudi? She say I shame all the women living in her street because I dress like . . . oh . . . you know the woman who has sex and gets money?'

'A prostitute?'

'Yes! *That* woman! She say I dress like a prostitute! You look at me, Trudi *Jan*. Do I dress like this woman?'

Shakila was an eclectic dresser—Muffy and I dubbed her the Carrie Bradshaw of Kabul—but still, she was covered from head to toe, and only her hands and face were visible.

'No, darling! You look decent and gorgeous. Was she old?'

'Yes! Very old! She was, I think, thirty.'

I smiled at this, despite feeling incredibly saddened by the knowledge that this beautiful young woman had been so cruelly attacked by one of her own.

In the provinces there are thirteen-year-old girls being married off to old men to settle debts; there are fathers who would never contemplate the notion of their female children attending school. A recent case—of a man who, together with his mother and sister, imprisoned and systematically tortured his fifteen-year-old wife for being disobedient—had even President Karzai speaking out.

In the eyes of many Afghans, being an actress is akin to being a sex-worker. Our actresses were often shunned by family members and harassed on the streets. The lead actress on *Secrets of this House* had recently fled to India because her uncle was threatening to kill her. And even when the actresses had initially enjoyed the support of their families, some seemingly innocuous storyline could turn all that on its head.

One of our actresses, Sahar, spent Season Four of *Secrets* embroiled in some of the most progressive, controversial narratives my female-heavy team had ever written. Her character, Laily, had fought against her parents' wish that she marry a drug-addicted cousin she had been promised to at birth; with the support of her brother, she took the matter to a council of tribal elders, who decided in her favour.

After that, Laily was sexually harassed by a university lecturer; when she reported this to his superiors and the police, she managed to get him fired from his job and arrested. Because she'd had a tough year, we decided that Laily should finish the season on a celebratory note—our storyline provided for her engagement to Manochehr, the man she truly loved.

When one of our producers outlined this scenario to Sahar on set, the very next day she arrived at our office with her mother, claiming that she could no longer appear on the program. Apparently her family felt that if she was to become engaged on television, it might spoil her chances of finding a husband in real life.

It seemed crazy, considering all the contentious issues Sahar had so bravely tackled on screen during the course of the year, but

I simply explained through Merzad that her decision would place us in a very difficult position. We had been working towards this engagement for months—surely she had noticed the blossoming romance between Laily and Manochehr?—and scripts had already been written (and approved by the client!) for their betrothal. But mother and daughter were immoveable—if we insisted on keeping the engagement in, Sahar would be quitting the show.

After they left, I hastily convened a meeting with Merzad and Hamid. With all the build-up it was implausible that Laily would reject Manochehr's proposal and, besides, the engagement party was meant to be our season finale. We ultimately decided to write her out of the show—her jilted cousin would run her down and kill her for shaming him, and the party would be replaced by her funeral.

I instructed Merzad to call Sahar and her mother back into the office so we could explain the difficult decision to axe her from the show. But both he and Hamid were adamant that we shouldn't reveal our plans to her. I argued that it was only fair to give her proper notice—that she needed time to start looking for another gig.

But Merzad just shook his head. 'Trudi *Jan,* this would be the wrong thing to do. You know, if she finds out that we are sacking her, she will just stop turning up for work.'

'Surely not!'

'Yes, Trudi *Jan.* This is exactly what she will do, I'm telling you the truth.'

Hamid nodded in agreement.

Against all my instincts, we kept Sahar's on-screen death from her. We actually filmed out of sequence the scenes where she got hit by the car and lay unconscious in hospital the following week, just in case she got wind of the fact that Laily was never going to wake up from her coma.

When, at the end of the run, Merzad told Sahar that she wouldn't be needed for the following season, she simply shrugged her shoulders and told him that she'd prefer to work in a bank anyway.

There were a number of occasions where I had to step in and fill the gaps when actresses failed to turn up for filming. My first appearance in an Afghan television show was on *Salam*. It also marked the first time that I'd seen our Pakistani actresses really laugh. Unfortunately it was a funeral scene, but the sight of me—wrapped in a headscarf, my back to camera, wailing and keening and howling with grief— made them all giggle uncontrollably. I ended up laughing too, but at least my mirth-induced convulsions, filmed from behind, could easily be interpreted as anguish.

My second appearance came in *Eagle Four*. An actress didn't show and I was enlisted to play the wife of a criminal and the mother of Roya, an extremely energetic, talkative six-year-old. In the scene, a police team bursts into our home to arrest my husband, and my daughter and I cower in the corner before being hurried out by one of the arresting officers. To mask the fact that I was clearly a fair-skinned, middle-aged, blonde woman, I had to wear a burqa.

We shot the scene about twelve times. It would be easy to now claim that it was the tigerish Roya who ruined every take, with her giggling and chatting and innocent refusal to look suitably terrified. But, in truth, I flunked more takes than she did. It was the bloody burqa. The mesh eye-panel afforded me little more than a blurry, blinkered view of my surroundings and, when I was moving, it had a tendency to slip away from my eye-line.

But it was running in the thing that really did me in. I tripped; I fell; I stumbled to the doorway. Take after take after take. There was talk at one stage of putting our sound assistant into the burqa, before I finally got it right. My respect for Afghan women grew enormously that day.

My next appearance on Afghan TV was as a blood-soaked corpse in a driveway; I was mother to another six-year-old girl, Rita. Rita was as patient and focused as Roya had been lively and rambunctious. The actress I understudied for *did* actually turn up for the shoot and was happy to film the scenes where she picnicked in the garden, chatted with her husband and hurried her daughter inside the front gate when the baddies turned up with guns. But when it came to lying on hard concrete for two hours in the scorching midday sun, she decided that acting wasn't really for her.

I patiently explained that she was under contract, and therefore professionally bound to finish shooting her scenes. I threatened not to pay her, and she just looked at me like I had four heads. She was going home, and there was nothing I could do to stop her.

Fortunately, she and I were around the same size. So I was able to slip into her outfit, turn my veil-covered head away from the camera and convincingly play her part. It was brutal. Rita and I were covered in sticky, sweet, fake blood and the flies just couldn't get enough of us. Also, I had to take regular breaks to shake out a sleeping foot or bend an aching elbow, but gorgeous Rita, enveloped in my bloodied arms, didn't move a muscle.

I think my favourite performance was as a Kuchi woman because it was just so inappropriate and absurd. Kuchis are traditional Pashtun nomads from southern and eastern Afghanistan, although many of them have now become farmers or settled in cities. In Kabul, Kuchi women can often be found in the bazaars selling bangles.

One of the storylines in *Eagle Four* centred on a group of bangle-sellers who also did a thriving sideline in child trafficking. We were shooting the scenes in the yard of a house on the outskirts of Kabul. Our main Kuchi actress turned up on time and was fully across her lines, but her three bangle-selling cohorts failed to show. They didn't have dialogue but they were essential to the set-up, as a solitary woman could hardly be held to constitute a criminal gang.

Our director, Sayed, suggested that Muffy, Shakila and I could fill out the posse. Muffy and I thought this was hilarious, and instructed him to come up with an alternative solution, but he failed to see what the problem was.

'Darling, we don't look like gypsy Afghan women,' I said.

'We have outfits for you to wear,' he replied.

'Even so, I mean, our skin . . . it's too pale. It will never work.'

'Trudi *Jan*, I can put brown make-up on your face,' Shakila chimed in.

The thought of going blackface on national television was simply outrageous, and yet nobody in our team could understand our reluctance to get on board. We finally agreed, on the proviso that they would only shoot us in extreme wide or side on. So Shakila daubed our faces in thick, muddy foundation and drew tiny Kuchi tattoos on our chins. With our headscarves and traditional dress, everyone agreed we looked perfect.

I had to ditch my glasses, so the next few hours were literally a blur, and when there was a commotion at the gate towards the end of the shoot, I had no idea what was going on.

'Muffy, Trudi, come with me. Quickly!' Shakila hissed as she scrambled to her feet.

We followed her inside the house, where Aleem soon joined us. 'The local mullah is outside with some men,' he told us. 'He knows there are foreigners here and is complaining that we didn't ask his permission to film.'

'Well, do we need his permission?' I asked.

'Not really—I think they just want money. I have told him to return to the mosque, and I will go there now and speak with him. But you must leave—you are not safe here.'

I didn't imagine that a couple of western women parading as Afghans would go down terribly well with the neighbours so, flanked by our local crew, we covered our faces, bowed our heads, bustled past the crowd gathered on the street and dived into an idling van. We laughed all the way back to work and spent the rest of the afternoon posing for photos as an endless line of amused kids filed into our office to check out the Kuchi queens.

Over the years in Kabul my TV roles included a foreign journalist, a terrified westerner in a suicide attack and the wife of an ambassador. My brother once asked me whether I was taking a huge risk, appearing so often on television, but whatever risks I was taking were nothing compared to those taken by the courageous Afghan women I worked with every day.

A lot of us in the expat community referred to people in Nilu's situation as 'Half-Ghans', a cute, catchy label that conveniently summarised their tale—born in Afghanistan then raised overseas before travelling back to their birthplace to help in its reconstruction. It was only when a heartbroken Nilu announced her intention to leave that I grasped how wholly inadequate the Half-Ghan tag was—how it failed to capture the constant struggle that people like Nilu faced in their attempts to straddle two worlds.

Nilu felt she could no longer stay in Afghanistan but didn't really want to go back to the States, and despaired at once again having to remould herself and adapt. I realised then that my fearless, extraordinary friend would most likely forever be a woman caught in limbo.

19.
It's All Just a Little Bit Wrong

It was March 2012 and the hot topic at our weekly supervisors' meeting was racism. It seemed that our music show, a singing competition generally fashioned on the *Idol* series, had managed to divide the nation. It was ironic because the program was originally devised as a way of connecting Afghan to Afghan. By featuring singers from all across the country, it was intended to unite the people through song.

But this particular season, its seventh, had proven to be a pernicious affair. Two Hazara singers and a Tajik made it to the top three and in that week's elimination round the Tajik was voted off. The clip of the elimination was posted on YouTube; before it was taken down, it attracted five hundred comments, the bulk of them threatening and ugly and frightening in their ferocity. There was common agreement amongst my team that the Tajik singer was, by far, the best and it seemed his backers were incensed about the Hazara voting bloc that saw him off.

On top of that, one of our best floor managers, Akram, had lost his job. One of the Hazara singers complained that Akram had made racist comments to him and, despite the fact that this poor Pashtun kid had a faultless record with the company, he was instantly let go.

There was now a zero tolerance policy in place regarding racism, and that day HR sent an email to everyone confirming this. Akram stood in my office that afternoon, choking back tears as he said his goodbyes.

There are four main ethnic groups in Afghanistan—Pashtuns, Tajiks, Hazaras and Uzbeks—together with a handful of smaller minority groups scattered across the country. Managing the bar had given me a pretty solid insight into the ethnic divisions that prevail in Afghanistan. My first experience of it at my current job had come just a month into my tenure, when I was called in to break up a physical fight between two of my writers.

I was at lunch at the time and it was a frantic phone call from Allie, one of our project managers, that alerted me to the melee. I raced into the writers' room to see Ramin, a hulking, bear-faced Pashtun man, holding a chair over his head, poised to smash it down onto the skull of Yosuf, a slight, bespectacled Tajik fellow who was yelling and flailing his arms about like a lunatic. I marched into the room, clapped my hands and yelled 'Hey! Hey! Hey!' As ineffectual as that sounds, it actually worked.

As I stomped inside, I momentarily wondered why a tiny western woman was stepping into the fray when at least half a dozen Afghan men were inside the room witnessing the violence, while another dozen spectators stood outside the door. I never quite got to the bottom of what the fight was about. Someone called someone a 'dog' . . . an insult about a mother may or may not have been thrown into the mix. The only fact that I could clearly establish was that the Dari and the Pashto writers no longer wanted to sit together in the same room. Tough titties. Space was a valuable commodity and they would just have to learn to get on as far as I was concerned.

Then, only a month or two later, as we were planning for our auditions in Jalalabad, Raouf confided to me that he didn't want Zahra along on the trip. I just couldn't comprehend Raouf's resistance. I was pleased and amazed that Zahra's parents were even letting her go—it is almost unheard of for an Afghan woman to be allowed to travel anywhere without being accompanied by a male relative.

She was a good worker, I argued; she was smart and well organised and I needed her there. It was then that he reached up and stretched back the corners of his eyes with his forefingers and declared, 'She too Chinesey.' I smilingly accused him of being a racist pig and then spent the next half-hour explaining to him through diagrams and charades exactly what that meant.

As the international carnival winds down, ethnic conflict is becoming more obvious and brutal. Hamid, who boldly declared that there is a little bit of Talib in every Afghan, explained it all to me as if to a child. Now that the 'foreign oppressors' had stated their intention to pull out, the power grab had begun in earnest. History had repeatedly demonstrated the difficulties in merging the tribal societies with a central government. In the vacuum that would inevitably exist once foreign troops withdrew from the country, Tajiks, Pashtuns, Hazaras, Uzbeks, Nuristanis, Sunni Muslims. Shi'as, conservatives, moderates . . . would all be staking their claims.

In our supervisors' meeting that day Christof was distraught. He made a long, desperate and, at times, rambling plea to our senior Afghan staff (an ethnically diverse bunch) to unite for the future of Afghanistan. He was close to tears, constantly clutching at his head, and his sincerity could not be doubted. But at times I found it hard not to laugh. His genuinely heartfelt speech was delivered in English and at least a third of the people in the room could barely speak the language, if at all. Even for those who spoke good English, his western perspective was undoubtedly lost on them.

'If you go to a disco or nightclub in Germany, you do not ask a woman if she is Catholic or Protestant! Imagine going up to a woman at a discotheque and your first question is "Are you Catholic or Protestant?" She would look at you and think: Cuckoo! You're crazy! Goodbye!'

I was pretty sure the scenario was beyond their imaginations. There were no discotheques in Kabul. Apart from in the workplace, there were very few opportunities for young Afghan men and women to mix freely. There were no Catholics. There were no Protestants. Christof's well-intentioned analogy—of a man not being able to pick up a chick at a nightclub because of his religious bias—fell on confused ears. Like so many other western initiatives that had occurred in Afghanistan over the past eleven years, it was all just a little bit wrong.

One week later, an episode of one of our serials was rejected for broadcast. Our foreign client, who had funded the show since its inception, had taken issue with the fact that a small Afghan flag that sat on a desk in two office scenes and three scenes at the police station was hanging upside down.

It had been brought to our attention two days ago. I then sat through endless edits as we attempted to cut around it and instructed our graphics department to slightly blur the flag in scenes where we couldn't.

My Afghan staff all agreed that the blurring was quite acceptable and that, due to the flag being folded over, its orientation was indiscernible anyway. But the client was still not satisfied and demanded that we reshoot all five scenes where the wretched flag appeared.

The reshoot would put us hopelessly behind schedule—for this particular program, we had to film fifty-two thirty-minute episodes per year. Yet we had no choice but to do what we were told.

This problem would have been nothing more than a tiresome affair except for the fact that the client's representative (who had only been in the job for six weeks and had never visited our offices, let alone the set) was inexplicably claiming over email that the flag had been deliberately placed upside down by one of our Afghan staff. It had now developed into a veritable scandal.

Eugene, who was managing the project and whose mother is Afghan, had taken great offence on our behalf. He had replied to the man and cc'd his superiors:

If you do not have any evidence to support your opinion, this comment is irrelevant, unprofessional, and extremely disrespectful to our entire Afghan staff and crew. Just as it is unfair for Afghans to accuse international peacekeeping forces of wrongdoing and harming Afghanistan, it is equally unfair for international peacekeeping forces to do the same of Afghans. Our Afghan staff and crew treat you with this respect—I ask that you treat them with the same.

Furthermore, I am not aware of your background so I do not know how much you know about Afghan cultures and sensitivities, but to even allude that an Afghan would deliberately hang his or her national flag upside down is unfathomable. It is a very revered national and Islamic symbol that is 'never' handled inappropriately on purpose. If you do not believe me, please verify with your Afghan advisors.

In response, there were numerous apologies made by the client, together with an assurance that the individual concerned would be receiving 'counselling' over the incident. Eugene was now my #1 hero.

Merzad couldn't have cared less about all this and informed me that the flag had probably been upside down for the last two seasons. The money the client gave us to make the show barely covered the wages of our cast and a skeleton crew, so nobody had the time or concern to notice the alignment of a crumpled, handkerchief-sized flag on a desk. We laughed about it, but I told him to keep this information to himself. Having leverage with a difficult client was a rarity and it was nice being on top for a change.

Most of our client reps were delightful people, who openly acknowledged their lack of understanding about drama production and were happy to leave it to the experts. A few of them even became close personal friends. What we called our 'show briefs' (consisting of a synopsis, episode outlines and character biographies) were often quite long documents, running anywhere up to forty pages, and we often wondered how carefully our clients read them. I once colluded with a very funny junior PSYOPS officer to tape together all the pages inside the perfectly presented folder of a particularly extensive show brief before handing it on to his superiors for approval. He laughed when he informed me that the series had been approved and fully funded—with the pages all still sticky-taped together.

But there always seemed to be the odd one or two who, for whatever reason, were intent on tearing us down at every turn. And even with great clients, their ideas about appropriate formats for delivering messaging could sometimes be a little out of whack.

One of them asked us to write a proposal for a thirteen-part drama serial on fistulas. I warily googled the term, a little uncertain as to what I'd find. I discovered that an obstetric fistula is an injury to the birth canal that leaves the woman constantly leaking urine. It is a devastatingly common problem in Afghanistan, often attributable to child brides bearing babies when they are not fully developed; communities routinely stigmatise women who suffer from the condition. While readily acknowledging the need for education around the problem, I wasn't entirely sure that seven-and-a-half hours of soap on the subject was the best way to go.

I also wrote proposals for a comedy show about a zany, likeable census collector and a twenty-five-part drama series based on the UK show *EastEnders* (kind of tricky when the action on that particular show centres around a London pub).

At the information session for the *EastEnders* series (where the client outlined its creative vision of the show for all the broadcasters and production companies interested in bidding on the project), the Afghan attendees sat in stunned silence as they viewed a clip from the UK original featuring a gay couple kissing.

We ultimately won the contract but had to decline it as the tender, based on a one-page synopsis, was offered in August and they wanted us to be on air by mid-September. A small Afghan production house ultimately received the funding; a friend who was writing for the series reported numerous breakdowns, showdowns and endless creative disputes as they scrambled to get the show up in time.

I sat in meetings and patiently explained why an Afghan version of *Doctor Who* was simply beyond our technical capabilities, and debated the feasibility of a local version of *Glee,* given that we couldn't actually show women dancing on Afghan TV.

But for every ill-conceived idea, there were many more great ones, and enough smart, dedicated clients to keep me sane and hopeful. And any initial reservations I had regarding the nature of my job had long since dissipated with the knowledge that we were preaching for positive change, and that hawking propaganda was keeping my wonderful team in work.

Eugene, Merzad and I had a meeting with Flag Man the following week and intended to play our hand for all it was worth. We would no doubt be punished for our smugness further down the track but the opportunity to bask in a brief moment of glorious self-righteousness was just too appealing to resist.

20.
The
Safe
Room

I was finishing up lunch with Nilu on 15 April when the attack began. It was our Last Supper together, in the Italian restaurant directly across the road from work where we'd sat so many times before, picking over life. I had arranged it only that morning, suddenly realising that we were running out of time to say our private goodbyes.

Nilu had just called a car and we were settling the bill when the first blast rang out. It was close, but not exactly on top of us; nonetheless, the manager herded us all down to one end of the room as everyone hit their phones for intel.

I had no network coverage, but Nilu managed to speak briefly with her driver—from across the table I could hear gunfire through her phone. Her office, just a few blocks away, was right in the middle of it all; before the line went dead, her driver actually apologised for not being able to pick her up. As a panicked Nilu tried in vain to reconnect, a skinny old Afghan dude in a shiny suit strutted in to where we were sitting and struggled to raise high a rifle circa 1898.

'Everyone will stay here. Nobody can leave,' he said. Then, heaving the ancient firearm even higher, just in case we hadn't noticed it: 'We will all be okay.'

I seriously doubted Slim's ability to take on the Taliban, but was quietly happy that I could at least have a drink or seven while we waited it out. But just as I was ordering my traditional neat whisky, my phone sprang into life. It was work, wanting to know where I was. They would send security over to bring me back to the office.

Slim was crushed to be losing two of his charges but, with Nilu in tow, the guards raced me across the street. The gunfire seemed to be everywhere and we both covered our heads with our hands, in some insane but instinctive bid to fend off any stray bullets.

Our protectors deposited us into the first building inside our gate, which houses our sales and marketing team. There was no safe room there, just a basement stacked high with water bottles and stationery. Only ten people could actually fit in there, while everyone else snaked up the stairwell and spilled out into the glass-fronted foyer. In two seconds flat, we'd had enough of that fruitless caper, plus there was no phone coverage in the bowels of the building and Nilu was anxious to check on her team.

So she and I made our way upstairs, sticking our heads out the door along the way so I could partake of a soothing cigarette, before landing in Eric's office. Eric was our head of sales and marketing—a loud, jolly New Yorker who was constantly wired. He told us there had been coordinated attacks across the city, but the main threat now was a group of militants who had made their way into a nearby building under construction and were firing on the presidential palace, various ministry buildings and several western embassies. It was a similar scenario to last September's siege and we knew it could rage on for hours.

'Oh boy, ladies! Hee, hee, hee! Looks like we're in for a long afternoon. Hee, hee, hee!' Eric exclaimed.

He was compiling a 'Terrorist Attack' playlist on his computer, which included such gems as 'Hate & War' by The Clash and U2's 'Sunday Bloody Sunday'. He didn't know 'Everybody Wants to Rule the World' by Tears for Fears, but I assured him it was appropriate.

Nilu switched the television over to her channel to try and get an update. She gasped as she viewed vision of her building—the stairwell on her floor was filled with rubble. 'Oh God no. God no . . .' she cried, as she tried once again to get someone on the line.

I tried to ring Muffy, who was meant to be flying out on leave that day. Her grandfather was dying in Los Angeles and her departure was time-sensitive. I finally got through on the fifth attempt. She and Eugene were together in the new safe room on the other side of the street. Because nobody knew where the key was, it had taken them twenty minutes to get inside. When the key was finally located (it was across the road, with the head of finance), they opened the door to find the room full of boxes of merchandise. And just a moment ago one of the security guards, morally affronted by the men and women all packed inside in such close proximity, had ushered all the local girls out again.

I could only laugh. If I'd let the security situation bother me, my tiny head would have exploded. And, despite now having found out that her colleagues were safe, I doubted poor Nilu was up for that.

Following the last big attack in September 2011, when my kids had stood outside sipping tea as bullets whizzed overhead, a handful of expats and I had taken it upon ourselves to sort things out. Patrick and David, who worked in business development, were both ex-military while I simply fancied being part of an exciting, strategic mission that would take me away from my desk for a few hours.

So one afternoon, Ahmad and I had trailed David around the place. I made notes and took photos as he pointed out security concerns and earmarked areas that could be used as safe rooms. I snapped away at broken latches on security gates, at basements being used as storage facilities, at rubbish-filled escape routes. Also low walls where ladders could be placed to lead us to safety.

I set it all out in a document and sent it to Dubai. To be fair, they responded rather quickly. A week later we had a siren installed in our compound that would signal us all to move to our safe area at the rear of the building. A drill was held that very same day. We all dutifully shuffled to the designated zone and hung around for a bit, not seeing the point of it really, as they hadn't yet installed the security grille on the door.

Ahmad also mounted a demonstration on how to use the fire extinguishers. He lit a fire in a bin, using gasoline to get it going. But then he discovered that the fire extinguisher was empty. A guard had to race around to the back of the building and grab a hose to put out the huge flames.

Still, over the next few weeks basements were cleared, first-aid kits were purchased and drills were conducted. And yet here we were, six months later in the midst of another attack, with no proper safe rooms to go to.

We all had to take responsibility for letting things lapse. I had been to the safe room on the other side of the street a dozen times since it was first cleared out, foraging through the jumble of boxes to collect T-shirts, stickers and DVDs, with no thought of reporting its dire condition to management. The first-aid kit in our building had been used as a prop on one of our shoots and was still sitting in a corner of our office minus bandages, Band-Aids and antiseptic cream. And poor old Ahmad had lost his initial enthusiasm for holding regular safety drills when people (myself included) simply failed to show up.

As for my Afghan friends, I had come to the conclusion that they were so accustomed to death that the thought of attempting to stave it off just didn't even occur to them. The simple truth was, we didn't spend our days waiting for the next bomb to go off.

By late afternoon on the day of the April attack, Muffy was still unsure as to whether she'd be able to fly out; the airport was open but she was told that she may not be able to get there. Having been in a similar situation with my mum, I felt her pain.

She finally managed to escape in a high-speed operation worthy of a Bond film. The guards allowed me into the car park for a brief goodbye, before she was spirited away. She went up and over Russian Swimming Pool Hill, where she was hurried into another waiting vehicle and then driven through the backwaters of Kabul, all the time being admonished by her driver for looking too western in her over-sized sunnies and with her visible blonde fringe. I'm guessing that her pale skin might have been the real giveaway. I was evacuated soon after and sat with my housemates in our compound, slurping on our drinks as the thunder of battle rolled all around us.

The next morning my phone woke me at 6am. It was Christof, telling me to stay home from work and to advise my team to do the same. When I asked him why, he positively squealed before marvelling at how I could not possibly know that the siege was still in full swing, seventeen hours after it had begun.

I had apparently slept through most of it. I had also slept through a missed call and three text messages from our house manager, Adiba. Because there was gunfire nearby, she advised us to stay away from the windows, to remain inside, and to come to the safe room if we were concerned. I also snoozed away soundly as a couple of panicked souls flapped around the compound for most of the night, certain we were being attacked. You've gotta love a Valium.

About an hour after Christof's call, the Afghan Security Forces took out the last of the insurgents and our management in Dubai had a change of heart. They decided that we could go to work after all, and HR advised us via email that we should make our way to the office as soon as possible. I had already spoken by then with Merzad, the first link in my chain of command; when I told him to remain at home, he promptly informed me that he fully intended to. He hadn't slept all night and, besides, his father wouldn't allow him to leave the house.

So I responded to Dubai, informing them that my team would not be reporting for duty. I ended with my usual sign-off in such situations: *You guys have no idea what we've been through over here!* Their standard apology and backpedalling reply (always quite genuine) arrived in my inbox five minutes later.

21.
The Drama Queens No More

It was towards the end of May 2012 that I had to perform the most difficult work-related task I had undertaken: I had to tell Muffy that her contract wasn't being renewed. Unbeknownst to her, Christof and I had been fighting to save her for almost a month, but, with a couple of lucrative projects either falling through or hanging in the balance, Dubai had finally decided that it was too costly to keep her on.

I cried when Christof and Shaikh, our head of HR, broke the news to me just after lunch. My tears were for myself as much as for her. I was not only losing my best friend, but also my most loyal work ally. I selfishly weighed up the myriad jobs I would now need to take on; I anticipated the workplace battles I would have to fight alone.

This wasn't the first time that Muffy's job had been on the line. Soon after Christof started with the company, he tried to oust her. He wanted to employ a guy called AK, who on paper presented as an experienced and competent director but certainly not as a supervising producer. The idea was ill conceived and grossly unfair to Muffy, and I threatened to resign in order to keep her.

When AK finally did join our team as a director a few months after this failed coup, he was stunned that he had even been considered for Muffy's job. He declared that he'd rather spend his days stabbing himself in the eye with a pencil than be tied to a desk, tackling her complex, Excel-heavy workload.

But in this current climate I feared that any dramatic threats on my behalf to resign might possibly be welcomed. News Corp had become a minor shareholder in the company earlier in the year; in the lead-up to that deal, new accounting systems were introduced requiring strict time-keeping practices and tighter control of expenditure. We all sat through a raft of mandatory meetings where fresh policies and procedures for the company were outlined.

Since then there had been a number of redundancies and an inevitable, commonsense shift towards transitioning Afghan staff into key managerial positions. Hey, I could have been wrong, but I sensed that the trimming of a relatively fat expat wage bill may have been viewed as a fiscal blessing.

I delivered the news to Muffy, who was out on a shoot, over the phone. That was not because I wanted to but because, when I called to tell her to return to the office, she immediately asked me what was wrong. She told me the arrival of Shaikh that morning on the first flight from Dubai had had everyone on edge.

'They're letting you go, sweetheart.' Hoarse and raw, my words caught in my throat.

But Muffy didn't cry. I think she knew it was coming, and this had manifested itself in her own longing to leave. Her sigh by way of reply signalled a release from months of indecision and angst.

Since early April she and I had been living together in a small villa at our new guest house. I struggled to remember a morning when she hadn't woken up crying or complaining of a sleepless night. Two years of incredibly demanding slog and hard living had exhausted her, while the recent cancellation of her lifestyle show—a popular program that was just finding its feet—had crushed her.

We decided to tell our team that she was jumping of her own accord because any suggestion that she was pushed would inevitably cause an angry uprising. Even so, she would have to endure a month of disappointed and disheartened people, from producers to security guards, asking her why—and begging her to change her mind.

From soon after her arrival, she and I had been known (affectionately, I think) around the traps as The Drama Queens. But in a matter of weeks The Drama Queens would be no more and that night we sat together on our private terrace, with generous G & Ts in our hands, trying to come to terms with it. There were tears, laughter, and a mixture of both, as we recalled our shared adventure.

Muffy arrived on the scene in early 2010 bristling with brio, determination and great plans for revolutionising the drama department. She quickly sized up my mental state and assessed me as 'defeated', and I couldn't convince her that I had simply become a realist.

I had squared off with management countless times over equipment, staffing levels and budgets; I had made erudite and reasonable arguments to back my various requests for a new monitor, an extra producer or an increased food allowance for my hungry crew. But I didn't always win, simple as that, and I eventually learnt to choose my battles wisely.

I had worked hard to earn the respect of my colleagues and to establish myself as a fair, albeit no-nonsense, boss, but for some people I was always going to be an invader—unwanted and disrespected for being a foreigner or a female, or both. What Muffy read as defeat was nothing more than acceptance, but she just wasn't buying it.

Shielded by naivety and armed with passion, she became a true soldier of production, crusading for causes that I wasn't even prepared to gear up for. Her battle fatigue set in after about six months, but during that time we enjoyed the spoils of some extraordinary and unexpected victories. Even after she laid down her arms, she refused to completely surrender.

Management's reluctance to sign off on much-needed equipment for *Eagle Four* saw her develop into a master negotiator. Tired old warrior that I had become, I would probably have agreed to shoot the show on a mobile phone, but she traded microphones for lights, sacrificed part of our wardrobe budget for make-up and orchestrated a last-minute deal to get Damian, our director of photography, on board.

I may have been captain of the ship, but it was so often my trusty first mate who kept us afloat. And that night, commiserating together after the news she would be leaving us, we traded war stories like the seasoned campaigners we had become. We struggled to recall a time when we had ever really fallen out, but then Muffy reminded me of a day in January 2011 when I had literally shaken her and screamed in her face. Indeed I had been an ogre, but we agreed she had had it coming . . .

We had just relocated to yet another guest house. It was about my sixth move and Muffy's third—we had been forced to find new digs when our previous house had shut up shop. We settled on the place because it had a bar, a squash court and a so-so menu. It was a huge, two-storey complex—hospital-like in appearance, complete with fluorescent strip lighting, linoleum floors and wide, empty corridors.

But the rooms resembled poorly decorated sets for a seventies porn film. The walls were covered in easy-wipe, pebble-textured plasterboard, which was festooned with bold geometric shapes. I had red triangles on a sky-blue background that clashed spectacularly with my shiny purple bedspread. The carpet was a mustard short-shag pile, the cupboards boasted a faux-teak veneer, and it was going to take tremendous effort and creativity to transform my garish boudoir into some semblance of a home.

During the course of our first week there I had hung a few pictures, draped a scarf or two over furnishings, and purchased a lamp for my bedside table, but the light globes I had bought were the wrong type. I considered mounting a shopping expedition to buy new ones on my Friday off but, as Muffy was heading out to the ISAF markets (a monthly bazaar held at the Headquarters of the International Security Assistance Force where Afghan women could sell their wares) I asked her to stop by the western supermarket, Finest, to pick them up.

I was pottering around in my room just after lunch when I received a text. Amy had managed to get me on to her company's security alert list, back when I first met her in Jalalabad, and it was usually through this that I got the first indication something had gone awry. The message was scant on details, simply stating that there had been an explosion at the Finest supermarket in Wazir Akbar Khan.

I immediately called our go-to man at work, Akmal, to see if he could enlighten me. He couldn't, but promised to talk to Ahmad and get back to me.

Then I tried to call Muffy. On my first attempt, her phone simply rang out. When I tried again, an Afghan man answered, barked briefly down the line and hung up.

My stomach dropped a little then, as I began to entertain the awful possibility that Muffy had somehow been caught up in whatever had gone down at Finest. But then Akmal phoned me back, informing me that it had been a gas explosion, nobody had been hurt and that there was nothing to worry about.

At worst, Muffy had lost her phone or had it stolen, but she is notorious for misplacing things, so I wasn't greatly surprised or terribly concerned. I tried to phone her one more time for good measure, but when the Afghan man answered again, I hung up, thinking I'd wander downstairs a little later and get one of the waiters to speak with him.

The hint of an attack made me realise that I hadn't yet devised a security strategy for my new home. I was just attempting to stuff myself into the cupboard under the sink when my phone rang.

It was Hamish. 'Sweetheart, where are you? Are you okay?'

'I'm home, I'm fine. Why?'

'You know there's been an attack on Finest.'

'Work said it was a gas explosion.'

'It was insurgents. Nine people are already confirmed dead. Is Muffy with you?'

I had to sit down.

'No. I've been trying to call her but some Afghan man keeps answering.'

'Same here. I just tried calling again and her phone's now switched off.'

'Oh Hamish . . .'

'Where was she going?'

'To Finest. Oh God, Hamish—she was going to Finest!'

'Just find her.'

'I feel sick!'

'Sweetheart, call your work and tell them that they have to find her. I've got to file a report, but let me know as soon as you hear anything.'

My hands were trembling with such force that it was an effort to dial through to Akmal and I struggled to suppress a sob as I demanded that he track Muffy down. Then I waited.

Even now, I find it difficult to fully relive that brief moment in time when I waited for news of Muffy. It was ten minutes, tops, but the overwhelming helplessness, the creeping sense of doom that threatened to swallow me as I paced around my room, was an acute and rare form of torture.

When Akmal's call finally came, I actually fumbled the phone and it fell to the floor. I was kneeling on the shag pile with my head to my knees when I received the news that Muffy was safe. She was out having a delightful lunch at the French bistro, but had accidentally left her phone in the car. It was one of our own guards who kept answering it.

I called Hamish and then stayed on the ground for quite some time, relishing the wonderful feeling of relief that now washed over me. I then phoned my mum in Australia and cried to her for a solid half-hour.

By the time Muffy arrived home, I was livid. When she airily tap-tap-tapped on my door, I yanked it open. I grabbed her by the shoulders and went nose to nose with the wretched woman.

'DON'T YOU EVER, EVER, EVER LOSE YOUR FUCKING PHONE AGAIN!'

She was genuinely confused. Despite having been driven home in a company car, she had been told nothing about the bombing, had no idea that she was apparently MIA, and had been enjoying a caesar salad while flicking through the latest issue of *Vanity Fair* as Hamish and I agonised over her fate.

In our post-mortem we figured out that she had been at Finest fifteen minutes before the attack, but it took around four litres of wine that night to settle us into sleep.

The next morning, I purchased a gaudy, jewel-studded phone pouch (the type that you hang around your neck) and made Muffy carry her mobile in it for the next two weeks. Ultimately it didn't cure her of her phone-forgetfulness, but her constant whining about how the ugly little bag clashed with everything she wore was a righteous payback I felt fully justified in administering.

Recounting the story over our final G & T that evening in May sent us both off to bed laughing, but I lay awake for a very long time thinking about Muffy's departure and my imminent loss. Yet another friend was leaving; my best mate's name would be erased for good from the Kabul expat chalkboard. By the time I finally closed my eyes, I knew that, for me, the dust from this deletion would never quite settle.

22.
Star-crossed Love

Our make-up artist, Shakila, was losing her hair. It wasn't a whole-sale shedding—just a handful of tiny, bald patches scattered across her head. They had first started appearing months ago. On my last trip to Dubai I consulted with a pharmacist and had returned with some drops that need to be applied twice a day. And Merzad and I had taken on the task.

He probably shouldn't have even been looking at her hair, so we huddled together in a corner of our office and we locked the door so no one could burst in on us. As I gently brushed back the strands I watched his face crease in concentration as he carefully applied the drops and I wanted to weep. The act was so simple but done with great love, because he did love her and she loved him back, and, if they had been born somewhere in the western world, they would inevitably have been together.

I'm not sure when I discovered that Shakila and Merzad were an item. There was nothing overt to really indicate they were a couple. Afghan men and women are typically not permitted to date, let alone hold hands in public or (God forbid) kiss, and our company had very strict policies about males and females fraternising.

I guess I'd heard whispers, and watched them deep in conversations that I couldn't comprehend. Or perhaps it was the day that we heard she'd fainted on set and a clearly panicked Merzad raced off in his car to rescue her. Whatever finally twigged me to it, I thought they were a perfect pair and, through my western-coloured glasses, I envisaged them one day getting married. The fact that Shakila was Hazara and Merzad was Tajik was blissfully lost on me.

I knew that, in the beginning, they too imagined they could be together. Early on in their 'relationship'—nothing more than incessant texting, lingering looks, secret chats on the phone at night—Shakila's parents approached her with a prospective husband. He was a doctor in Germany—a worthy catch who would provide her passage out of Afghanistan.

When Merzad found out, he begged her to refuse. Most Afghan women wouldn't have had a choice, but Shakila's parents were extraordinarily progressive—she was allowed to work, could stay out for night shoots and travel abroad unchaperoned. And, despite being disappointed that she was knocking back her chance of escape, they accepted her decision not to wed.

I know that around that time Merzad made some kind of overture to his father about marrying Shakila, but his dad, a widower, had definitively shut him down. He would be marrying a Tajik girl, a relative no less, and there was no room for debate on the matter.

I guess love made them believe they could work it out—that they would maybe one day run away to Iran, India or Pakistan, and live out their lives together. And I believed it as well. They had time on their hands and the whole world was changing around them. Perhaps Merzad's father would change his mind too. At that stage, I couldn't have foreseen the part I would play in cutting this time so cruelly short.

In 2010, the company had announced that it would be granting scholarships for two employees to study in America. It was an eight-week film course and I was asked to select suitable candidates from my department. Muffy and I narrowed it down to six young men, all worthy of the accolade, before finally settling on Hamid and Merzad. They were thrilled with the news, but apparently their families failed to share their joy. Hamid's wife wasn't overly keen on being left with sole care of their newborn baby while he flitted off overseas, and Merzad's father was worried that his son would do a runner.

It's quite common for Afghans to run away if they manage to get themselves out of the country. From our department alone, we had lost four people; when Muffy had gone to America to film a documentary the year before, she left with three crew members and returned with one.

But I never saw Merzad as the running-away kind, especially not in the US, where he didn't have any family or friends to run to. Still, in the weeks leading up to their departure, the thought that Merzad would fail to return haunted his dad, and he hounded him daily about going away. My assertion that Merzad should just put his foot down, and politely tell his father where to get off, was met with a look of surprise, even disapproval. It was his father—he couldn't disrespect him like that.

Then I received a text from Merzad one morning just a month before lift-off:

> Dear Trudi Jan. I will not come to the office today. There is some personal problem that I have. Sorry. Merzad.

I texted back that I hoped he was okay and asked whether I could do anything to help. He didn't reply.

When Muffy and I arrived at work the next day, we found Merzad and Shakila sitting together at his desk. It was clear she'd been crying and that we were obviously intruding, so we left them to it, giving them time to sort themselves out while we wondered over coffee and cigarettes what could possibly be the matter.

When we returned thirty minutes later, Shakila was gone and Merzad looked up at us and attempted a grin. 'Well? Where is my treat? You should be giving me sweets—I'm going to get married.'

We somehow guessed that it wasn't to Shakila.

Then he told us what had happened. In a final desperate bid to ensure that he would return, his father had yoked him to his cousin. Merzad had arrived home from work on the night in question to discover his family and relatives all preparing for a party—his engagement party, more precisely. He confessed to us that he felt indifference towards the girl he was marrying—they had exchanged no more than a dozen words in the past five years—and now he was going to spend the rest of his life with her.

My first feelings were entirely selfish. I felt guilt; I felt overwhelmingly responsible for what had occurred. In rewarding Merzad, I had ruined his life. Muffy asked whether there wasn't something he could do to change his father's mind, but it was all too late and too far gone. I boldly suggested that his father was a fool—surely, if anything, it was *this* that would encourage his son to stay in the States.

But Merzad was adamant that wasn't the case. If he failed to return, his cousin would be 'shamed' and no other man would want to marry her. Despite his lack of real affection for his fiancée, he would never subject her to that.

Shakila's initial despondency quickly gave way to rage. She was now certain that Merzad had never planned to marry her and that he knew all along his father would not allow him to wed a Hazara girl. For the next few weeks, our office became a battleground. Her work posse—a group of fiercely vocal females—also entered the fray, pulling Merzad aside for lectures and abuse whenever he ventured from the sanctuary of his desk.

Merzad's trip away gave us considerable respite and allowed Shakila some time to heal; when he returned they seemed to find their amiable groove again. There was an air of defeat about them both but, like the resilient Afghans that they are, they simply pulled themselves together and soldiered on.

Once an engagement has gone down, Afghans don't waste time mucking around, and Merzad's father had decided that the wedding would be two months after his son's return. Merzad struggled with this, as he wanted more time to get to know his wife. In all honesty, he wasn't making much of an effort.

'That was my fiancée. She texts me all the time!' he'd announce after checking who was messaging him on his phone.

'Well, are you going to text her back?' I'd ask.

'No.'

'Why not?'

'I have nothing to say to her. I hardly know her.'

'Well, how are you going to get to know her if you refuse to communicate with her?'

'What is there to talk about, when I don't know her?'

'Sweetie, you're telling me that you *are* going to marry this girl and spend the rest of your life with her. So maybe you need to get to know her. Text her, talk to her on the phone.'

And on it went. He and I talked in circles about the inevitability of his marriage, and his refusal to try to make it work.

A month out from the wedding I was awoken at 6am by a text from Merzad. He could not come to work; he was again grappling with a personal problem. I rang him at 9am to find out what the deal was, given that the last 'personal problem' had been a doozy.

He explained that he had fought with his father the previous night over delaying the wedding; he had begged to be allowed six months more to prepare himself. He didn't yet love his fiancée and needed more time to take it all on board.

It had raged on for hours, punctuated by long bouts of storming off to separate rooms and sulking; it finally ended when his father just walked out the door. He hadn't returned and Merzad was frantically trying to track him down. His father's phone was switched off and none of his family knew where he was.

His dad had a heart condition and needed medication and Merzad was certain he had no money on him when he left. I was privately enraged that a seventy-year-old man would behave in such a way, but wished Merzad luck in his search and promised to keep in touch.

His father hadn't returned that evening and by the following morning, when he continued to be a no-show, Merzad feared the worst. It took forty hours for his father to finally emerge. He had gone to Mazar, a ten-hour bus trip from Kabul, to stay with some relatives and had 'lost' his phone on the journey there. I met Merzad across the road from work, to slip him some cash so he could go and fetch him. His eyes were raw, his skin was grey and he bubbled with remorse. He would never argue with his father again and in four weeks' time he *would* be married.

I'm not a huge fan of Afghan weddings. For starters, the men and women are usually segregated, a flimsy partition dividing the room. And while the chicks sit on one side, staring dumbly at one another because the music blaring from pastures greener is deafening, next door the men dance and whoop and make regular trips to the car park to swig back booze.

Muffy and I had taken to smuggling in our own vodka supplies to keep us smiling and engaged, because there were usually around two hundred sets of eyes and a smattering of mobile phones set on 'record' continually pointed in the direction of the foreigners.

At wedding receptions, the bride and groom are conspicuously absent for most of the evening since they eat in a completely separate room. They do a sullen walk-through about three hours into the evening, with the bride actually forbidden to smile because she's meant to be in mourning over leaving her family; then they pose for some joyless photos on a gaudily dressed stage.

The gloomy pall over Merzad's nuptials had Muffy and me knocking back stiff drinks right up to the arrival of the car that was going to take us there. Despite loving Merzad, we had genuinely considered pulling out, but we knew that Shakila would be there and needed our support. She, in turn, was only going because she wanted to be there for her friend Merzad.

The day before the wedding, I'd been mulling over some scripts when Shakila asked me why I wasn't married. I began trotting out my pat answer—because I don't have to be—when I looked up at her. The concern, the hint of fear, that I read in her eyes made me realise that my standard response would be plainly inadequate and entirely inconsiderate.

At twenty-five years old (positively ancient in Afghan terms), she'd wanted to know whether I was truly happy, whether a woman could really be all right if she didn't have a husband. I assured her that I was a very contented woman. She suspected as much, because I was always laughing, but she'd wanted some assurance that it could all be okay.

Muffy and I arrived at the wedding more than a little cut, and oohed and aahed like proud mothers at the sight of Shakila. She looked beautiful, but possessed an air of fragility we had never seen before. I sat next to her and, when the bridal party swanned into the room, I gripped her hand under the table.

'Oh Trudi, I think I am going to be sick . . .' she whispered in my ear.

I squeezed her hand as we dutifully smiled. After the bride and groom had swept by, we looked at each other for a very long time, before a tiny nod of her head and a blink of her eyes told me she was okay.

In time, Shakila found another boyfriend. Merzad, although growing increasingly fond of his wife with every month that passed, still ignored the text messages she regularly sent him. Even Shakila joined in the cry for the hopeless man to make more of an effort.

'Shakila and I love each other,' Merzad explained to me one day. 'But just like friends. People in our country don't understand that men and women can just be friends.'

I assured him that I, at least, understood

Merzad and I finished off the hair-growth ritual and, as I tenderly fluffed Shakila's hair back into place, he unlocked the door. She asked me why I thought she was losing her hair. I told her that the pharmacist thought it could be due to stress or anxiety, and Merzad nodded his head knowingly.

Shakila, whose grasp of English wasn't as good as his, asked him to translate. He bent close to her ear as he explained it in Dari. She looked up from under her fringe, nodded her head and simply blinked her eyes at me. It would all be okay.

23.
All for a Good Night's Sleep

There are many reasons why you don't sleep well in the Ghan. It's a noisy place for starters; then, with the local staff and neighbours rising for prayer at the first sign of sun, and the early-morning garbage guy wailing for refuse from the street outside, you can easily lose valuable, pristine snooze-time on a daily basis.

If you live in a party compound, an impromptu mid-week knees-up may prove to be the culprit. In winter, you can be woken up prematurely, freezing because the power has gone out in the middle of the night. In summer, you are dragged from sleep in a lather of sweat because ... well, the power has gone out in the middle of the night.

It can be the noise of a gun battle nearby that has been going on for hours, or an argument between the couple in the next room that has been raging for half the night, or simply obsessive thoughts about how you are going to survive another stressful day at work.

Most of my posse was on something to help them sleep. Alcohol was perhaps the chief enabler, followed closely by hash, and then prescription drugs bought over the counter—*sans* the prescription, cheap as chips. I myself started a little love affair with Valium.

I had never taken any kind of sleeping medication in Australia and it was a good nine months before I dabbled in it in Kabul. I was at a party one night, talking to a security contractor who is an ex-army medic, complaining that I hadn't properly slept in weeks.

'You need to pay a visit to Mujeeb's,' he replied.

'Who's Mujeeb?'

'It's a chemist over in Shar-E-Naw. The guy's got everything.'

After he'd carefully talked me through the assortment of sleeping aids on offer, setting out their various pros and cons, we settled on Valium.

'You don't want anything stronger than that. You're only a wee thing—I reckon half a tablet will knock you right out,' he assured me.

It took Muffy and me the entire week to build up the nerve to visit Mujeeb's, primarily because, once news got out that we were doing a pharmacy run, people started popping up all over the place with personal orders to add to our single-item shopping list.

Within days, we had instructions from housemates and friends to purchase everything from Tramadol to Viagra. What we were doing wasn't illegal, just all rather sad, really. So, at 4pm one Thursday, we finally took the plunge.

We climbed into a car and, pointing at my throat as I coughed a few times, we indicated to our Dari-speaking driver that I had either some cold-like affliction or a fur ball. Whatever. I needed a chemist.

'Mujeeb's? Shar-E-Naw? Butcher Street,' I offered.

Traffic in Kabul is a nightmare at the best of times, but on a Thursday afternoon, with Afghans all rushing home to prepare for their Friday off, it can come to a standstill.

'Nay, nay. No Mujeeb's,' said our driver. 'Here. Pharmacy, here,' pointing out the window in reference to the pharmacy just up the road.

It took considerable effort to convince him that we simply *had* to go to Mujeeb's and it was a decidedly grumpy Ayub, our security guard, who trailed us into the chemist forty minutes later. Our discomfort was only magnified by the fact that the shop assistant was barely in his teens.

Muffy and I fussed over cough medicines and fiddled with tubes of antiseptic cream, all the while non-verbally egging each other on to go for the hard stuff. After assembling our irrelevant pile of medical supplies on the counter, Muffy finally dived in. 'So do you ... um ... have ... um ... do you have Valium?'

'How many boxes?' Without missing a beat.

'Just one, I guess.'

'Three!' A little eagerly from me. I didn't relish the thought of going through this again anytime soon.

Three boxes were plucked from the cabinet and casually plonked on the counter.

'How about ... oh, what's it called again? Viagra?' Muffy ventured.

'Three?'

'Make it two.'

Boxes of Normison and Ritalin were added to the heap. When the boy went out the back to fetch the Tramadol, Ayub picked up a box of Viagra and examined it. I did my throat-pointing and coughing routine again, feeling emboldened by the fact that he couldn't read English, but his knowing smile, by way of reply, made me blush.

Drug deal done, the assistant began to tally it up. But then he stopped mid-calculation. 'Would you like some Xanax as well?'

Having a twelve-year-old kid try to upsell me on prescription drugs was not one of the high points of my life but, after a nanosecond of silent consultation, Muffy and I agreed to buy it.

Muffy had to stop doing the Mujeeb's run during her final months in Kabul. We had both appeared in what we thought was going to be a corporate video for a newly opened, four-star hotel. We were helping out AK, who needed some western bodies to make the place look chic, and I personally felt obligated to assist as I had just about destroyed the hotel's business.

Only the previous month, we had used it as a location for *Secrets* and had staged a terrorist attack there. Unfortunately for the owner, two days before the initial episode went to air there was a real attack in the streets surrounding the hotel. It went on for almost two days and having it re-enacted on one of the country's most popular soaps wasn't the best publicity. The poor man came to the office, begging us to pull the follow-up show. The best I could do was edit it all in tight, so as to try to make the place unrecognisable.

For reasons still unknown to us, the 'corporate video' found its way on air, appearing on prime-time TV during every ad break. I was just one of many diners in their 'luxury' restaurant. Muffy played the receptionist and was prominently featured not wearing a headscarf.

As soon as the ad started airing, Muffy began being recognised. A waiter at our favourite Chinese joint asked her what time the dining room closed; an assistant at the local shop wanted to know how much the rooms cost. With every enquiry, Muffy patiently explained that she was not, in fact, the receptionist at the Kabul Star Hotel. Afterwards, discussing it with me, she would wonder what kind of desperate foreigner *would* be working front desk at a hotel in Afghanistan.

Being celebrity-spotted by an assistant at Mujeeb's finally saw her break. 'Listen! I am not the receptionist at the Kabul Star Hotel. I have never worked at the Kabul Star Hotel. I'm a TV producer—I work in television, okay!'

'Which station do you work for?' he asked.

She grimaced at me, suddenly realising that she had given too much away. I scooped up our stash, ushered her out the door, and turned to smile at the boy behind the counter.

'Darling, she *is* the receptionist at the Kabul Star Hotel. And there *is* a swimming pool on the roof.'

On the set of *Secrets of this House*—our huge cast outnumbered our tiny crew.

Filming on location for *Secrets of this House*. Guns, police, bad guys—the usual fodder for an Afghan soapie.

Shooting *Eagle Four* on the mean streets of Kabul. We didn't have to worry about adding any gritty authenticity.

Lynchy, me and Muffy with one of our actors on *Eagle Four*. Shakila's fabulous handiwork is hard to miss.

Our *Eagle Four* lead actors busting their moves.

The rubbish-dump shoot. Scratch & sniff would give you a better appreciation of this photo.

Muffy and me as Kuchi bangle sellers.

An Afghan take on the *Charlie's Angels* pose. With Lynchy, Damien and two of our *Eagle Four* crew.

Salam, Season 2: Extras gone wild—it was truly terrifying watching them laying into each other.

The Commandos arrive to save the day! . . . And everybody stops to watch. The guy dashing out of shot is the director.

The Ministry, Afghanistan's take on *The Office*. Courtesy of Wakil Koshar

Sir William Patey on the set of *The Ministry*.

A fun day out for the girls organised by Moby—an afternoon of bowling at Kabul's only bowling alley.

Expat life: A glam night out with my girls Sophie and Erin—an evening of wining, fine dining and dancing at the British Embassy Ball.

On stage with the winners at the Seoul International Drama Awards. COURTESY OF
SEOUL INTERNATIONAL DRAMA AWARDS 2011

With Sal and Fran at Darulaman Palace, watching Kabul wake. One of my last
days in paradise.

24.
The Acting
Ambassador

Season One of *The Ministry* was one of the few drama productions
we ever produced without external funding. Conceived by Saad,
the eight-part comedy series centred on the day-to-day running of
a government ministry and tackled corruption, nepotism, sexism,
violence, and collusion between the government and major criminals.

The actors all spoke Dari, the topics we covered were all transpar-
ently relevant to Afghan society, and we constantly referenced local
current events and scandals. Mindful of the fact that the show would
undoubtedly offend the government and wary of having it yanked
off air by the conservative Ministry of Culture, we set the show in
the fictional country of 'Hichland' (Nothingland). This device, also
masterminded by Saad, made us untouchable.

I appointed AK to oversee production. We had a minuscule budget, so he suggested that we shoot the show on one camera as a mockumentary. This would be an invaluable time saver, and would cover for the boom mikes and lighting stands that invariably found their way into so many takes on all of our shows.

None of the writers, cast or crew had ever seen a mockumentary, and conveying the concept to them took considerable time and explanation. In an early rehearsal with the wonderful actor Abdul Qadir Farookh, who played the minister, we asked him to improvise a little spiel about his 'job' (as the Minister for Garbage, of course), but he launched into a personal discourse about his early days as an actor in Afghan theatre. However, AK had assembled a cracker ensemble cast; the scripts were hard-hitting and funny, and the show proved to be a huge hit when it aired in August 2011.

It also garnered interest from around the world. Saad tweeted a link to a three-minute trailer for the show and, within thirty-six hours, we had over fifty thousand hits on YouTube. Suddenly journalists from everywhere wanted to know about Afghanistan's version of *The Office*.

A dear friend, Jerome Starkey (writing for *The Times* in London), was the first journo to visit the set and, blessedly sensing the excitement of our team, stayed with us for two hours as he patiently interviewed everyone from the lead actors to the lighting man.

After the UK *Sun* ran a piece pointing out the similarities between *The Ministry* and *The Office*, Ricky Gervais even got on board, blogging: 'They found a fat, middle-aged bloke with a beard. That bit was easy. The difficult part was finding a town in Afghanistan as grim as Slough.'

Muffy and I celebrated that night—a mention from The Master was as good as it got. But after our thirty-seventh drink, we were suddenly struck by the thought that Ricky Gervais might have thought that we'd actually ripped off his show. After a rambling, repetitive and dreadfully slurred discussion between us on the matter, we were quite certain that he intended to sue the company.

At 4am, and quite oblivious to the fact that it was 11.30pm in London, we decided that the only course of action was to call him immediately and plead our case against plagiarism. Mercifully, we only got as far as his agent's answering machine and, thankfully, they never returned our call.

We quickly launched into creating a second season, again under our own financial steam, and I gave the two local writers free rein to devise episode outlines. They were coming along quite nicely, save for the fact that three of the eight episodes ended with everyone fainting; but, with a fair bit of polish and a little less swooning, we were ready to start scripting in December.

Then one night I ran into Daniel, the press officer for the British Embassy, at a party and he proposed an idea that turned all our hard work firmly on its head. Apparently the ambassador, Sir William Patey, was a huge fan of *The Ministry* and, as he was leaving his post in the next few months, wondered if he might do a wee cameo in the second series—a kind of swansong to Afghanistan. I immediately agreed.

We would have to work closely with the embassy to come up with a suitable and acceptable storyline to accommodate his appearance; we would need to rework all our outlines and shoot his scenes out of sequence, but it would be worth it to get him on the show. I had met Sir William on many occasions. Easy-going, funny and a natural performer, during our first meeting with him regarding his cameo, he made it abundantly clear that he wanted us to take the piss out of him.

I sat with my writers and mapped out new outlines, incorporating a storyline where the 'Borland' (British) Embassy gives funding to the ministry to clean up the city and the minister embezzles the lot. I took on the job of personally writing the two scripts featuring the ambassador and we sent them to the embassy in mid-January for approval.

Daniel liked the four scenes featuring Sir William, but would have to get the nod from him before he could agree to anything. And if the ambassador was happy, it would then still need the go-ahead from London. We pushed on with scripting the rest of the show, trusting that Sir William and London would come through.

He was due to leave the country at the end of March but, as February drew to a close, we still didn't have a firm commitment regarding his appearance. I got Saad on board at that stage—he was a personal friend of Sir William's and could perhaps give the process the nudge that it so desperately needed. He forwarded me Sir William's succinct reply in early March: '*The Ministry* has three weeks to get organised.'

We were ready to go but still didn't have formal script approval, and it took a further two weeks to finally sort it out. The scenes I had written would take a good half a day to shoot but, due to the ambassador's busy schedule, he could only spare us an hour of his time. This was entirely understandable, but a little prior notice would have helped.

It took a couple of hours of pacing around and some solid chain-smoking to devise a solution. By the end of the day I had confined his cameo to one short scene, where the minister briefly meets the ambassador before Sir William blows him off in favour of a tennis game with another foreign diplomat. I wrote in an advisor to the ambassador, who could take on the bulk of his dialogue in the remaining scenes, and had no other option than to cast myself in that role.

We seemed genuinely set to go—the only conceivable problem I could see was me mastering a plummy English accent—but, the day before the shoot, a whole new drama erupted. Much of the comedy in the scene derived from the minister (at the prompting of his PR man) wearing a kilt to the meeting, in order to impress the ambassador. When Farhad sheepishly informed me that Abdul was refusing to wear the kilt, I almost swallowed my tongue.

Abdul had been to the tailor for fittings and was fully aware he was going to wear the thing, so I struggled to comprehend this last-minute backflip. Farhad explained that it was actually Abdul's family members who were against the idea; he had told his sons about our wardrobe choice the previous evening and they had convinced him that he would bring great shame upon them all if he appeared on television wearing a 'skirt'. I argued that Afghan men wear salwar kameezes—effectively 'dresses'—all the time, but it seemed it was the exposing of his bare knees that was the shameful part.

I immediately advised the embassy of this latest development, begging their understanding and promising them a fresh scene within the hour. I ultimately decided to write the minister's refusal to wear the 'skirt' into the episode and, after assurances from Abdul that he had no problem sporting elaborate jewellery on TV, had him turning up to the meeting wearing a sporran around his neck. Hey, it wasn't comedy genius, but the clock was ticking and I still had an English accent to perfect.

The morning of the shoot was rather manic. We had the ambassador from 11am until noon, and had to be set up and ready to go as soon as he arrived. And, because we were shooting at the embassy, we would be subjected to extensive and time-consuming body and equipment checks before we could enter. There would be no time to rehearse with Sir William and the scene was a complex beast—it was in both Dari and English. In a quick read-through at the office, the actors struggled to find their cues.

While the crew set up, Tahir took us through rehearsals; Muffy stood in for the ambassador, and we ran through it over and over and over again. We were as good as we were going to get when Sir William finally made his entrance.

He proved to be a one-take wonder. He didn't have his lines down pat, but he improvised his way through what turned out to be a very funny scene. We wrapped at 11.50am and the actors and crew spent the final ten minutes all getting their photos taken with the British ambassador, before he graciously took his leave.

This was the first scene we shot for the second series and we left the embassy all very excited about the project. Then the very next day, Adiba in business development called me for a meeting where she recommended that we include *The Ministry* in a massive proposal promoting 'good governance and civil society' that we were currently bidding for.

I was honestly surprised by her suggestion. We had previously canvassed the idea with another big client and had been shot down in flames. Ridiculing the government went against everything NATO was trying to promote, and that particular client wanted nothing to do with the show. Still, I agreed to meet with this new potential funder the following morning.

I had a pretty good grasp on 'good governance', but was a little lost when it came to 'civil society'. I rocked up to the meeting completely unprepared and a little overwhelmed. When I was asked to detail how I intended embedding its messaging into the show, I threw out some random idea about the secretary, the only female character in the series, having a four-sided cardboard enclosure constructed around her desk in order to segregate her from the men in the ministry.

President Karzai had just endorsed a restrictive code of conduct issued by an influential Council of Clerics; this code forbade women travelling without a male guardian or mingling with men in schools, marketplaces and offices. I offered that the secretary could turn to local civil society organisations for support in her fight against segregation, before ultimately speaking out against corruption in the ministry.

The client, and the four representatives from various local NGOs also present at the meeting, loved it. The contract would be signed in May, and I returned to the office burdened with the task of telling my writers that we once again had to rework our outlines.

We spent the next two days mapping out a new narrative that accommodated both Sir William's storyline and our new client's agenda. I assured Saad that we could include the messaging without diluting the comedy, so I worked very closely with the writers to keep my promise. And when one of them did a runner to Germany two weeks later, I effectively took the lead on the project.

The remaining writer, Ashraf, had been with our team for two years and was excellent at scripting drama. He was studying Medicine and was earnest, clever and very clued-up on current affairs. He was obviously the brains behind the show's political content because, to be honest, comedy writing was not his strong point.

With Hakim as our go-between, Ashraf and I argued over scenes that lacked any real humour, over story set-ups that fizzled out to nothing and the fact that the soldier (a minor character in the show, but a good friend of Ashraf's) seemed to dominate every episode. Hakim was also a very good friend of Ashraf's; when I would privately ask him whether he thought scenes his mate had written were funny or whether, perhaps due to cultural differences, I was just not getting it, I know it pained him to have to betray his friendship and side with me.

The final episode of *The Ministry* went to air in mid-August 2012, and the buzz around the show was phenomenal. But I derived my greatest joy from knowing that my team produced this incredibly popular, 'must-watch' series all by themselves. My role in the scripting process was necessary, due to the ever-changing landscape of the narrative and a client-mandated deadline that meant we had to work fast, but, apart from that, I had very little to do with production. Sure, I visited the set a few times and dutifully did a spot of acting, but essentially I was able to let my team roll along alone.

I'd started this job fully intending that, one day, I would do myself out of it. And it made me so proud, after three years, to know that I was almost there.

25.
A
Skinful
of Bliss

Dick Willy had just flown out of Kabul. Again.

He had been threatening to return to Afghanistan ever since his inglorious exit in 2010. Because he'd been complaining of feeling heart-sick and lost back home in the States, his best friend there, having grown tired of his constant crying jags and his endless expressions of yearning for his 'spiritual homeland', finally demanded that he come to Kabul and make peace with his past.

The triumphant return lasted a little over three months and ended in another messy, emotional departure. In fairness to Dick, his ruin coincided with a sort of *Lord of the Flies* scenario at our guest house, where he had been living since July. We had all turned feral and hostile and loopy, and Dick was cast as the doomed Piggy.

I had lived at the Bliss Guest House since November 2011 and it was my ninth residence since arriving in Afghanistan. I knew about Bliss long before I moved in, as it was renowned for its parties. With a beautiful garden, a well-stocked bar and a friendly ambience, its regular social gatherings were legendary affairs, and there was a lengthy waiting list to become a tenant.

Muffy and I lucked our way to the top of the tree when the manager of Bliss, Adiba, came to work for our company. At the time we were living in the crudely fortified guest house run by Bela. I suspect the poor woman had stayed in the Ghan way too long. She was always stressed and exhausted; she was perpetually at loggerheads with the Afghan owner, whose nephew supervised the operation on his uncle's behalf. She was also a little too interested in the private lives of her guests.

I awoke one morning to find my sheets a little worse-for-wear due to an unexpected head start on my menstrual cycle—it honestly looked like I'd been massacred in my sleep. I decided to save the poor laundry woman from having to deal with the mess and, instead, folded the sheets up. I placed them in a garbage bag in my wardrobe, with the intention of washing them myself that evening, and remade my bed.

Muffy and I returned home that night to find a furious Bela stalking around my room. She had found the sheets in my wardrobe and wanted to know why I was 'hoarding' her bedding.

Despite imagining that the situation was fairly obvious, I mumbled out embarrassed apologies and attempted to explain my intentions. I had just managed to reach my massacre analogy when Muffy boldly waded in; she demanded to know what Bela was doing going through my wardrobe in the first place. Did she go through our drawers as well? What gave her the right to be in our rooms at all? Bam! Bela half-heartedly attempted to blame it on the cleaner, but that backfired spectacularly. Muffy shot back by asking why the cleaner would need to be poking around in our things. This was all absolute bullshit, she declared. Wham!

Backed solidly against the ropes, Bela folded and, I guess by way of apology, recounted all her woes around running the guest house. We comforted her and forgave her, and she left the room wearing my only pair of wedgie shoes, which she had evidently tried on earlier and believed would help her enormously with her aching back.

But it wasn't dear Bela who drove us to seek refuge at Bliss. I guess it started with the four Russian pilots who moved in on our floor and who left for work at five o'clock each morning, talking loudly and laughing in the corridor while they waited for their car to turn up. I had asked them politely over dinner one night to reduce their pre-dawn decibels; when that failed, I pleaded with Bela to have a word with them. I finally resorted to sticking my shameless bed-hair head out the door each day and bellowing at them to please shut up.

Then there was the time when Bela went on holiday for three weeks and the owner's nephew seized the opportunity to turn Reception into his own private playground. Every night he and his mates would take over the space, getting stoned and drunk and leering at us whenever we ventured from our rooms. The assistant chef, who was meant to be assuming Bela's cooking duties, also took advantage of her absence and, after the fourth night in his new role, just stopped turning up.

Then came the edict from the owner—enthusiastically enforced by his nephew, with Bela powerless to overrule it—that Muffy and I were not allowed to have any male visitors in our rooms. When Hamish dropped by one night on his way out to dinner, the nephew and a security guard came to Muffy's room and demanded that he leave. We had a solid argument to counter his inference that we were up to no good (or, as one of my Afghan friends describes it, 'touching his fuck'), but making a case based on our gentleman caller's sexual orientation was neither wise nor safe.

And finally, there was the great heist, when my brand-new iPod (still in its packaging), $400 (hidden between the pages of a book, inside a shoe box, under a pile of jackets at the back of my wardrobe) and my camera (which could no longer autofocus, so the thieves were sucked in there) all disappeared in the space of a day. Somewhat typically, the nephew claimed that I must have lost the lot when I was out 'drinking alcohol' or that one of my western friends had executed this brazen burglary.

But I was beyond bothering to argue anymore. Instead, the next morning we begged Adiba to let us move into Bliss and she obligingly secured us the next available rooms, in the process skipping over two French UN workers, a German woman stationed at ISAF and an Italian advisor to the government.

Communal living can be exacting, but Bliss felt like a real home. We already knew many of the seventeen people residing there, and Adiba managed to get Eugene into a room soon after. It operated like a collective: there were regular house meetings, where everybody got their time with the conch and where we voted on important, pressing issues such as whether we could smoke in the bar if it was snowing, what quantities of spirits, wine and beer we ought to order in our next grog purchase and whether we should spend our bar profits on a new barbecue.

There was a tradition of holding tequila breakfasts when we were in lockdown (days when, due to some security threat or actual attack, we were forbidden to leave home) and, in accordance with the hippy connotations around the compound's name, everyone pretty much slept with everyone else. Usually it was just an innocent crash out in a friend's room—a snuggle and a cuddle on a lonely night—but at other times it was the real deal, with no shame or strings attached.

We had pork-rib and lobster-tail barbecues; we wandered in and out of each other's cribs at whim. It was a feel-good community and Adiba oversaw it all with a steady hand and a clear vision of what the 'Bliss Vibe' was truly about.

Then in June 2012, Adiba accepted a job in Southeast Asia. Her partner, Pedro, who had just signed on for twelve months with a government ministry in Kabul, was appointed to manage Bliss until his contract expired.

Pedro was a genuinely good bloke, and by all accounts he did an incredible job when it came to setting up systems for government departments. But running a guest house was just not his bag, and he was grateful when a jobless Dick joined the family a month later and offered to help him out.

It seemed hardly surprising to us Blissers that the Beast that led to our downfall was alcohol. Over the previous six months there had been a government crackdown on indulging the foreigners; even restaurants that had legitimate licences to serve alcohol had now taken to serving wine and beer in teapots and teacups, fearing raids by local police.

Booze was now harder to come by and more expensive to buy. Our last big delivery had come courtesy of an Italian diplomat who was leaving the country for good; but, with a household full of hardy drinkers, stocks didn't last long and with each bottle drained we collectively grew a tad edgier.

We always managed to get our hands on enough alcohol to stave off a drought. John in Room 7 shipped a case in from Germany each month and would miraculously produce a bottle of spirits just when we thought we were completely dry. Steve in Room 9 made weekly visits to the US Embassy (where alcohol was in plentiful supply) and always left there with a bottle or four of something. We had a friend at ISAF, a frequent visitor to the house, who somehow was always able to get his hands on cases of scotch and red wine. And an R & R trip to Dubai could deliver a fairly healthy bounty, so long as you were happy to risk being caught smuggling grog into the Islamic Republic of Afghanistan.

The rules around bringing alcohol into the country were a little vague. The official line was that foreigners could bring in a 'reasonable amount', which was peculiarly subjective. I have known people to have a single litre of spirits confiscated at customs; others claimed to have swanned through with four or five bottles clearly on display.

My personal strategy was to buy the permissible four litres of duty free on my way into Dubai, which I would then decant into water bottles and hide in my checked-in luggage. I would then purchase three litres of vodka on my way back out of the UAE and, in the unsavoury confines of a toilet cubicle at the airport, pour one litre into water bottles before placing them in the duty-free bag with my 'official' two litres.

So far it had worked. I once had some cheeky, junior official chase me out of the Kabul terminal to tell me that his boss wanted me to hand over one of the legitimate bottles of vodka they had just allowed through. I politely informed him that if his boss wanted it then his boss could come and get it, before shooing him back inside and bolting to the car park.

The latest sting entailed you getting safely through customs, but then being stopped by the police just as your car hit the road leading from the airport. More than one friend chose to smash the bottle on the ground rather than surrender it to some dodgy cop, who would either drink it himself or sell it on for a handsome profit.

As a last resort, there was always Vodka Man—an enterprising young Afghan who would deliver alcohol straight to your door. He had a false bottom in the back of his jeep but no doubt had some kind of deal going with the police at the various checkpoints he needed to pass through as he wound his way around the city.

Vodka Man swore that his vodka was genuine Stoli and, at sixty bucks a bottle, you would have liked to believe him. But the skewed labels, complete with spelling mistakes, were a bit of a giveaway. Everyone knew it was Tajik vodka, and you always half-expected to go blind after your first couple of sips, but, mixed with a generous dose of pomegranate juice, it slid down a treat.

At various times, but generally on a Wednesday, Vodka Man would flash up on your phone screen; when you answered his call, he would, in his halting English, hit you with a 'very special deal, too special'. It may have been Johnny Walker Red, the 'real stuff' (naturally) at

$100 a bottle. One week it was white and red wine at $480 a case. White wine is scarce in Kabul, so Eugene and I ordered a couple of cases. It was Russian (I think) and arrived in 600-millilitre Tetra Paks; they were four months past the use-by date that was clearly stamped on the side. We figured we could always arrive at a party with it, hide it at the back of the booze table and then drink someone else's superior drop.

Bizarrely, our domestic upheaval began with news that one of our new housemates was flying in a planeload of alcohol from Italy and that we could order whatever we liked. We quickly convened a house meeting to figure out how much cash we had in the bar kitty and to decide exactly what we wanted to purchase. Talk turned to each of us supplementing the bar fund, in order to buy more booze, before someone suggested that we should also each order individual supplies to imbibe at our own leisure.

The discussion around this last proposal drifted on for an hour and, after a lot of symbolic conch-holding, almost everyone was in agreement that we should go that way. Pedro was the only person holding out. He argued that the bar was a communal area that encouraged housemates to mingle and socialise; he was concerned that personal stocks would result in seventeen sad, sorry people drinking alone in their rooms each night. He also reasoned that the bar fund—which bought us much-needed items, such as an above-ground swimming pool and a plastic jacuzzi that had fritzed out on its first run—would be severely depleted if we stopped buying from the house.

We all assured him that his fears were unfounded—we enjoyed each other's company and would personally pitch in for any luxury goods that we might decide to buy—and voted to try out the proposal for a month or two. Pedro responded the next day with an email stating that, as house manager, he was vetoing the decision.

It was pretty much a declaration of war. Some of the more vocal house members accused Pedro of being a dictator, and worse. Night after night we sat on the terrace debating the issue—Pedro calmly repeating his two slim arguments and holding himself up as the only true champion of the Bliss Vibe, while others simply shouted him down.

Dick, who was now officially the bar manager and who was struggling to straddle both camps, constantly appealed to Pedro to see good sense: 'If 18,260 people are telling you the same thing, then maybe it's time to listen,' he reasoned.

Factions were starting to form—some were pro-Pedro, some anti-Pedro, and then there was a handful of short-termers who couldn't be arsed to get involved. Despairing over the constant confrontations, Dick called an official bar meeting to try and sort out the issue once and for all. He wrote up an agenda and people who couldn't attend gave other house members their proxy votes.

Then, on the day of the scheduled meeting, Pedro vetoed it. We held it anyway and wrote up a bar constitution, which he subsequently declared null and void.

Dick was in constant contact with Adiba at this time, assuring her that he was doing everything he could to try and soothe house tensions:

Subject: Chat with Adiba

I am doing my best to right the ship and steer clear of the rocks.

Adiba, it is all a bit wonky (to say the least) but I'll get it as straight as possible and resolve to keep all in order to the best of my ability going forward. I'm good with people and can handle this joint (even the big egos Afghanistan seems to attract).

I prefer peace and understanding and this is always my first approach, but I can 'put on the face of the father' when needed!

When Pedro went on leave over Eid, we discovered that he had changed the lock on the liquor cabinet. Someone smashed down the door and, in a furious act of anarchy, we held a party and gave away *our* alcohol for free. A mannequin was burnt that night, a dressmaking doll that Dick had discovered in storage. It was outfitted in one of my corsets, so it was most certainly *not* an effigy of Pedro, but, as its synthetic body burst into flames, ignited by who knows who, it was Dick who hurled water onto it and extinguished the fire.

Post-Eid saw the simmering feud erupt with alarming regularity and Dick finally appealed to Adiba to intervene in some way and resolve the matter. He had lost all patience by now and showed little restraint in describing the discord in the house. 'There was a better "vibe" on the train to Auschwitz than there currently is at Bliss!'

But Adiba was settling into her new job in Laos and, understandably, declined to enter the fray from such a distance.

Then two nights later it all kicked off again. There was yet another debate on the terrace and I quickly retreated to my room like an overwrought littl'un, declaring that I simply couldn't sit and listen to it anymore. The whole argument was now meaningless anyway as, due to the dwindling bar supplies, everyone had sourced their own alcohol. Dick didn't like confrontation, and so settled himself into the lounge room to listen to music.

Through my window I heard snippets of various contributions to the 'discussion'.

'Pedro, this household is made up of intelligent, responsible people. Can't you at least try and understand our point of view?'

'You, sir, are nothing more than a bloody tyrant! You are fucking up this house and you'll have nobody living here in a month's time!'

'Pedro, dude, you have a serious psychological problem. You seem to like the fact that everyone is against you. That is some seriously fucked-up shit, man.'

I drifted off to sleep somewhere in the middle of it. I only learnt of its bloody conclusion the next morning via an email Pedro had sent at 4.48am. In it, he informed all residents that due to Dick's 'threatening behaviour', Pedro had ordered him leave the guest house by 4pm that same day and had banned him from visiting ever again.

I went straight to Dick's room. He hadn't slept, and was clearly unhinged and honestly confused. He had just wanted to shut down the fighting and the noise. He had just wanted peace.

Apparently the terrace discussion had raged on for hours, ironically fuelled by the last of our communal booze and becoming increasingly irrational and abusive. At some point, Dick snapped. He marched outside, grabbed Pedro by the collar and demanded—in his loud, menacing, Texan drawl—that the man see reason.

As Pedro hollered for security, others stepped in to drag Dick away and he was quickly led off. Pedro declared that this behaviour constituted a 'red-card infringement', which he confirmed via an email to Dick as soon as he retreated to his room. I slept through the lot, but then again, I can sleep through bomb attacks.

Dick didn't make his 4pm deadline. By 2pm he had booked a flight out of Afghanistan, but he hadn't found alternative accommodation for his remaining night in the country nor packed his bag. He was anxious, sleep-deprived and paranoid about the Afghan house manager, who he believed was spying on him. So I raced home early from work to supervise his departure.

I helped him shove his scant possessions into his suitcase and finally found him a room in the guest house Muffy and I had most recently escaped from and which a pleasant English fellow was now managing.

Dick was determined to leave Bliss with his head held high and, with encouragement from his former brothers-in-arms and a bottle of expensive tequila, courtesy of John, he got splendidly wasted before Steve and I finally dragged him into a taxi and off to his new temporary home at 7pm.

I masqueraded as Dick's PA and went in ahead of him, to let the new manager there know that my 'boss' had indulged in a few drinks before his flight in from Pakistan and was a little fruity.

'Not a problem, darling. I've seen it all before,' he assured me.

I'm sure he had. We all had.

It shamed me at that moment to think that our idyllic, communal existence was being eroded away by alcohol; but that was the truth of it. We used it to compensate for the tedium of compound life and as a salve for the stresses of living in war. It helped mend broken hearts and took the edge off a hard day at work.

And that night I would be cracking open a carton or two of rancid white wine, as we sat on the terrace to dissect Dick Willy's demise and toast the angry peacemaker's last goodbye.

26. My Most Difficult Meeting

I had just come out of a meeting with Saad where the awful man made me cry. I was in such a state that, even after our get-together ended, I had to sit in his office and compose myself for a good five minutes as the last of my tears slowly drained away.

It was 4 September 2012 and I had just officially resigned from Moby.

It was a decision I had been wrestling with for months; in fact, I sent my original resignation letter to Christof and Shaikh (our head of HR in Dubai) at the start of August. I announced my intention to leave via an email sent at 2.30am, because it had taken me most of the evening to compose it and then a good two hours to find the guts to finally hit 'Send'.

They were having none of it. Christof professed that he couldn't possibly carry on without his one remaining Drama Queen, and Shaikh confessed that he was too scared to pass the news on to the Mohsenis. They both counselled me to please reconsider my decision, but, after close to a month of conferring with expat colleagues, friends and family, I was determined to go. Saying it out loud to Saad in the meeting I'd just emerged from broke my heart.

Saad also asked me to rethink the matter, assuring me that any fears I might have about being surreptitiously shuffled out of my position or the organisation were entirely misplaced. He talked about how hard my team would take the news and his certainty that Afghanistan was now in my blood and would be impossible to shake. He was, of course, right. About everything. But I had seen mates leave Afghanistan so burnt out and deranged that they could barely function; I wanted to exit while I was still laughing every day.

So many factors figured in my decision to move on. Losing Muffy was a terrible blow that I didn't ever fully recover from. Results from a recent medical check-up I'd had in Dubai reported that 'clinically significant amounts of mycoplasma pneumonia antibodies were detected'—I wasn't entirely sure what that all meant but I was a little anxious about spending another winter in Kabul.

I guess my most significant concern was my mum—she had turned eighty-two, had continuing health problems and needed her girl closer to home.

A few weeks before, she had again been bedridden with some strange muscle virus that took her out every few months and had first attacked her in October 2011. It had been five o'clock on a Friday morning when my brother phoned me from Sydney to say that Mum was sick. I had just spent the evening at yet another farewell party and was rounding off the night (or more precisely, the very early morning) back at my mate Tahir's house—sipping red wine and yarning about films. My brother had woken that morning to discover Mum still in bed and unable to move. She was immediately taken by ambulance to hospital and the initial diagnosis was that she had probably suffered a stroke.

As I cried and fretted over mum, darling Tahir (who himself hadn't slept for twenty-three hours) got straight online to find me a flight home. With the internet going on and off all the time and site pages constantly timing out, it took him most of the day to get me the ticket that would ferry me via Kuala Lumpur and on to Sydney. Tahir was a saint but, to his splendid credit, Christof sorted out and paid for my flight from Kabul to Dubai.

News of my dilemma spread fairly quickly and I spent much of the day fielding phone calls from friends wanting to know whether there was anything they could do to help. Then at around 4pm, with my travel plans only having just been settled, the Big Juice called, demanding to know where I was. When I told her I was still with Tahir, and hadn't even thought about preparing for my 7am flight the following day, she immediately came and picked me up. We went back to my guest house, where I hastily packed a bag, and then she took me home with her—for dinner, a Valium and my first sleep in thirty-eight hours.

BJ had one of her producers going out on the same flight as me from Kabul; once we got on the plane, the wonderful woman swapped her boarding pass with me so that I could grab a snooze in the comfort of her business-class seat.

I had a six-hour stopover in Dubai and passed out near the Malaysian Airlines counter, feeling relaxed after the staff there assured me that somebody would wake me up when it was time to check in. They did.

I was feeling kind of human by the time I hit KL. I fell asleep while getting a back massage at the airport, only to spring awake again when I realised that the male masseur had his hands on my bosoms. It shames me to say that I'm not entirely sure how long he'd been lingering there, as I had incorporated the sordid scenario into a rather rude dream.

My good friend Maree had arranged for my lovely mate Alman to pick me up from the airport at Sydney and take me straight to the hospital. By then I knew that Mum hadn't suffered a stroke, but she was clearly weak and unwell. However, one look at me after twenty-nine hours of travelling had her more concerned about my well-being than hers.

I stayed at my brother's home that night. I walked in the door, headed straight for the bathroom and had the longest shower I think I have ever taken. I barely found the strength to unzip my suitcase but, upon examining its contents, thought it a thoroughly adequate representation of the previous few days' madness—I had packed precisely nine pairs of undies, two bangles and one belt.

Saad understood all my reasons for needing to leave. He was pleased to know that I had faith in my kids to go it alone, and was relieved that I would stay on for a few more months to facilitate the handover. He ended our discussion by advising me to go back to Australia and take a nice, long break.

'Trudes, we'll have you back next week, next month, next year. Your job will be waiting for you whenever you decide to return. We all love you.'

And then came the tears. The awful man.

27.
Someone to Watch Over Me

I was ambling along Main Street on a mid-October morning when one of our security guards, Mukhtar, spotted me and jogged up the road to meet me. He looked worried and at first I thought he was going to deliver some bad news about his two-year-old daughter, who'd recently had surgery on her nose. He spoke very little English but in our own way, and with a great deal of gesturing and facial antics, we generally got one another. However, his concerned expression had nothing at all to do with his daughter.

'Al Qaeda . . . ?' And he motioned with his hand to indicate a plane taking off. He had evidently just found out that I was leaving. I sadly nodded my head and he simply lowered his, shook it slowly and said: 'This no good.'

I started to cry (something I was doing with increasing regularity at that time) and he squeezed his eyelids with his fingertips to hold back his own tears.

We stood like that for a moment before he again muttered, 'This no good.'

He quickly turned and walked away.

Out of all the Afghans that I worked with and loved, my personal security guards probably knew me the best. They were the people who escorted me in the car to bars and parties, and who knew when I turned up to work the next day wearing the same clothes I went out in.

They took me to the doctor when I was sick, ensuring that the driver went slowly and carefully along the bumpy roads, and followed me around the supermarket as I shopped. They had a fleeting but rare insight into my life that my staff weren't privy to, and for the past three-and-a-half years they had been literally guarding my life.

I'd scored the nickname Al Qaeda after my stint on *Salam*. Al Qaeda operatives were usually Pashtun, so when I arrived back in Kabul after the *Salam* shoot with a smattering of Pashto words and phrases under my belt, the security guards and drivers all thought it was hilarious. Many of them were Pashtun themselves but, for some reason, I became the evil insurgent. They called Muffy 'Malaka', which translates to 'Princess', so I felt rather ripped off in the nickname department.

Whenever there was a terrorist attack, they jokingly wagged their fingers at me, muttering something along the lines of: 'Al Qaeda. Bad. Boom!'

I simply winked, smiled conspiratorially and nodded my head. Yes, it was entirely logical that I would mastermind a bombing that I was caught up in the middle of.

If we arrived at a police checkpoint, they would turn to me and, by way of indicating that they were about to expose me, whisper something like: 'Police, Al Qaeda. You . . .' Before feigning tossing me out the car door.

They chased me down Main Street hurling imaginary grenades in my direction; we drew pretend guns and staged bloody shoot-outs. They accelerated towards me in the parking area, and grabbed me when we were crossing the road and teased at throwing me into the traffic. And once, on a routine trip from work to home, I was driven through the backstreets and up and around an isolated hill as I half-jokingly enquired whether I was actually being kidnapped.

The games were a little twisted, but we played them every day and it always made us laugh. And when I finally returned to Australia, many of my happiest memories would be courtesy of these brave, mad men who were some of the lowest-paid workers in the company and who routinely lived away from their families for weeks at a time to look after me.

Usually, if an expat has security in Afghanistan, it will be of the western variety—highly paid professionals, typically ex-army, who wear body armour and carry nifty little Russian pistols. With the exception of a Brit, who earlier that year had been appointed as our head of security and who operated out of Dubai, our entire security detail was comprised of Afghans.

There were security guards who spent their days (and nights) at the office, perched on rooftops with machine guns trained on the streets below. There were others who manned the boom gates on Main Street and a handful, both male and female, who guarded the various entrances to all the different sections of our huge, sprawling compound. The latter did body searches on local staff and visitors, checked bags and confiscated contraband—anything from USB sticks to aerosol cans.

Then there were around ten men who worked on rotation and provided personal security for expat staff. They occupied the front passenger seat whenever we were being ferried around town, and one or two—sometimes more—would accompany us on our shoots.

The first security guard I really got to know was Zarhawar and I just adored him. After Tiggy and Jose left Afghanistan, there were a good few weeks of just me and my shadow while we finished filming *Salam*. Zarhawar would carry my bag around for me; he would guard the bushes (at a discreet distance) where I'd hidden to relieve myself, and sit alone with me in rooms the size of broom closets, shielded from the men, when we ate at local restaurants. Barely a word ever passed between us; but we rubbed along together like an old, married couple until he finally delivered me safely back home to Kabul.

There was the wonderful Omar, who still laughs with me about our treacherous bus trip to Mazar.

Then there was Naveed, a fit, young guy who, in between trailing expats around, could generally be found working out in the makeshift gym behind the CEO's office. I heard from the others that he was particularly handy with a gun; however, his powers of observation were a little lacking.

On our army shoot in Jalalabad, Nilu and I had decided to play a trick on him whereby I snuck away, lay down behind a sand dune, and waited for him to panic when he discovered I was missing. After thirty-five minutes, Nilu called for me to come out.

Parched and covered in sand, I crawled away from my hiding place to see Naveed wrestling with the producer. He was blissfully oblivious to the fact that he was one man down and that an unaccounted-for expat might, at that very moment, be holed up in a cave somewhere, waving her wedding band around and rehearsing the answer to her 'proof of life' question.

Still, I was mad about the man and our bonding moment came over a game of golf.

Allie, one of my Moby housemates, had organised a group of us to play at the Kabul Golf Club on a muggy, hot Friday. Despite the fact that there were western security contractors in our party packing pistols, our company insisted we take along one of our own guards. Naveed volunteered to escort us and was actually quite happy to tag along, as he had never seen a game of golf played before.

I'm not much of a golfer myself—I think I've played a handful of games in my entire life—but even I could see that calling the ditch-riddled piece of dirt we were playing on a 'golf course' was a stretch. There were bumps and lumps everywhere, and clumps of bushes and big, nasty thistles plagued the landscape. I blame my lack of knowledge about the game for imagining that rubber thongs would make appropriate golfing shoes.

The first hole was a hoot. I swung three times before I actually hit the ball; but, when I finally connected, I managed to send it high into the sky and was delighted when I saw it hit the ground in a puff of dust away in the distance. However, it was walking to where the ball had landed that did me in.

As the others strode off in their fancy, closed-in footwear, I gingerly picked my way along the course, where prickly chunks of flora latched onto the sides of my feet. The thistles were so fierce that they actually embedded themselves into the flimsy soles of my thongs, each step bringing them closer to my flesh. Naveed dutifully sauntered along beside me, no doubt envisaging a rather dull afternoon of having to lag behind with the dim-witted western woman who couldn't even dress properly for golf, let alone play it.

At the second hole, I hit the ball about a metre and pretended to admire a tree as a grinning Naveed picked it up and hurled it further down the 'fairway'. As we slowly set off in pursuit of it, I turned to him, laughed and shook my head in unmistakable defeat. He hesitated for the briefest of moments, before pointing to his back and indicating that I should jump on.

For my part, there was no wavering—I happily got on board and also gladly let him finish playing the remainder of the round for me. Piggy-backing me for eight holes didn't seem to affect his game at all, and he actually ended up coming in third.

Ayub was a relatively recent recruit to the security-guard fraternity, but he had very quickly become one of my favourites. He was the chief instigator of the Al Qaeda bomb-hurling-and-finger-blasting battles, and thought that I was genuinely crazy.

Our friendship was sealed over an ATM at a western supermarket. He had just received his very first debit card and indicated to me that he needed to use it to withdraw his pay. He was driving to his village that same night and wanted to give money to his family.

When the machine asked which language we'd like to use, I instantly hit Dari. He was surprisingly reluctant to enter his own

PIN—I assumed it was just beginner's nerves—and so I took to the keypad myself. Ayub didn't speak English and, to my great shame, I had only managed to master one to five in his native language, so figuring out his PIN became a great charade of holding up fingers and vigorous head nodding.

PIN safely settled, I stood back so he could select the transaction. He just looked at me and shrugged his shoulders. I pointed at the various options on offer and indicated that he should choose one. Still nothing. It was then that I realised that Ayub was illiterate—the squiggly writing on the screen meant as much to him as it did to me.

There were two Indian guys standing behind us by this stage; as Ayub and I started all over again in English, I apologised to them for the delay. We were going great guns until we had to decide on the amount of money he wanted to withdraw. There were upraised digits all over the place, with the machine eventually tiring of our antics and cancelling the transaction.

We retreated to the back of the lengthening queue, giggling and snorting and maniacally gesticulating at one another. Until we had to give up. I slipped him some money from my wallet instead, and we finally withdrew his cash a week later with the assistance of an English-speaking driver.

Despite being young enough to be my son, Ayub hovered over me like a protective father. He could sense when I was having a bad day and didn't feel like playing, fussed over me when I was sick, and wouldn't leave my side if he was assigned to me.

A few months before I left, we had a meeting with a US colonel at a commando training base and he gave us free rein to try out the obstacle course before we left. Ayub followed me up ladders; he held up netting as I crawled along the sand underneath it and lifted me up so I could take on the climbing bars . . . before we both retreated to separate simulated bunkers and had the mother of all simulated shoot-outs.

The day I met Mukhtar out in the street and confirmed to him that I was leaving, he appeared again that afternoon in front of my desk. I assumed he was after some form of painkiller. Our office had become the workplace pharmacy; people regularly popped in and presented with headaches, stomach ailments, body aches and abrasions. If we didn't have anything on hand to dispense, we went to the western supermarket to pick something up.

Early on, Muffy and I had learnt to be very careful to get our diagnoses correct. I once gave one of our drivers a cream that I understood was needed for a sore shoulder muscle. It took me two days to discover that the poor man had been regularly rubbing an anti-inflammatory gel into a very nasty cut.

But that afternoon Mukhtar was healthy and, through Merzad, told me that he was very sad that I was leaving. He was also worried that he wouldn't be able to repay me the money I gave him for his daughter's surgery before I left Afghanistan for good. I told him that I didn't want the money, but he argued that, if he had to repay me, then I would have to return one day to collect it.

I laughed through more tears and assured him that I would come back. How could I leave Afghanistan forever?

28.
Motherly
Advice

Finally I was meeting Aleem's mum. The meeting had been coming forever, but shamefully it was only in my final week that I found time to make it happen. Aleem would have liked it to be an entire afternoon's worth of catching up at his family home, but I had so little time to spare that, instead, we opted for a quick lunch at his married sister's apartment close to work.

Aleem had always called me his second mother. Mum-Number-One and I had constantly communicated over the years through our shared son—sending greetings back and forth, hopes from my side that her ailing health had improved, enquiries from her as to the well-being of my family in Australia.

I was greeted at the apartment by a giggling gaggle of children, all dressed in their Friday best and shyly shaking my hand as I greeted them in Dari. Aleem's two twenty-something brothers were there, also scrubbed shiny and fresh; his sister made a fleeting appearance early on, self-consciously tucking her hair under her scarf and barely able to raise her eyes to meet mine, before scuttling back to the kitchen.

Despite the fact that I was ostensibly there to meet Aleem's mother, she failed to appear so, as I sat on the floor with her three sons, I asked Aleem where she was. He told me that she was cooking our lunch and I would meet her later. The food arrived, and Aleem's nieces and nephews carefully laid down plates of oily, hot bolani before us on the floor. I told Aleem to go and get his mum from the kitchen, but he was adamant that she wouldn't come out; it was her job to feed the men and the western woman, but she would be sure to join us once we'd had our fill.

I had been in this position before and on other occasions I had made my way to the kitchen, to smilingly coax the womenfolk out to join us to eat. But Aleem was from conservative Pashtun stock and so I didn't feel comfortable pressing the point. It was probably for the best anyway, as Aleem was anxious to update me on his cousin's marital situation and, despite knowing that his mother didn't speak a lick of English, I didn't think I'd be entirely comfortable discussing the rather delicate subject in front of her.

The cousin had married four days ago, and Aleem and his family had all travelled to a small village in the east of the country for the wedding. It had been a huge affair, with hundreds of people in attendance; indeed, most of the village had been invited to celebrate the union. The morning after the big event, Aleem's aunty and assorted interested women had gone to the marital bedroom to inspect the sheets for blood.

The sheet inspection is still a widely practised custom in Afghanistan, as many Afghans believe that blood-stained bedding is the only certain proof that the bride was a virgin. When Muffy was producing her lifestyle show, she workshopped a segment on women's health with her female producers that ultimately evolved into a discussion about S-E-X. When one of the producers, who was studying to be a doctor, tentatively asked Muffy what a tampon was, she took one from her bag and delicately explained what it was and how to use it. The girls were intrigued and thought it a great device for dealing with menstrual flow, but they unanimously acknowledged that they could never use one, for fear that it might prevent them from bleeding on the marital sheets.

Aleem's aunty and friends arrived at the honeymoon suite (no more than a curtained-off section in the family home) to discover the bride in tears and the sheets perfectly white. But any doubts as to the seventeen-year-old girl's chastity were quickly dismissed when Aleem's cousin admitted that he had failed to perform—an inopportune bout of erectile dysfunction had hit him and he hadn't even come close to probing his bride's virginity.

There was outrage, of course, and savage declarations from the bride's mother that the groom wasn't a real man and had always been a hopeless, effeminate weakling. But the outrage wasn't confined to the appointed bed inspectors; over the next few hours, husbands, brothers, sisters and cousins were all informed. Very soon the entire village knew about the poor man's misfortune.

The second night saw a similarly pitiable showing from the hapless hubby (not surprising, considering the enormous public pressure he was now under to deflower his wife) and it was communally decided that the local mullah should be consulted.

The mullah had some interesting insights into the dilemma, declaring that the solution lay in the husband boiling an egg and then eating it with his wife. I wasn't greatly surprised when Aleem informed me that the mystical cure had failed to do the trick.

The utter shame of the third strike-out had compelled the family to falsely declare that the deed had been done. But the cousin was not in the clear—a disgrace to his entire family, he now turned to Aleem for advice.

Over the phone, Aleem had questioned the mullah's advice: 'How can eating an egg make your "thing" work? You need to take off all your clothes, lie down beside each other and start kissing.'

I had naively imagined that this would be the natural start to any such proceedings, but apparently not—Aleem was roundly berated by his cousin for being a shameful, shameful man and a very bad Muslim.

'So what to do?' Aleem asked me with upraised palms and a grave shake of the head.

I shrugged my shoulders and shook my head too . . . until I realised that he and his brothers were genuinely looking to me for an answer. After gnawing on my bolani for an inordinate amount of time, I conceded that Aleem's advice was as good as it got (privately harbouring my suspicions that the unfortunate fellow may, in fact, be gay) before venturing into territory that I was loath to explore. 'There are tablets he can take. To help with sex. Have you ever heard of them?'

Aleem admitted he knew something about it, while his brothers just stared at me, slack-jawed and mute.

I took a deep breath. 'Okay. The tablets are called Viagra and you can buy them at any pharmacy. My male friends here get them all the time.'

'And what will they do?' Aleem enquired.

'Well, they will . . . make your cousin's "thing" work.'

The two brothers looked at each other and giggled, while Aleem tore a piece of paper from his nephew's notebook and instructed me to write down the name of this wondrous drug. I was insistent that his cousin seek some kind of medical advice before embarking on this course of action. I was quietly wondering about the effectiveness of Viagra with a man who refused to disrobe to have sex, when Aleem's mum entered the room.

Our meeting was brief but moving. Using Aleem as our translator, we chatted like sisters. Mum-Number-One was younger than me, but raising six children and years of struggling with kidney and heart complications had taken their toll on her sweet-natured, delicate features.

As our time together drew to a close, she presented me with a scarf. Then, with her eyes fixed firmly upon me, she spoke softly to Aleem for a very long time. She was thanking me for looking after 'our' son, for guiding him through his career and for helping our boy grow into a beautiful young man.

As my eyes filled with tears, I noticed Aleem absent-mindedly fingering the piece of paper that he had hurriedly shoved into his top pocket when his mother had appeared. I hugged her tightly to me as we said our goodbyes, wondering what she would make of the motherly assistance I had given our son just that afternoon.

29.
Farewell to Days Like These

I was sitting on a bus at Dubai Airport, being ferried to the plane that was finally taking me home. I looked like a strung-out junkie— bleary-eyed, dishevelled and coughing up the nasty remnants of a two-day surprise farewell party that, due to a nagging cold, I really hadn't been fit enough to attend. Naturally I had, which is essentially why I'd missed my scheduled flight out of Kabul; instead, I'd taken to my bed, my lips wrapped around my asthma inhaler for most of the day.

I could sense that my fellow business-class passengers were wondering why the hell I was here with them on the first bus to hit the tarmac. So was I really—the free upgrade had been granted to me just as we were boarding.

The stewardess who informed me of this fortuitous turn of events looked puzzled too. She checked my boarding pass, consulted some list, scrutinised my passport, looked at my boarding pass again and then quietly conferred with a colleague before confirming that, yes, this wreck of a woman now leaning on the counter in order to stay upright *was* the 'Trudi-Ann Tierney' that the airline had deemed worthy of turning left as she entered the aircraft.

And just to reinforce my clearly disturbed and fragile state, I was now crying as well. The exquisitely fragrant, perfectly groomed woman sitting next to me on the bus made an almost imperceptible move to the edge of the seat as I again read over the text I had just received from Dave, who was now living in Dubai. He and Sienna were getting married in New Zealand in a month and I was already booked in as best man. He had just messaged to tell me that Sienna was pregnant.

My last days in Kabul were chaotic. So many goodbyes to be said, so many send-offs to attend—the endless tears and beers undoubtedly responsible for my state of extreme dehydration. And somewhere in the midst of all of this, I had to finalise transitioning my work duties to Merzad.

Just that week we'd signed the contract with our client for a second season of *Eagle Four*. It had been in negotiation for two years, with endless plot rewrites as the funder grappled with what exactly it should be propagating to the Afghan populace.

I, of course, wasn't going be there to see it swing into production and Merzad was nervous about doing it without me. He'd asked me on a daily basis whether I could stay and see it through. I promised him that the team could pull it off and excused myself with talk of my failing health and needing to see my mum. But the truth was: I simply didn't have the energy to take that ride again.

Alka, Wassi, Ali, Sidique, Shakila, Ashraf . . . all of my kids had stolen a quiet moment in the past few weeks to ask me to stay. Khan and I looked at old photos from the *Salam* shoot and both of us cried. Raouf quite confidently told me that he could have the Attorney-General issue an order to stop me from leaving Afghanistan. And Farhad genuinely wanted to know what they had done wrong to make me go.

It was Hakim, the boy who had never left Kabul, let alone the country, who found the words to express the real meaning behind their despair. 'I knew you would one day go, but then you kept on staying. So I thought it might never happen. And now you are going. Everyone will one day leave us. What will happen then? That is what I can't stop thinking about.'

I assured him that he'd be fine; that Afghanistan would thrive. That, with wonderful, intelligent people like him, determined to see the country progress, there wasn't any need for us crazy foreigners to hang in there. But to be honest, I really didn't know what would happen and much of *my* despair over leaving had been the constant, awful thought that in a few years' time my young friends could be caught up in some kind of hell that would be beyond their control to change.

Khalid had come by to visit. He'd heard that I was going for good and wanted to say goodbye. His English had improved considerably since I'd last seen him and he needed me to know that there were no hard feelings about his undignified exit from the company.

He told me that he was now making a very good living from dressing as a woman and dancing at weddings. But he'd recently got into a scrape with the police when a brawl erupted at a reception and the cops turned up to find everyone drunk. He proudly informed me that he managed to avoid jail by 'connecting' with the arresting officers.

I couldn't help but laugh. And in truth, there had been as much joy as there had been despondency in my final days.

When my girl posse from the office took me out to lunch, we played Spin the Bottle and the bloody bottle seemed to be constantly pointing at me.

'So Trudi *Jan*,' Alka began. 'How many boys have you had?'

'Do you mean boyfriends?'

'Yes, boyfriends,' she replied.

'Boys who you have done "you-know-what" with. *Real* boyfriends,' added Rukhsar (who, as a married woman with two children, had both the authority and confidence to venture into the 'you-know-what' territory).

It all got a little complicated when I attempted to explain that 'you-know-what' boys didn't necessarily constitute 'boyfriends'. And my subsequent feeble attempt to count the 'you-know-what' boys on my fingers had them shrieking with shocked but delighted laughter.

They would have happily probed my 'love' life all afternoon, but they had to go after a couple of hours to distribute pens and books at a girls' school that their women's group supports.

There was an enchanting dawn excursion to Darulaman Palace on the outskirts of Kabul with two members of my expat chicks' posse—Sal and Fran—and some sweet chap I still only know as

Random Italian Dude. We were the last ones standing at a Thursday-night shindig when Sal decided that she wanted to take photos of the palace at sunrise. A huge, sprawling European-style building constructed in the 1920s, Darulaman was ravaged by fire during the communist coup in 1978 and almost completely destroyed by the Mujahideen at the end of the Soviet invasion. And, with its blown-out walls, its tangles of twisted metal hanging from the ceiling, and its crumbling marble floors, it is indescribably magnificent.

The first blush of light was just staining the horizon when the taxi arrived that was going to take us there. As we raced out to meet it, I grabbed my terry-towelling dressing gown for warmth, Sal grabbed her camera, while Fran grabbed a bottle of vodka. Somewhere along the way, Random Italian Dude (RID) made us stop at a street stall to buy cigarettes and a soccer ball.

The palace was surrounded by a wire fence and guarded by security, but it only took us ten dollars to gain admission for the grand tour. The soccer ball proved to be a genius move because, as RID and our heavily armed tour guide kicked it back and forth across the enormous reception area, we ladies climbed all over the place, marvelling at the shapes and shadows, sitting together sipping Stoli in the massive arched windows and watching the sunrise over Kabul. I had never loved the city as much as I did that morning.

And my official farewell party—held a few weeks back so as to be a joint affair, since my good mate John was also leaving—was a riotous celebration that felt a little like an end-of-high-school do. We drank, danced and sang to our favourite summer songs of 2012. I indulged in emotional deep and meaningfuls with all my besties, before retreating to my room to make out with my good mate Mick.

291

He was a man I had an impossible crush on, primarily because he was ten years younger than me and at that time, the most popular boy on the Kabul campus. Still, as queen of the prom, it was a fitting and deserved end to a glorious night.

Just before I left I caught up with Jahid, the Mohseni brother who was CEO when I arrived. He hadn't been to Kabul in months and we spent hours together talking about the 'good old days'. We laughed about *Salam,* recounting all the hilarious mishaps and calamities we endured to get the show made and on air. When I thanked him for having such faith in me to manage the project, he sheepishly informed me that nobody else had been crazy enough to take the job on.

Hiking off to the Badlands with a bag full of money and no idea was now just some notional, romantic relic. The stuff of nostalgia, of wistfully murmuring 'Remember when...' and 'Can you believe...?' And I felt blessed for having been there, because I sensed I would never see days like these again.

Epilogue

From: Hakim

To: Trudi-Ann

I'm fine, and everybody is doing well here.

Oh, you're great. I'm really happy hearing this.

Thanks for my word too. I'm not in the office and unfortunately i can't get any word for you now. Anyway, as i always
get a good one on behalf of you, so if i were in the office,
you'd definitely get JOY today. that is why i can ensure that
your word of the day is JOY.

I hope you don't laugh very very loud.

thanks,

Hakim

I don't laugh very, very loud. I cry until my throat aches.

In the weeks leading up to my departure, when I was barely holding it together and feeling such incredible guilt about abandoning my team, I was advised by an expat old-timer that, for the sake of my sanity, I needed to cut the cord as soon as I left Kabul. But I simply can't. The adorable Hakim sends me a Word-of-the-Day each morning and I send him one in return. We're six-and-a-half hours out in our timings, but it works for us.

We have all stayed in touch, desperately holding on to one another via email, Facebook and phone. My Afghan friends' need for constant contact is as acute as my own. There is expected baby news from Merzad and from Aleem's cousin (it seems like the Viagra did the trick); there are engagements, weddings and office gossip. Truth is, I gather they are coping with the separation far better than me.

I sit here now, shuffling through my pack of Word-of-the-Day cards searching for the good stuff and thinking about Hakim.

During our last week together, I gave him one final job. My laptop had packed it in (something I took as yet another sign that it was truly time to go) and the cursor kept jumping all over the screen. I actually can't touch-type and so I had to keep my eyes glued to the keyboard as I bashed away at it.

So, in the difficult, dying days, when I felt that I still had so much to fix before I left, Hakim had to stand behind me and tell me every time the cursor moved. After thrashing out an exceptionally long email to management, with Hakim at my shoulder, I thanked him, hugged him and told him how wonderful he was.

He lowered his head and, when he looked up, his eyes had turned to liquid brown. 'There is a saying that you never realise what you have until you've lost it. But we know *now*, Trudi *Jan*. We already know.'

And I think I know now too.

Acknowledgements

Thanks to my wonderful mum, Coral, who instilled in me my spirit of adventure and my remarkable dad, Rog, who, although now gone from this world for twenty-seven years, is still with me everyday. To my brother, Adam, and my sister, Jenny, and my beautiful extended family and friends (too many to name) who have always supported me in my many crazy escapades.

Special thanks to the wonderful, wise Richard Walsh who held my hand and guided me through the initial writing process. You patted me on the head when I deserved it, kicked me up the backside when I needed it and never panicked when I went MIA (well, not much anyway).

Thank you to the team at Allen & Unwin, including Claire Kingston, Angela Handley, Amy Milne, Christa Moffitt and Karen Ward, who have been so helpful and enthusiastic about my work. And to Jo Butler, who helped to make perfect sense of my chaotic tale.

And an incredibly heartfelt thanks to my Afghan and expat 'family' who made my time in Afghanistan so extraordinary.

Finally to my niece Amy—here's the shout out I promised you when on that morning not so long ago you said: 'Trudi, why don't you write a book about Afghanistan?' You went out that same day and bought me my first journal, and it came as no surprise to either of us when just a few hours later an email from a 'Richard Walsh' arrived in my inbox asking me the very same question.